Civil War in Russia 1917-1920

Civil War in Russia 1917–1920

J.F.N. Bradley

St. Martin's Press
New York

St. Martin's Press, Inc., 175 Fifth Avenue, New York, N.Y. 10010
Printed in Great Britain
Library of Congress Catalog Card Number: 75-18594
First published in the United States of America in 1975

12-19-78

Contents

Preface

It has always been difficult for historians to write histories of any civil war from the 'outside'. Naturally such historians have no access to primary sources on the inside, and consider themselves fortunate if they can consult the sources of the defeated side, which are usually scattered all over the world. Despite these difficulties some remarkable accounts of recent civil wars have been written by historians who have had enough courage to face these drawbacks: Hugh Thomas's *Spanish Civil War* is the most contemporary example.

It is also true that several more or less competent versions of the Russian civil war have already been written and they certainly provide us with the basic knowledge of this event. Moreover, the policy governing archives in the USSR has not been altered, so nothing fresh and revealing can be expected from that source. However, the 50 years that have elapsed since the battles of the Russian civil war were fought have brought to light important new material and evidence particularly outside the USSR, and they alone warrant another, more accurate, version.

Three important sources of primary documentation have been opened to historians in the past ten years. First of all, the Trotsky archive as well as many other Bolshevik or former Bolshevik collections of documents, among which figures most prominently the captured Smolensk archive. Secondly, the personal papers of the White leaders and the 'official' documents of anti-Bolshevik movements have become accessible: General Denikin's diaries, journals and correspondence in New York; General Wrangel's in California. The Miliukov papers can now be consulted as well as the papers of many minor White figures, scattered as they are all over Europe and North America. The third new source, and perhaps the most important one, is the declassified official papers and archives of the Western Allies, France, Great Britain, the United States and Italy. Since these Allied powers attached military missions to the White movements and had observers on the spot on both sides, these papers serve mainly to verify the Red and White versions of events, to clarify political, economic and military situations during the civil war; without any doubt they throw a new light on the Red and White leaders, armies and organisation.

In the past historians had to use the conflicting Red and White versions of the civil war and often tried to reconcile discrepancies by means of their personal bias. Though Western official papers help to sort out many discrepancies, they also create new complexities: in some instances they even give us a third version of events, fresh dates and even provide entirely new facts about leaders or events, especially those in which the Western Allies had been directly involved. The German and Austrian official archives, also accessible, are another foreign source of some importance. This study of the civil war takes advantage of these new sources to correct misinformation and bias. Otherwise it owes much to three particular accounts of the civil war which have appeared in the West: those of Chamberlin, Footman and Zaytsov. It also relies to a great extent on three studies which have appeared in the East: the two 'official' histories of the civil war and Kakurin's. Even these limited improvements have entailed the most exhausting enquiries: sources had to be consulted all over the world, continents had to be traversed and inhospitable climates suffered. Above all, these exertions required financial resources far beyond the means of an academic historian. Thus I feel that I must acknowledge my gratitude to all those who have helped me in this historical enterprise.

First I must beg indulgence of my publishers, particularly Mr Peter Kemmis Betty who has suffered patiently all the delays that my globe-trotting caused. Then I must record my gratitude to the various foundations and institutions whose financial support made this study possible: the Humboldt-Stiftung, Centre National de la Recherche Scientifique, Astor Foundation, Hayter Committee Fund (Manchester University), Osterreichisches Institut, Akademische Austauschdienst and the British Council. I must also thank many colleagues for advice, help and encouragement: Professors Renouvin, Nove, Grenville, Scheibert, Hillgruber, Hanham, Erickson, the late P. Moseley, George Brinkley and Schapiro. The following librarians and archivists have proved most helpful and must be thanked: Dr Blaas, Dr Peball, Monsieur Laloy, Monsieur Miramon-Fitzjames, Mr C.J. Child O.B.E., Dr Magerovsky, Dr Sworakowski, the late Colonel Koc, the librarians of New College, Oxford, Houghton Library, Harvard and the university libraries of Istanbul and Helsinki. Last but not least I am indebted to my wife who researched for me all over the world, and my children, Catherine and Christopher, both reading history at Cambridge University and Bordeaux University, whom I have shamelessly exploited as copyists of Russian, French, German and English documents. They all helped me with this book, but I alone am responsible for its defects.

JOHN F.N. BRADLEY
Manchester University

Bibliographical Introduction

It is extremely difficult to study objectively the Russian revolution and the subsequent civil war, for although some 50 years have elapsed since these events, they still remain ideologically so topical and politically so controversial that not only politicians and ideologues but also historians tend to take up philosophic positions and quarrel among themselves. They accuse each other of being 'bourgeois falsifiers' or 'political time-servers' and in the heat of their arguments forget that the very ground for these disputes is most uncertain: neither side has at its disposal the evidence that historians normally require to establish plausibly historical facts, not to mention truth. Official documents have only just become available in the West, but even then, for those with security implications, Western historians will have to wait another hundred years. In the USSR historians will have to wait even longer for official documents *in toto:* they suffer from the added disadvantage that most of their documents are security labelled, and embargoes are applied much more strictly than in the West.

Thus absolute objectivity (if it exists at all) will perhaps be impossible even in this study given the unevenness of available historical evidence. However, it will definitely not be consciously biased, as, for example, the pre-war official Soviet work, *The Civil War, 1918-1921.*[1] This pioneering study, apart from being a useful collection of documents and memoir material, is a 'history of victors' justifying and glorifying themselves, and explaining their success without any corroborating evidence. The post-war Soviet effort, *A History of Civil War in the USSR,* is only slightly better.[2] Justifications are taken for granted, but many of the Stalinist historical excesses, which, for example, removed the majority of Bolshevik leaders from the civil war, are left uncorrected. At this stage Soviet historians had at their disposal White memoirs and documents, and still failed to produce a fuller picture of the civil war than their predecessors: Trotsky was practically left out, the Allied intervention was a plot against the Bolshevik revolution and the Czechoslovak Legion a tool of the Allies. Since this work extensive summaries of the civil war have been published, along with numerous collections of documents, monographs and memoir material.

Still, no basic concepts nor interpretations of the civil war have been developed, improved or elucidated.

Trouble stems from Lenin's interest in the civil war, both as a politician and as an historical organiser. Even while the civil war was being fought, Lenin gave orders that documents be collected and historical writing preserved. He was instrumental in establishing the Military Historical Commission whose first publication, *Civil War in Russia 1918-1919*, appeared in 1919. However Lenin was primarily a political theoretician and political leader and his interests were not historical as such. He elaborated the theory of class struggle and proclaimed civil war as its most acute form. This simple political idea caused inestimable confusion in subsequent historical research and interpretation. To this day Soviet historians have not cleared up the havoc raised by Lenin's thesis that 'on the 25th of October 1917 civil war in Russia was a fact'. In Lenin's theory Bolshevik victory in the *coup de Petrograd* on 7 November 1917 meant the start of the civil war. It was more difficult to justify this ideological assertion empirically and Soviet historians, especially those who understood Lenin's concepts ideologically and not historically, advanced a selection of dates for the beginning of the civil war. Only the 'official' historian, N.I. Nayda and his collective, considered that civil war started with the Bolshevik uprising in November 1917. Others thought it started with the Kerensky-Krasnov expedition or the officer-cadets' rising in Petrograd a few days later. For some the Japanese landing at Vladivostok and the British takeover at Murmansk in April 1918 was the real start of the civil war. For others it was the revolt of the Czechoslovak Legion in May 1918. A fortuitous date, 18 June 1918, was chosen by other Soviet historians as the start of full-scale civil war.

Unfortunately Lenin made the Soviet historians' task even more precarious, when as a good politician he decided to exploit the struggle to justify and make popular his current policies. Thus, for example, he applied to the civil war his innovatory 'class analysis' and determined that without imperialist intervention there would have been no real civil war in Russia at all. He admitted that after the Bolshevik victory in November 1917 which was brought about on behalf of the working and peasant classes, thus having the support of the majority of the nation, the defeated bourgeoisie continued to resist (non-acute class struggle) by means of mutinies and economic sabotage. However, this was no civil war and Bolshevik sailors were perfectly capable of dealing with this problem. It was at this point that the imperialist Allies conceived a plan to destroy the Bolsheviks and Soviet power with them. They were making ready immense military forces against Russia and the plan came to nothing only thanks to the separate peace treaty with Germany and the German offensive on the Western front. After this 'immense' plan had failed, the Allies replaced it by smaller plans of intervention: the Japanese landed in the Far East, the

British and others in the North, then the Czech Corps mutinied and acted as the Allied shock troops against the Bolsheviks. The British also moved directly against Soviet Central Asia and the Caucasus, while the French landed in Odessa and the Ukraine. After initial successes, because of class wavering among the Russian peasants and the petty bourgeoisie, all the 'small' plans also failed, because the Red Army proved too strong and Allied units quickly became demoralised.

It was at this stage (in spring 1919) that the Allies dropped the idea of a direct intervention and began to organise and arm the domestic counter-revolutionaries and subject nationalities, especially the Poles. Though the fighting in 1919-20 was undoubtedly fratricidal, Russians killing Russians, civil war was declared by Lenin to be a succession of Allied marches (*Pokhody Antanty*) against the Bolsheviks. The temporary successes of the counter-revolutionaries at this stage Lenin explained by class wavering of the small peasants: but when the small peasants began to predominate also in the armies fighting the Bolshevik Red Army, they in turn collapsed and melted away. As for the Allied motives for the intervention they were on the whole 'preventive' – the warring imperialists wanted to smother the Bolshevik revolution to prevent it from spreading. Needless to say they also hated the revolutionary Soviets because they had left the war, would not pay back war loans and would not protect Allied economic interests in Russia. These were the reasons for which they wanted to plunder Russia in the habitual colonial fashion.

All this theoreticising served Lenin well politically. In this life and death struggle he led the majority of Russians against foreign conspirators and imperialists, who were bent on the destruction of Russia with the final aim of turning it into a colony, Lenin rebutted most vigorously social revolutionary claims that the civil war was a fratricidal struggle fought by sections of the working class and peasantry. Everything was done by the Allies, even the timing of the White offensives: Denikin-Yudenich in 1919, the Poles-Wrangel in 1920. The civil war was, according to Lenin, a national resistance against international imperialism. In this way Lenin was able to justify his tough policies and measures at home and by producing a determined leadership and superior organisation against the foreigners and their agents, he was able to win the struggle.

However, Lenin's political theories and justifications put Soviet historical writing into an intolerable position: historians could not produce historical analyses but *romans à thèse*. Thus the first histories of the civil war proved to be eccentric ideological exercises. However at this stage Lenin and his Bolshevik party could not enforce compliance in ideological matters and soon unorthodox, deviationist histories began to appear: Kakurin was the first historian to advance his own interpretation of the civil war. He questioned practically everything that Lenin claimed was at the root of the civil war and reinterpreted a great deal. He was joined by

Anishkin and Popov, each of whom put forth his particular explanation of the civil war. Still the 'official' *Civil War 1918-1921* was orthodox (more or less), and only military monographs and memoirs could differ and follow their own line of interpretation.

Lenin's ideological impositions on Soviet historiography were removed in the 1930s only to be replaced by even cruder ones. As early as 1929 Voroshilov launched the cult of Stalin in the civil war and the terrible struggle was rapidly reduced to a personal affair conducted by Stalin. Stalin himself wrote down his 'theses' simplifying even those of Lenin: there were only three marches of the Allies against the Bolsheviks and Stalin was always there to beat them off: at Stalingrad (on the South East front), Perm (on the Eastern front), Petrograd (on the North West front), in the South and finally in the South West against Poland. S.E. Rabinovich wrote up these ideas as a history and the book·remained the authorised version (abridged to make it simple and clear) of the civil war, while Stalin was alive. During this era of the personality cult only monographic studies were allowed to appear and the projected 15-volume 'official' *chef d'oeuvre* never saw the light of day. Only after Stalin's death could Soviet historians publish documents and histories, and revive the study of the civil war, albeit with the old Leninist version and with many Stalinist ideological limitations still remaining in force.

In the late 1950s and 1960s Soviet historians published a tremendous number of useful monographic studies, especially on Bolshevik leaders. Lenin's role in the civil war was more realistically assessed, and Stalin's, Voroshilov's and Minin's criticised. Still not all the purged leaders were rehabilitated and Trotsky continued to be ignored.[3] The Bolshevik party's role in the struggle was analysed in all the areas of the USSR and the Latvians were singled out for special praise.[4] This was a great advance on previous efforts and helped in the understanding of the Bolshevik side. Collections of documents which began to appear in the late 1950s were even more useful to both Soviet and Western historians.[5]

With the appearance of monographic studies of Allied intervention in the West, Soviet historians renewed their interest in this old bugbear. However, possibly for ideological reasons no new interpretations were attempted; instead, western elucidations were seized upon and used to support old arguments and provide fuel for new controversies.[6] Whenever a study could not be exploited for these purposes it was condemned as imperialist 'whitewashing', therefore this field of research remains the most barren.[7] Sadly also, even when the Czechoslovak archives became available, Soviet historians refused to revise Lenin's views on the Czechoslovak Legion which continues to figure in the civil war as the tool of the Western Allies.[8]

Perhaps the most useful monographs to appear in the USSR since Stalin's death are those concerned with the civil war in the various regions and territories of the USSR, such as Kazakhstan, Uzbekistan, the Far East, Siberia and the Caucasus. However these regional studies become much less useful when they deal with Poland, the Baltic republics, Moldavia or Finland.[9] Still, the wealth of detail revealed in them helps to break new ground. Nationalist tensions within the Bolshevik camp gain new dimensions; at long last we discover how the Bolsheviks dealt with them more effectively than the Whites.[10]

The most recent publications give a more penetrating insight into Bolshevik military organisation in the civil war: the use of the Red Army, various shock troops, partisans and the *Cherezvychaynaya komissiya*, the secret police. We now have the decisions and instructions of the Soviet High Command (1917-20) as well as a systematic treatment of the Chinese units, Yugoslav internationalists, and sailors. The importance of the *Cheka* becomes apparent both in the armies and the rear, and above all in the newly acquired territories.[11]

All this accumulated Soviet bibliography, materials and publications now available in the West must lead to a better understanding and a more balanced interpretation of the Russian civil war, which is the avowed aim of the present study.

conclude
summary

1

Bolshevik Uprising

It can be argued, even without accepting fully Lenin's definition of civil war, that the political and military conflict which is termed the Russian civil war was started in the moment when the Central Committee of the Bolshevik Party accepted and endorsed Lenin's demand for an armed uprising in view of seizing power from the Provisional Government. While the Provisional Government was only a feeble successor of the tsarist government and the country was really ungoverned, it did represent as far as was possible in Russia the political majority of the Russian people. On the other hand, the Bolsheviks were only a small minority and had practically no following among the non-Russian nationalities. It was clear that if this resolute faction came to power through the uprising it was organising, it would necessarily clash with the vast majority of the people and, if it persisted in clinging to power, civil war seemed inevitable. Still, given the total anarchy and paralysis of the majority, Lenin's gamble had just a slender chance; initial successes seemed to indicate that there might not even be a civil war.

In March 1917 the collapse of tsarism was so unexpected and complete that all Russians, even those who had plotted its downfall, were at a loss what to do next. Those who gained power soon recognised that Russia was in the grip of anarchy and could do nothing but 'swim along the anarchic current'. But Vladimir Ilyich Lenin (Ulyanov), while equally surprised by the unexpected windfall, showed no hesitation as to the next step. Very shortly after his return to Russia from Switzerland he publicly announced his 'theses', which were in fact instructions for further action to his followers. Lenin thought that the March Revolution was unfinished, that the working class represented by his Bolshevik faction of the Russian Social Democratic Party should come to power, and he proposed that he and his government would wield power effectively and not just drift like the Provisional Government. This was a declaration of intent and Lenin never wavered in his determination to carry it out, though he had to modify certain details. In the end he convinced other Bolsheviks and ultimately the whole party, but one of his first and independent 'converts' was a 'Mezhrayonets', L.D. Trotsky. As the traumatic shock of the March Revolution wore off, other individuals and groups began to think of seizing power. They were mainly right-wing elements and they realised the simple truth: in the prevailing anarchy whoever succeeded in acting in an organised way would come to power. When the right (General Kornilov, for example) began to think of a coup d'état, Lenin was already on the way to convincing his Bolshevik faction that power should be seized in an armed uprising, but in July 1917 he suffered a serious setback. Some of his followers thought of putting his 'April prescriptions' into practice in an unorganised and spontaneous way: they tried to exploit the Bolshevik conference and street demonstration in Petrograd to spark off a riot and ultimately a coup d'état. Incredible as it may seem, they came within a hair's breadth of success. In the end the Provisional Government managed to muster a battalion of loyal troops who dispersed the rioting Bolsheviks with machine-gun fire. Lenin had to run for his life and many other Bolsheviks, among them Trotsky and Stalin, ended up in prison. However, Lenin learned a lesson even from this failure; he bacame absolutely convinced that an organised coup would bring him power. He continued to bombard the remaining Bolshevik leaders with his instructions to organise a coup d'état against the feeble Provisional Government.

On 23 October 1917 the Central Committee of the Bolshevik Party finally yielded and voted overwhelmingly to execute Lenin's idea of the armed uprising and risk their personal and the party's political future in this dangerous enterprise. This decision meant that this time there would be no spontaneity, but all would be planned and well prepared. However, already in September 1917 the Bolshevik plotters were forewarned that their coup would have to be better organised than that of General Kornilov, whose attempt had just collapsed. But while undoubtedly impressed by this failure, Lenin and the Bolsheviks were convinced that they could stage-manage their coup much better than the general. Militarily they did not have to be more efficient – all they needed was the neutrality of the Russian army. September was for them a turning point.

On 11 September, after his release, Leon Trotsky, who had joined the Bolshevik Party and shared Lenin's ideas, was not only elected President of the Petrograd Soviet of Workers and Soldiers but also personally took on serious preparations for a coup. Curiously enough, despite Trotsky's advocacy of a coup, at the decisive party meeting he was not included in the party revolutionary centre which was to prepare the uprising.* Bubnov, Dzerzhinski, Sverdlov, Stalin and Uritsky, who formed the committee, could not hope to pull off a successful uprising. Nonetheless, aided by Trotsky, who was in charge of revolutionary preparations in the Workers' Soviets and among soldiers, and prompted by Lenin, they were all to play an important role. However, Trotsky's role was to be decisive. He gained

*In 1967 Soviet historians asserted that the centre existed, but it is still unproven.

the neutrality of the Petrograd garrison and enabled the Bolsheviks' tactical plans to be carried out.

The size of the garrison troops under the command of the Petrograd Military District appeared most intimidating; when thinking of the numbers no one in his right mind could even contemplate an armed coup. However Trotsky, as Chairman of the Workers' and Soldiers' Soviet, knew the military situation well enough to become convinced that all this might was really a wooden giant with clay legs. Nonetheless, garrison troops amounted to some 350,000 men, and to neutralise them all would require an excellent pretext. Trotsky immediately found a most convincing one. Petrograd garrison troops feared only one thing, namely a transfer to the fronts for active duty, and this was precisely what the Provisional Government was planning for them. Trotsky therefore decided that they should stay in Petrograd to defend the revolution instead. After a campaign of agitation along these lines only two regiments refused to act on Trotsky's orders. Only some 63,000 guard reserve troops remained to be dealt with, and they were deeply demoralised; but Trotsky was convinced that they would neither heed Bolshevik orders nor support the Provisional Government. Then there were some 25,000 infantry, 5,000 women volunteers and 7,000 officer-cadets. The task not only of neutralising them, but also of converting some of them to the Bolshevik cause, was infinitely more difficult than dealing with the garrison. However, again the strength of these forces was impressive only on paper. Soon Trotsky found out that they were quite leaderless and would never act positively; they had one common hatred, and that was the Provisional Government. Thus Trotsky and the Bolsheviks made the right but risky deduction that their opponents would cancel themselves out.

For the purpose of the uprising, Trotsky decided to mobilise and make use of the Petrograd Soldiers' Soviet and its special sub-committee, the Revolutionary Military Committee. The Bolshevik Party heavily infiltrated both the Soviet and its committee with its military experts, including Antonov-Ovseyenko and Podvoysky. Antonov was secretary of the sub-committee and completely eclipsed the chairman, a Left Social Revolutionary, P.E. Lazimir, who proved rather naive and later joined the Bolshevik Party. Though the Bolsheviks were a minority on this committee they made it a most prestigious and pliant tool. There were, however, other forces on which Lenin, Trotsky and the Bolsheviks could call: some 10,-12,000 Red Guards who, under the command of I. Yurenev, had only just been armed by the Provisional Government itself. But the most important source of armed power for the Bolsheviks was the Baltic Fleet which contained some 60,000 shock troops of the revolution, tough sailors. The political basis of Bolshevik power in Petrograd was the factory committees and the 11 districts of the city which they controlled, but above all the Soviet of the Workers and Soldiers dominated by Trotsky.

Power was to be seized on behalf of the Soviets, and the opening meeting of the All-Russian Congress of the Soviets became the target day. Lenin was to announce the seizure of power to the Congress and then form the new government on its behalf.

When on 29 October 1917 Lenin returned clandestinely to Petrograd from Finland to take part in the actual uprising, all the organisations and forces went into preliminary action. However, though simple and clear the Bolshevik plans also contained flaws. Antonov-Ovseyenko, who was in charge of military planning, envisaged the occupation of the Winter Palace, the seat of the Provisional Government, as well as the Maryinsky and Tauride Palaces which housed the Pre-Parliament and Duma respectively. This was logical, since the symbols of power had to be liquidated. But he also wanted to occupy points of strategic importance, such as railway stations, telegraph offices, the main post office, the state bank, the telephone exchange and even the electricity and water works. But these tasks were beyond his means and they should have been reduced in numbers. Above all he forgot about the defence of the Smolny Institute itself. This was the seat of the Petrograd Soviet and henceforth the headquarters of the armed uprising. In this institute, originally for young noble ladies, the All-Russian Congress of Soviets was to take place. That such a vital centre should be left undefended until the last moment was a dangerous oversight. For really effective military forces Antonov-Ovseyenko had to rely on the Baltic Fleet which was outside his immediate control at Kronstadt and Helsingfors (Helsinki). In fact he could not start the revolutionary machine without the sailors and they all arrived very late. All these flaws made the outcome of the uprising rather problematic. Nevertheless on October 27 the central committee and Lenin decided to go ahead. Lenin and Piatnitsky informed the committee members that Moscow would rise simultaneously with Petrograd. This made the uprising in Petrograd inevitable despite the flaws. Two days later, at another central committee session, Lenin made sure that everyone thought of and prepared for nothing but the insurrection. Though the central committee continued to meet frequently in order to retain its grip on the plans and actions, politically it was the Soviets, above all the Petrograd one, which were struggling for power.

Since the Bolshevik Party also put into action an elaborate plan of military deception, the insurrection itself was to be directed by the Revolutionary Military Committee. On 2 November 1917 the sub-committee was finally established and firmly put under Bolshevik control. On that very day Lenin met the Bolshevik military organisers and reprimanded Zinoviev and Kamenev for opposing the uprising. Next day the Revolutionary Military Committee established its staff and appointed commissars who were detailed to various regiments to keep them neutral or gain them to the Bolshevik cause: Kiselev was sent to the 1st Reserve

Car Company, Zaitsov went to the Egersky Guard Regiment, Gorbatchenko to the Volynsky, Ter-Arutiunyan to the Peter and Paul Fortress, and so on. On the same day the Revolutionary Military Committee issued an ultimatum to Colonel Polkovnikov who wanted to transfer Petrograd garrison troops to the front. The troops would not go in spite of his orders. Thus the neutrality of the Petrograd garrison was founded on self-interest, not on loyalties or ideological adherence.

Throughout November 4 the Revolutionary Military Committee continued its preparations for the uprising. It detailed many more commissars to other regiments, railway stations and ships moored on the Neva. Yet Trotsky was not happy with developments so far: several delays and half measures were upsetting his plans. Thus the Social Revolutionary members forced the Revolutionary Military Committee to declare publicly that it was not the Headquarters of a revolutionary rising, but a defence organ of the Petrograd garrison. Though obviously a paper declaration not binding on the Bolsheviks, it was nevertheless confusing. In the evening Antonov's report on the measures taken by the Revolutionary Committee were approved by the Petrograd Soviet, which was a political success for the Bolsheviks. But the move succeeded in confusing and deceiving the Left Social Revolutionaries who helped the Bolsheviks to control the Soviet sub-committee; at the same time Trotsky found out that the Peter and Paul Fortress was not quite neutral and its control remained a condition for any armed rising.

The following day was spent in final checks on the Petrograd garrison. Soviet representatives, and Trotsky personally, had to visit and convince the Fortress and 'recalcitrant' units, above all the Bicycle Battalion which had already once before checked Bolshevik ambitions. After this final round of inspections, all was ready for the ultimate *coup de force* planned for the next day. However, at long last the Provisional Government saw through the facade of feints, and decided on counter-measures. It is clear that these came too late and only slightly delayed the Bolshevik success.

On November 6 at 1.55 am the Military District Headquarters began to counteract the orders of the Revolutionary Military Committee, which inevitably led to insurrection. Since the command could not be sure of the loyalty of the Petrograd garrison, it called for élite units stationed in the vicinity of the capital. The Rifle Regiment at Tsarkoe Selo was ordered to Petrograd, and an hour later so was the 1st company of the Peterhof officer-cadets. Early in the morning the Pavlovsk Battery was called to Petrograd as well as the Women's Battalion. At 5.30 am the Provisional Government Commissar arrived with a picket of soldiers at the printing plant of the *Rabochy put,* a Bolshevik newspaper, and after some resistance closed it down. This action seems to have exhausted further determination of the Provisional Government to oppose the Bolshevik coup and nothing else was done.

In the meantime the Bolsheviks were putting the finishing touches to the preparations for the rising itself; at 8 am (or 9 am) the central committee met again and detailed Kamenev and Berzin to work politically with the Left Social Revolutionaries. Bubnov was put in charge of railways and Dzerzhinsky of post and telegraph services. Since the Smolny Institute, the political and military headquarters, could easily be raided by government troops, it was decided to set up a reserve HQ in the Fortress. Afterwards the central committee members dispersed for action. At the same time the Revolutionary Military Committee issued its defiant Order No.1: it appealed to everyone for aid, claiming that the Petrograd Soviet and the committee were in danger; government armies were marching on the capital, the *Rabochy put* was closed down as well as the *Soldat* and it was clear that reactionary elements were plotting against the scheduled Soviet congress and the Constituent Assembly which was to be elected shortly.

After this tactical appeal which was, of course, quite without foundations, the commissars and the Revolutionary Military Committee went into full action. To start with the commissars persuaded some units of the Litovsky Regiment to go to the Bolshevik printing press and reopen it. It was considered politically vital that the Bolshevik Party should maintain open communication with the Petrograd public. The operation was easy: the police guards at the *Rabochy put* went off most willingly when it was explained to them that the order of closure was issued without the authority of the Revolutionary Military Committee and was therefore invalid. When shortly afterwards the District Military HQ riposted with an empty declaration that only its orders were to be obeyed, it became clear that the coup would be smooth. General Bagrateni then issued another futile order: arms and ammunition were to be issued from the Petrograd arsenal on his orders only. Subsequent sacking of the' Bolshevik commissars was not only futile but theoretical, for they controlled the situation on the spot and did the sacking themselves. The Bolsheviks had made a good start.

But all was not lost yet for the Provisional Government. It still found itself obeyed, and put into operation several counter-measures. Thus the Smolny Institute's telephones were disconnected and consequently communications between the HQ and the men in action were considerably slowed down. The cruiser *Aurora*, which was ordered back to its Kronstadt base from the Neva mooring, the very centre of Petrograd, started preparations for sailing. Above all three officer-cadet units and the Women's Battalion which arrived to protect the Provisional Government began to execute their orders: they lifted the bridges across the Neva so that no outside force could enter the city itself. It was abundantly clear that the Bolsheviks would have to bring in their Red Guards from the outer suburbs and sailors from the naval bases across the bridges, and this measure was intended to stop them. The Bolsheviks themselves suffered a setback when the Helsingfors sailors, without whom they could not possibly take the whole capital and keep it, failed to arrive. All the same they proceeded with their final measures: Trotsky told a meeting of some of the available central committee men that the Provisional Government would simply be arrested and a new government elected by the congress of the Soviets. Last but not least Lenin arrived in person (heavily disguised) to supervise the coup and assume political leadership afterwards.

While the coup d'état was properly to start the next day, throughout 6 November 1917 both sides were busy with measures and counter-measures which obscured the beginning of the coup. It is not even clear who started first. The Bolsheviks began to load their Red Guards in the suburbs onto requisitioned lorries and concentrate them around the Smolny. But to do it they had to cross the bridges and enter the city. According to government orders they should have been unable to reach the Smolny, for the bridges were controlled by government troops. However, considerable confusion surrounded the bridges: the Liteyny Bridge was not lifted because the cadets who arrived to perform the operation were disarmed by an unidentified unit, presumably from the Petrograd garrison, and sent back to their barracks. The Troitsky Bridge which was to be raised by the Women's Battalion remained down, presumably because the operation proved too difficult for the brave women in military uniform. But the Nikolayevsky Bridge went up and Red Guards trying to cross the Neva this way were stopped and disarmed, though not arrested. The Dvortsovy Bridge was also under strict government control. Thus Bolshevik operations must have been disrupted even by these inefficient counter-measures. However, in the evening, when the women and cadets were to be relieved, no relief came and they departed, all the bridges passing under the control of garrison troops dispatched there by the Revolutionary Military Committee. On the eve of the coup the city was wide open for the revolutionary forces.

During the evening of the same day the Provisional Government suffered further reverses. The units of the élite Cyclist Battalion which guarded the Winter Palace, the seat of the government, decided to leave their posts and withdraw to their billets. Then it became known that the officer-cadets from the military academies outside Petrograd refused to obey orders to move to the capital: the Pavlovsk Battery would not come either. Next came a Bolshevik reverse. When at 5 pm Commissar Pestkovsky arrived to take over the Telephone Exchange the employees refused to cooperate with him and his soldiers, and for the time being at least the Bolsheviks did not really control this means of communication, for the Commissar and his troops could not work the exchange on their own. The same evening Trotsky attended the meeting of the Petrograd Soviet and reported on the situation in the city and measures taken by the

Revolutionary Military Committee. He carried on with the Bolshevik deception plan and disclaimed any knowledge of a military uprising, saying that this would take place only if forced on the Soviets and its committee which was peacefully awaiting the congress of the Soviets and cared for nothing else. Simultaneously with this meeting Bolshevik commissars held meetings in all the barracks of the Petrograd garrison requesting the soldiers to protect the Soviet and the congress against any reactionary threats. At the same time Bolshevik units beat off two desperate actions by the Provisional Government: they sent off a police detachment which had turned up to close the *Rabochy put* down again and disarmed cadets who attempted to do the same with the Petrograd Soviet journal. Commissar Stark and some Kronstadt sailors, who began to arrive during the day, peacefully took over the Telegraph Exchange and later Commissar Katz and his unit occupied the Baltic Railway Station to make sure that Bolshevik reinforcements arrived safely, and government forces, if any, not at all. At 10 pm Lenin finally reached the Smolny and at midnight the Red Guards were sent out to patrol the city streets and take over control from government police and troops.

In the early hours of November 7 the meticulously prepared coup (or armed uprising) swung into full action. Units of the Sapper Battalion led by their commissar took over the last railway station, Nikolayev; at the same time Commissar Feirman (not a Bolshevik but a Left Social Revolutionary) seized the Central Electricity Station and cut off power to government buildings. It is clear that Commissar Feirman and many others, both leaders and men, were completely deceived by the Bolshevik tactics. The commissar thought he was acting in the interest of the Petrograd Soviet and the Revolutionary Military Committee supposedly controlled by his Left Social Revolutionary comrades. He was under no deception when he occupied the Central Post Office, but when he ordered the cutting off of the telephone lines from the Winter Palace and the Military District HQ, his orders were not obeyed.

While many people were deceived by Bolshevik tactics, it is obvious that the preparations for a Bolshevik coup were known to their opponents, and above all to the Provisional Government which still attempted counter-measures. Yet the coup caught the Provisional Government in complete disarray. At about 3 am on the morning of November 7 the Pavlovsky Regiment patrols, which acted on the Revolutionary Military Committee's orders, stopped a car and arrested its two occupants. They turned out to be Minister Kartashev and the chief of the Provisional Government's counter-espionage, Lieutenant-Colonel Surin. Neither had any idea of what was going on and why they were arrested. They were taken to the Smolny where Dzenis, one of the Bolshevik commissars, put the two men under arrest, released the Minister immediately and detained the colonel for only a short while. There were no other arrests during the coup except at the end, when ministers were put under arrest and conducted to the Fortress prison.

The see-saw struggle over the bridges finally came to an end. The Kronstadt sailors began to take an active part in the coup and proved very efficient. The *Aurora,* which failed to sail up the Neva, now moved up to the Nikolayevsky Bridge, landed a party and lowered the bridge so that it could be used by Bolshevik forces. Amazingly the government succeeded in sending an élite unit to the bridge to try and lift it up again, but the move failed. In the meantime some 200 Red Guards arrived to guard the bridge, and such numbers could not be dislodged without bloodshed; both Bolshevik and government forces shrank from it. The effects of the Bolshevik occupation of various strategic points in the capital began to be felt. Officer-cadets from Peterhof, who had shown willingness to come to the aid of the Provisional Government when the other academies had refused, could not depart, for the railway line and stations were under the control of the Revolutionary Military Committee which would not let them through. Trotsky's estimate that the Provisional Government would find precious little with which to defend itself was proving right.

However discouraging all this must have seemed to the Provisional Government, it was far from giving up the struggle. The pattern of the coup was becoming clear and Kerensky decided to act personally. After all the élite 1st, 4th and 14th Don Cavalry Regiments were part of the Petrograd garrison and could be called upon. These Cossack troops alone could put an end to any coup in strictly military terms but despite their anti-Bolshevik feelings they were also deeply demoralised. Three days before the coup they wanted to cross-march through the capital (the cross-march was a traditional religious ceremony) but were forbidden to do so by the Provisional Government. Now the same government in the person of the Prime Minister was appealing to them to protect it and die for it. Kerensky forced the commanding officer of the Petrograd Military District, General Bagrateni, and Commissar Malevsky to send telegrams to these Cossack regiments ordering them to come to his aid. But their reply was a blunt 'no'. Trotsky's other prediction was proved right.

After this failure Kerensky became frantic. He telegraphed to General Cheremisov, C-in-C of the Northern Front, to send his élite formations to the defence of the capital in order to suppress the Bolshevik coup. Once again Cossack regiments were called for, but they proved very slow and in the end never arrived in the capital. The Bicycle Battalion and the Oranienbaum cadets, who were ordered to come to the Winter Palace to protect the government, also failed to arrive. During this time of desperate bungling, Bolshevik forces, aided by confused Social Revolutionary commissars, occupied the National Bank, the Telephone Exchange and the Warsaw Railway Station. Commissar Kislyakov-Uralov, detailed to take over all the printing presses in Petrograd, completed the operations by 11 am. The Bolshevik central committee was in continuous session, or better was actively participating in the coup. On instructions from the central committee the Revolutionary Military Committee moved out of the Smolny and formed their field HQ. Antonov, Bubnov, Podvoysky and Chudnovsky moved out to conduct operations in person. At 10 am Lenin, who was at the Smolny through the night, felt strong enough to issue his first political declaration, which was plastered all over the capital and told the Russian citizens that the Provisional Government was no more. Although this was strictly speaking inaccurate, the Provisional Government was certainly on the way out.

Frantic telephoning and telegraphing went on through the morning, but there was very little to show for it. Colonel Polkovnikov was forced by Kerensky to request aid not only from General Cheremisov but also from the Generalissimo of the Russian armies in the field, General Dukhonin. But their response proved disappointing too, and by 11 am Kerensky made his own decision. Leaving the government in the Winter Palace he requisitioned two American cars and left for the northern armies' HQ. The idea was to bring back loyal troops who would suppress the Bolshevik uprising, but it was clear to friend and foe alike that he was abandoning the capital to the insurrectionists. After this departure no one attempted any counter-measures and everyone waited passively for the inevitable conclusion. Needless to say, Kerensky never returned to the capital.

Even though the Bolsheviks did not know of Kerensky's departure, it became clear that the crowning success of the coup would come with the taking of the Winter Palace where the headless Provisional Government was in session. At noon Bolshevik sailors and units of the Lithuanian and Cuxholm Regiments politely dissolved the Pre-Parliament, the last political body supporting the Provisional Government, took over the Admiralty and began to move against the Winter Palace itself. As they began to encircle the Palace, Trotsky, presiding over the Petrograd Soviet meeting, once again declared that the Provisional Government was dead. He was, however, absolutely right when he said that the 'revolution' was a peaceful one without any bloodshed so far. Lenin also addressed the meeting, and told the members that power was theirs and bade them to form a government. The session then passed Volodarsky's resolution which praised the successful uprising, urged the formation of a new government which would immediately open peace negotiations, order wholesale nationalisation and land distribution. At 2 pm the decisive moment of the uprising had arrived: the Winter Palace was finally sealed off and surrounded by Bolshevik forces. Antonov-Ovseyenko took personal charge of the forces concentrated against the Palace, the bulk of which was the Kronstadt and 2nd Baltic Fleet sailors who had finally arrived in the morning. He also had units of the Pavlovsky and Keksgolm Regiments which joined the uprising and the Petrograd, Vyborg and Vasileostrov Red

Guards. But even with these relatively 'huge' forces Antonov hesitated and decided to attack the Palace at 9 pm under the cover of darkness. Paradoxically, after Kerensky abandoned the defence of the capital as hopeless and before the Bolsheviks isolated it, the hapless government managed to muster its defence forces. Despite their previous refusal, units of the 14th Don Cossack Regiment did after all arrive at the Palace. They were preceded by various groups of officer-cadets and the Women's Battalion. The Government appointed a three-man defence committee (Kishkin, Palchinsky, Butenberg) and Colonel Anayev became officer-in-command. However, the vigour and determination of Kerensky was missing and nothing but desperate telephoning was done after these measures. Commissar Stankievich again asked General Dukhonin's aid but was told bluntly to help himself. The Generalissimo asked the commissar what had happened to the loyal Cyclist Battalion and could not be answered because no one knew anything about it. Then the Bolshevik forces took the last important centre of administration, the Ministry of War next to the Winter Palace. When Antonov-Ovseyenko issued his ultimatum for surrender, and was bravely answered by the Provisional Government, the defence of the Palace began to crumble. Once again confusion favoured the Bolsheviks: Commissar Akashev ordered the artillery cadets and their four guns back to their billets and was obeyed. The commissar and two other cadets were caught in time and arrested, but the unit got away, considerably weakening the defence.

As the evening drew near the defence forces began to feel terribly demoralised, but their opponents also lacked resolution. No one wanted bloodshed and it became clear that whoever persevered longest would win. The élite Cossack units which did turn up at the Palace regretted it deeply. They felt offended at being ranged side by side with the Women's Battalion. Most of the officer-cadets felt like following their Michael Academy comrades, and other army officers in the Palace, in the euphoria of the place, got hopelessly drunk. General Palchinsky had very little to coordinate and the defence of the Palace rested in fact in the hands of the old tsarist commissioners who controlled the gates and the lights. After a good evening meal, the ministers once again refused to surrender and made it known that they were prepared, if necessary, to face heroic death. After this demoralising declaration, they ordered the lights to be put out. The unexpected darkness caused considerable commotion among besiegers and besieged alike. In the resulting confusion the first shots were fired and four officer-cadets defending the Palace were hit, probably by their own fire. Seeing their comrades slightly wounded the Constantine Academy cadets decided to return to their quarters and left without telling anyone.

When the news of their departure finally filtered to the Smolny and to the anxious ministers it elicited two different reactions. Lenin urged his forces to take the Palace immediately; the ministers began frantic telephoning again for aid. They succeeded in getting in touch with the Petrograd Duma (Municipal Council) and drew encouragement from that quarter. The Duma apparently was also under attack by Bolshevik forces but it succeeded in beating them off, and presently would undertake negotiations with the Bolsheviks to relieve the besieged government. A Duma delegation then actually left for the Smolny, but its mediation was rejected. The delegates were told to go to the Winter Palace and talk the Provisional Government into surrender. When the *Aurora* and the Fortress garrisons also refused to receive Duma delegations, the Duma leaders called on some 300 followers who had gathered outside the Municipal Building to form a marching column and led them to the Winter Palace. Their intention was to relieve the besieged rather than persuade them to surrender. But they were an unarmed column: they were halted several times and when they reached the Palace perimeter Bolshevik units dispersed them. The besieged knew nothing of the outcome of this abortive attempt, but could see that no relief was coming. The GHQ of Mogilev telephoned late in the evening to say that the Cyclist Battalion and three other regiments were on the way to Petrograd. But General Cheremisov stopped all troops moving towards the capital pending further orders.

More immediately around the Palace the Bolsheviks began to feel restless when the time fixed for the assault approached. At 9.30 pm the first fusillade burst out, but no one seems to have been wounded. Ten minutes later the *Aurora* was finally persuaded to fire at the Palace to cow it into submission. Most of these shots, however, went wide and missed the target. Then the 300-strong Cossack contingent, led by its colonel, negotiated a free passage through the ranks of the Pavlovsky Regiment, which was among the forces besieging the Palace, and left for their billets. Once again, no one was told of this desertion, but when it became known and after another salvo from the *Aurora*, the Women's Battalion tried a sortie, then surrendered and was disarmed. After them another small unit of cadets was let through the ranks of the besiegers to their academy: defence forces were rapidly melting away, but Antonov-Ovseyenko still did not give orders for the final assault. Wild unsystematic shooting by both sides was always followed by negotiations and this game continued throughout the hours of darkness. But the Palace continued to defy Bolshevik forces. Bolshevik agitators who penetrated into the Palace were disarmed and interned in various rooms within the Palace. As time went on the defending forces became so weak that they felt unable to cope with such numbers of agitators and parliamentarians.

Around 11 pm Chudnovsky who had been to the Palace as a negotiator realised that there were no defenders left and ordered the final assault. The excited and restless Red Guards, garrison soldiers and sailors broke through the gates and began a cautious but systematic penetration of the

Palace, room after room fell to the advancing Bolsheviks in search of the Provisional Government now defended by a mere handful of young cadets. Finally at 1.50 am on 8 November 1917 Bolshevik forces reached the Malachite room where the government sat waiting. Antonov-Ovseyenko was quickly told of the discovery: he arrived and arrested the ministers in the name of the Revolutionary Military Committee. Ten minutes later, he telephoned the Smolny Institute that the Winter Palace, the last bastion of the Provisional Government was under Bolshevik control. He then had plenty of trouble getting the arrested ministers safely to prison. The incensed victors wanted to lynch them. Perhaps as a result of this disappointment or to celebrate the accomplishment of the last important task of the coup, Bolshevik forces in turn melted away in one immense drunken orgy.

Even before this final military victory in the capital, Lenin began to act as if he were master of the whole country. At 10.45 pm, when most of the delegates for the 2nd Congress of the Workers' and Soldiers' Soviets arrived, the Bolsheviks found out that they controlled a clear working majority. The Menshevik President Dan, knowing this, refused to open the Congress and Lenin therefore seized the initiative and proposed to the assembled delegates the election of a new praesidium to take over the management of the Congress. The 515 delegates present voted 14 Bolsheviks onto the new body; Lenin naturally led the Bolshevik faction and Trotsky, Zinoviev, Kamenev, Antonov-Ovseyenko and Krylenko were among the newly elected members. The Left Social Revolutionaries had seven members, the Mensheviks three and there was one Menshevik-Internationalist on this important body. The Bolshevik-dominated praesidium then threw out all resolutions condemning the Bolshevik uprising and proposed their own agenda which was to deal with more immediate tasks: the formation of a new government, problems of war and peace and the Constitutional Assembly.

Smarting under this defeat all the opposition delegates left *en masse,* abandoning the Congress to the Bolsheviks. After the walk-out and in order to consider the agenda and resolutions more fully, the Bolsheviks adjourned the session. Shortly after the adjournment Lenin heard that the Winter Palace had finally been taken, and the Provisional Government was on its way to prison. He could form a new government. At 3 am when the Congress reassembled, Lenin personally gave the news of the Palace's fall. Subsequently it was decided to form revolutionary committees on the Northern Front and in all army units. Before the session adjourned once again the delegates overwhelmingly sanctioned the uprising (only 12 voted against). The Congress was reconvened for 9 pm on November 8. By then Lenin was Prime Minister (Chairman) and his government (the Council of National Commissars) was warmly applauded by the delegates. Among other things, the Congress approved decrees presented to it by the chairman of the council: the decree on immediate peace was passed unanimously, as well as that regulating the distribution of land. The Congress also approved the composition of the new government, which included Trotsky as Foreign Commissar and Stalin as Commissar of Nationalities. Then the Congress closed and the delegates dispersed.

Lenin was in power as a result of the uprising, but at this stage he controlled only the imperial capital, and even that was not certain. The Bolsheviks also rose in Moscow, but there the fighting was for real and they had to use artillery to defeat their opponents. Only on 16 November did they succeed in putting down and reducing all the pockets of resistance. In several other cities attempts were made at takeovers, but they were unsuccessful. Only the faraway Krasnoyarsk became Bolshevik on November 11 and Krasnovodsk followed the next day. The almost bizarre coup of 7 November 1917 was but a bloodless beginning of a bloody civil war.

Not unexpectedly the first serious threat to Bolshevik power came from the trade unions: the railway workers and civil servants. The first one was particularly dangerous, for without the railways the Bolsheviks would have been isolated in the capital and could not have expanded their control. A railway strike would disrupt their operations against centres of military and political opposition as well as threaten food supplies for the capital and the towns which were gradually coming under their control. Moreover, if the striking railmen let through military units sent to suppress them, the very existence of the Bolshevik government might be in balance. Both Lenin and the Bolshevik central committee understood the situation quite clearly and while Lenin was too busy with military matters, the central committee in his absence decided to respond to the railway union's ultimatum. Sokolnikov and Kamenev were detailed for negotiations and they met the railwaymen's representatives and other socialists on 12 November 1917.

The railway unions knew that they were in a strong position and therefore advanced far-reaching political demands. They demanded an immediate armistice lasting three days and then a new coalition government with the Bolsheviks and without Lenin. Kamenev, Sokolnikov and Ryazanov went tactically too far when they accepted these proposals. At this stage, when the Bolsheviks had to cope with cadet uprisings in Petrograd and fight a battle with the advancing Cossacks under General Krasnov, Lenin was ready to broaden his government at least while these dangers and the railway threat lasted, but he was most unwilling to resign. On 14 November Lenin persuaded the central committee that Kamenev and his friends were 'capitulators' and politically quite wrong; instead of continuing negotiations the central committee in turn issued an ultimatum to the railway union and pronounced itself against any cooperation with the Mensheviks and Right Social Revolutionaries. Further meetings were simply boycotted and Kamenev and his group had to resign from their offices when they refused to comply with the decisions of Lenin and the central committee. However dangerous these internal dissentions were, they were certainly less ominous than a railway strike which in the end was never declared. Lenin gained some breathing space to sort out internal party problems as well as the railway challenge, and the Bolsheviks could turn to the other strike issue.

Civil servants went on strike in protest against the Bolshevik coup d'état and Bolshevik leaders found out about the strike when they arrived to claim ministries and start administering the country anew. The People's Commissars had to stay in the Smolny Institute and run their department from there. On 17 November Trotsky arrived with a group of sailors at the Commissariat of Foreign Affiars and found it deserted. Councillor Tatishchev was apprehended and forced to hand over the keys to safes containing cyphers and archives. On 21 November when Menzhinsky tried to take over the Ministry of Finance he had to use armed guards and arrest senior civil servants. On 27 November 1917 the Bolsheviks acted more decisively: the civil service strike committee was arrested, strikers drafted into the army and immediately sent to the front. The civil service strike, which paralysed Bolshevik attempts at administering the country from the capital through the old administrative machine, never really ended. Bolshevik Commissars had to build Commissariats from scratch: they hired a few strike-breaking officials and in most cases had to employ their wives and relations. Thus the Commissariat of education was staffed by wives: Krupskaya heading one section, Mrs Menzhinskaya another. In the confusion and chaos that reigned everywhere it was clearly much less important to administer the country through central Commissariats than to control it politically and militarily. The Bolsheviks therefore decided to divert their attention to this dual control.

Bolshevik Takeover of the Armies in the Field

It became imperative to neutralise the Russian armies, if they could not be controlled and gained over to the Bolsheviks. The Northern front, because of its proximity to Petrograd, was the most important. But because of general demoralisation, combined with internal dissention among the officers, it proved the easiest to control. Pskov, in which the front HQ was situated, came under control of the newly formed Revolutionary Military Committee on 7 November 1917. The committee, dominated by Bolsheviks, immediately stopped all movements of troops and attempted to take over the town. The Pskov Soviet went Bolshevik after an improvised election and soldiers and officers released from the local jail joined the Bolshevik units which finally drove out the loyal units, especially from the railway station. In any case General Cherimisov, commanding the Northern front, was against helping the Provisional Government, and in particular Premier Kerensky. Miraculously, despite this dual opposition, units of General Krasnov's Cossack division managed to pass through Pskov and leave in the direction of Petrograd. Commissar Voytinsky also left for the 'march' on Petrograd, but he and Kerensky seemed far from popular with the Cossack troops coming to their aid. The railways proved unusable and the Cossacks drove on with their horses. Without any opposition they took Gatchina, but then found their way barred by hurriedly erected defences at Pulkovo Heights. The Bolsheviks concentrated here all their military might from the capital: Baltic sailors, Red Guards and all sorts of units led by a Left Social Revolutionary, Lieutenant-Colonel Muravyov. The Bolsheviks also succeeded in placing into position a number of guns which then decided the ensuing engagement. Krasnov sent his horsemen against Bolshevik positions four times and when their attacks were beaten off he withdrew to Gatchina to await reinforcements. This was militarily a decisive moment: if an advance continued the Bolshevik uprising could be nipped in the bud and the Provisional Government re-established. Else, it was the final act in the defeat of the Provisional regime. General Niessel, head of the French Military Mission in Russia, was at Gatchina and asked both Premier Kerensky and General Krasnov about their subsequent plan of action: they had none. On 14 November 1917 Bolshevik negotiators, led by Dybenko and Trushin, suddenly arrived at Gatchina and began to talk to Cossack soldiers. It became clear that an armistice would be arranged: the Cossacks would hand over Kerensky to the Bolsheviks and the Bolsheviks promised to exclude Lenin from the government. Neither side kept the conditions of the armistice: Kerensky disappeared, and Lenin sorted out problems to his own satisfaction. The Cossacks were allowed to proceed home, but for good measure they did hand over their general to the Bolsheviks. However, Krasnov was soon released on a word of honour that he would not fight against the Bolsheviks again, and followed his soldiers to the Don.

This was the only serious military threat that Petrograd and the Bolsheviks had to face from the Northern Front armies. Nothing else materialised although the commanding general of the 5th Army, V.G. Boldyrev, tried hard to send to Petrograd an armoured unit; Bolshevik soldiers intercepted it and sent it back to Dvinsk to the hapless general. General Yuzefovich, commanding the crucial 12th Army, could not prevent the Bolsheviks from taking over, when they succeeded in sending round the Latvian Rifles who went over to them *en masse* . The 1st Army was against helping the Provisional Government even before the Bolshevik uprising; subsequently it offered units for the protection of the Petrograd Soviet. On the whole the Northern Front was neutralised from the very beginning and passed under Bolshevik control without much delay. As everywhere else the Bolsheviks showed political initiative and backed it skilfully by elections or re-elections, as well as loyal military units, or even divisions. The anti-Bolshevik Committees for the Salvation of the Motherland and the Revolution never got off the ground politically; militarily they could never muster enough soldiers to back them.

Such development and *dénouement* repeated themselves at all the remaining fronts, the Western, South Western and Rumanian, though with local variations. The Western front command remained loyal to the Provisional Government and even managed to beat the Bolsheviks at Minsk, when they formed a revolutionary committee and tried to take over the front. On 8 November 1917 Cossacks re-took the city, the Menshevik commissar Kolotukhin formed a Committee for the Salvation of the Motherland and then waited. The Bolsheviks convoked congresses in the three armies which formed the front and managed to gain control quite peacefully through the vote. By 19 November 1917 they also controlled an armoured train which arrived at Minsk and re-took the city and the front for the Bolsheviks. On 25 November General Baluyev was under arrest; Orsha, a railway junction, stopped reinforcements sent to Moscow to suppress the Bolsheviks there and units of the Western Front began to converge on Mogilyov to take over the GHQ of the Russian armies.

The Stavka, as the GHQ was called, remained loyal to the Provisional Government, and General Dukhonin, who was temporarily in command, refused to comply with Bolshevik orders. He continued to send troops against the Bolsheviks in Petrograd and Moscow but without significant success. Dukhonin also refused to obey Lenin's order to start armistice negotiations with the Germans, and was replaced by Ensign Krylenko, who was sent from Petrograd to take over. On 1 December 1917 Mogilyov was surrounded by units of the 2nd Army led by R.I. Berzin and after two days of manoeuvering and fighting, the town and Stavka were taken. The soldiers lynched Dukhonin and Krylenko immediately sent off a delegation to negotiate with the Germans. Henceforth the Bolsheviks controlled the high command of the Russian armies but it did not help them much in the takeover of the remaining armies.

On the South Western front the struggle for power was complicated by the Ukrainian (nationalist) factor. The armies' committees rejected Bolshevik proposals to recognise the Sovnarkom, the new government, after the Bolshevik uprising. In Kiev, however, the Ukrainian Rada proclaimed itself the supreme organ of power in the Ukraine and accepted local Bolshevik support. Only at Vinnitsa did the Bolsheviks rise and were later defeated by loyalist troops. On 10 November 1917 the Rada suddenly turned on the Bolsheviks, expelled them and gradually won recognition all over the Ukraine. However, the Bolsheviks decided to organise their power basis in the Donets basin and Kharkov, in which they established the alternative Ukrainian government to the Rada. The front command hung uneasily between the Rada and the Bolsheviks, but the armies were neutralised; they were never really brought under Bolshevik control, but dissolved themselves and went home. The Rada continued to defy the Bolshevik central power and on 17 December 1917 Lenin issued his ultimatum: the Rada must submit or accept the imposition of Soviet power.

By January 1918 the Ukraine was a cauldron of chaos and the Bolsheviks launched their drive against the Ukrainian nationalists. Led by Colonel Muravyov of Pulkovo fame Soviet units began to penetrate into the Ukraine without much resistance from the nationalists. Odessa fell on 31 January and on 8 February 1918 Soviet forces drove into Kiev to be joined by the Ukrainian Bolshevik government from Kharkov. The Rada, however, appealed to the Germans, whose armies in turn invaded the country and forced the Bolsheviks to retreat back to Russia.

The Rumanian front proved the most difficult to take over. There army discipline remained reasonably good, officers acted with vigour and political commissars with determination. The front committee protested against the Bolshevik uprising, but also wanted an armistice when the Bolsheviks proclaimed it. General Scherbachev tried to keep his armies going by dissolving units which were showing signs of revolutionary ardour or disloyalty. But he had difficulty in finding a political authority to be loyal to: only the Kishinev Soviet recognised the Sovnarkom and he had the Ukrainian Rada or the far Don Cossack Union to choose from. The Bolsheviks finally succeeded in convoking a Rumanian Front Congress to Odessa and the newly elected leadership joined them. On 10 January 1918 the new leaders arrived at Kishinev for a final takeover, but had to fight for control with nationalist Moldavians. By 16 January 1918 the Bolsheviks controlled not only the towns but also most of the armies of this front. Three days later the Rumanian army took advantage of Russian dissension and struggle, invaded Moldavia and chased out both the Bolsheviks and their opponents. Only General Scherbachev stayed behind, but he also soon left for Paris and émigré diplomacy.

Provinces and Regions

As early as 8 November 1917 the Petrograd Bolshevik committee sent out important telegrams to all the regional and rayon party committees urging them to 'agitate' for the new government and Bolshevik power. To help them directly and back up the paper telegrams, the Petrograd Military Committee sent to 41 *Guberniyas* (provinces) simultaneously some 644 'agitators'. In the first month after the coup d'état the Petrograd committee dispatched to the provinces 106 commissars, 61 instructors and 600 agitators. On 14 November 1917 Lenin appealed to the Bolshevik

Party to take over the whole country; at the same time he sent out experienced party leaders to help local leaders. Ordjonikidze went to the Ukraine and the South; Chudnovsky to the visibly anti-Bolshevik South Western front; S.G. Roshal left for the Rumanian front and A.S. Bubnov for the Don. Voroshilov organised the takeover in the Donets basin, while Volodarsky reinforced the Ukraine, Bessarabia and the Black Sea region. Skrypnik and Kotsubinsky were also helping in the Ukraine, while Slutsky was in the Crimea. All these were essentially political moves and almost invariably they had to be backed by naked power.

Lenin personally insisted on the formation of shock units consisting mainly of Baltic sailors who had proved themselves in the Petrograd coup. In the first three weeks after the uprising some 200 sailors were sent out to various parts of the country to help with the establishment of Bolshevik power. Sometimes their very arrival and show of force were sufficient to achieve the change, as happened at Mogilyov, Syzran, Penza, Kaluga, Gomel, Rybinsk and elsewhere. At other times they had to help local Bolsheviks in armed struggle and their discipline and enthusiasm usually decided the issue.

Thus, for example, in Moscow the arrival of these shock units (some 500 of them) tilted the balance of power in favour of the Bolsheviks. Moscow Bolsheviks found out about the Petrograd victory on 7 November, when the Moscow Bolshevik leader, Nogin, telephoned for action. The Soviet immediately voted for a Bolshevik takeover and formed a Revolutionary Military Committee to effect it. However the mayor of Moscow, Rudnev, received orders from Petrograd to resist the Bolshevik seizure of power in the city. Since the garrison troops proved unreliable Rudnev appealed to Colonel Ryabtsev to 'maintain public order'. The colonel who only had officer-cadets under his command issued a strong declaration, and immediately began to negotiate with Bolshevik leaders who arrived from Petrograd. Neither side wanted to give in and Colonel Ryabtsev had a temporary advantage as his forces succeeded in occupying the Duma itself, several strategic points in the city, as well as the Kremlin, which was the regional military headquarters. On 10 November Bolshevik forces launched attacks on Colonel Ryabtsev, although neither party was ready to fight and both were waiting for reinforcements. The Kremlin was besieged and inconclusive fighting occurred throughout the city. Then Petrograd detachments arrived to reinforce the Bolsheviks, while army units failed to get through to the city. After an abortive attempt at negotiations the Bolsheviks opened artillery fire on their enemies and on the 15th Colonel Ryabtsev's forces surrendered and handed the city to the Bolsheviks.

All round Moscow, in the province, the takeover was on the whole peaceful. At Podolsk, Koloma, Serpukhov and Bogorodsk the Soviets were in Bolshevik hands and they automatically accepted the new Bolshevik government; in fact they were then able to help the Bolsheviks in Moscow who were in danger from the advancing Serbian troops.* The Serpukhov Soviet persuaded the Taruss railwaymen to stop these reinforcements and Moscow became Bolshevik. At Ivanovo (Voznesensk) the Soviet organised a strike on 3 November in support of the Bolshevik uprising in Petrograd, and the takeover there was smooth. At the railway junction Shua M.V. Frunze became chairman of the Revolutionary Committee, thus making it safe for the Bolsheviks. On 8 November 1917 the Bolsheviks took over power quite smoothly at Vladimir and Yaroslavl.

At other places the Bolsheviks had to exploit political confusion to achieve power. Thus at Smolensk the Bolsheviks established a revolutionary committee to take over the city and then the whole province on 8 November. However, the City Council (Duma) which was not Bolshevik refused to submit, formed a Committee for Salvation and even scraped together enough Cossack troops to issue an ultimatum to the Bolshevik Soviet to surrender. The Smolensk Soviet had no choice but fight for power. The demoralised Cossacks were defeated in an armed clash, the city council and the Committee for Salvation dispersed and on 13 November the Bolsheviks controlled another provincial capital. By political manoeuvres and a little fighting the Bolsheviks took over Pskov, which they had to paralyse previously so as not to let through troops against Petrograd. Tver came under Bolshevik control on 10 November after the local liberals (*Kadets*) had been disarmed. In the Volga cities, where the Bolsheviks were in a minority, power was seized surprisingly smoothly. At Nizhny Novgorod the non-Bolshevik majority refused to acknowledge Bolshevik power, so I.P. Romanov and local Bolsheviks immediately formed a revolutionary committee, carried out another election in which they gained a majority and then simply declared themselves Bolshevik. At Kazan the city liberals decided to fight, but surrendered on 8 November. At Samara Kuybyshev and Shvernik were in charge and carried out the changeover by one vote. Tsaritsyn became Bolshevik on 17 November, but at Saratov the Soviet had to fight. The city Duma hoped that the 2nd Orenburg Division (Cossacks) would help it to remain in power, but the Cossacks refused to fight and on 11 November the local Bolsheviks were in control.

In several provincial cities local Bolshevik leaders failed to understand the power takeover effected by Lenin and instead continued to share power with Social Revolutionaries and/or Mensheviks. At Ekaterinburg, where the Bolsheviks were particularly strong, I.M. Malyshev effected the change of control on 8 November. Although the city had also a central committee emissary, P.D. Khokhryakov, for consultation it surprisingly formed a coalition Revolutionary Military Committee, 'throwing power away'. Only on 5 December 1917, after intervention from Petrograd, did the committee become purely Bolshevik and this Urals province came decidedly under Bolshevik control. Similar political difficulties occurred

*A Serbian division was attached to the Western front.

for example at Tula and Kursk and decisive Bolshevik control was established only late in December. Archangel, Viatka, Olonets and Vologda came under Bolshevik control in early 1918.

So far political manoeuvering and a little fighting allowed the Bolsheviks to obtain power. However, in the more distant provinces, where the Bolsheviks were in a tiny minority, or had no Russian troops to fight for them, local powers were strong enough to assert themselves and to refuse submission: in such cases fighting for power went on for some considerable time. At Astrakhan and in that province, where the 156th Regiment joined the Bolsheviks, real fighting lasted some four months; the same happened on the Don, Kuban and Terek. The struggle for the Don was resolved only in February 1918; Kuban and Terek submitted in March 1918. In the Caucasus only Baku went Bolshevik on 15 November, while the rest of Adzerbeijan, together with Georgia and Armenia, turned nationalist and mainly for international reasons escaped Bolshevik seizure of power.

In the huge areas of Central Asia there was no obvious successor to the Provisional Government. The Bolsheviks' only stronghold was Tashkent, but even there General Korovichenko and a few officer-cadets prevented them from taking over power peacefully. However, on 14 November, after heavy fighting around the fortress in Tashkent the Bolsheviks became masters of the city. On 28 November they convoked the 3rd Territorial Soviet Congress and formed a government of Turkestan, but had to share power with Left Social Revolutionaries. In Central Asia the Bolshevik victory was not unqualified, but all the same, after this political compromise, principal cities turned Bolshevik in quick succession: Samarkand, Ashkhabad, Skobelev. The Transcaspian Government was formed shortly afterwards and at Fergana the Soviet also declared itself Bolshevik. In December 1917 two revolts perturbed Turkestan's Bolsheviks: at Samarkand General Dzhunkovsky managed to persuade returning Cossacks to take the city, but then suddenly wavered and surrendered. Then the Kikand National Government claimed autonomy for the territory but was easily defeated by Bolsheviks from Tashkent. At Orenburg the Alashorda government which also claimed autonomy for Kazakhstan never got off the ground. When in January 1918 Kronstadt sailors began to arrive all this vast area passed under Bolshevik sway: Kustanay, Semipalatinsk, Akulinsk, Pavlodar, Ust-Kamenogorsk. In March 1918 the Bolsheviks took Verny and in April at the 5th Soviet Congress Turkestan was proclaimed an autonomous republic with two important exceptions: the Khanate of Khiva and the emirate of Bokhara remained under their monarchs.

In the Southern Urals the Bolsheviks encountered expected resistance from the Cossacks and their newly elected leader, Ataman Dutov. Dutov declared war on the Soviets, gained the support of nationalist Bashkirs and

Kazakhs, and cleared Troitsk, Verkhne Uralsk and Chelyabinsk of the Bolsheviks. However the Bolsheviks, led by P.A. Kobozev, managed to put together enough troops to defeat Dutov's Cossack army and on the last day of January 1918 they captured Orenburg. Although it took them more than a year to clear the Southern Urals they hung onto Orenburg, menacing permanently Dutov's rear and maintaining contact with Bolshevik Turkestan.

In Siberia the Bolshevik takeover was slow because of the distances and scarcity of men. At Krasnyarsk, which became Bolshevik three days after Petrograd, Bolshevik forces consisted mainly of radical-left prisoners of war and elements of the 15th Siberian Regiment. Lazo, the Hungarian, presided over this one red spot on the white vastness of Siberia. At Omsk local Bolsheviks, aided by prisoners of war, had to fight for the city, but when they convoked the regional West Siberian Congress of Soviets, they were smoothly acknowledged. Tomsk, the seat of the All-Siberian Soviet, was under Social Revolutionary control. It was only in February 1918 that the Tomsk Soviet decided to disperse the Siberian autonomous Duma; the Provisional Siberian Government together with its Premier, Derber, had to move to Mandjuria. At Irkutsk Bolshevik takeover was peaceful, but late in December 1917 Russian officers and caders suddenly rose and tried to seize the city. However, Lazo and his prisoners of war were at hand and the uprising was suppressed. At Chita Bolshevik units had to dissolve the National Soviet to seize power and Ataman Semenov, leader of the local Cossack army, retreated into Mongolia. The nationalist Buryats were expelled from Ulan Ude only in February 1918, while in the Far Eastern province at Vladivostock and Khabarovsk Bolshevik power was recognised in December 1917.

By March 1918 Lenin and the Bolshevik party controlled to a great degree the greater part of what used to be the Russian Empire. Incredible though it may seem, Lenin was quite right to plan the seizure of power in and from Petrograd. He was also right to base his strategy of gradual takeover on the paralysis of his opponents and military neutralisation of the armies. Politically the coup was excellently stage-managed: the Bolshevik minority took over power from the Provisional Government on behalf of the Congress of Soviets. Henceforth it could shield behind the Soviets. After they had seized political and military initiative their inevitable momentum enable the Bolsheviks to control the whole country. Although the coup d'état was not an example *par excellence* of a coup, the very fact that Bolsheviks could act and make tactical moves, coupled with political initiative, led them from one military victory to another. Though Lenin and the party were far from secure in power they had achieved relatively easily and in a short time what they set out to do: they wielded power and the overwhelming majority of their opponents was ostensibly crushed and defeated.

2

Interlude, 1917-18

After Premier Kerensky's escape from Petrograd no-one seems to have bothered about political leadership or initiative. However much the Bolsheviks were disorganised on the military front, it was their opponents' political errors and indecision which proved decisive in the confused situation following the coup. Since the Provisional Government was under lock and key in the Peter and Paul Fortress, the Social Revolutionaries (the right wing only) decided at long last to take some political intiiative. In reply to the Bolsheviks' proclamation that they were the new government of Russia and their action in consolidating their control of the country through Revolutionary Military Committees, Chernov, Gots and Avksentiev formed a counter-government, the Committee for the Salvation of the Revolution and Motherland, and urged their Social Revolutionary followers to set up Committees of Salvation to counteract the influence of the Bolshevik ones. Perhaps a little unexpectedly the movement for the salvation did spread in the country, but the Social Revolutionary counter-government faced immediate problems on the spot. It was not in possession of sufficient military forces to ensure its security in Petrograd, so it decided to go into the country in search of armed backing and real power basis.

The departure was precipitated by an abortive attempt at taking control of Petrograd. This operation was mounted by Gots and Braun, two leading Social Revolutionaries, who asked Colonel Polkovnikov to order his officer-cadets to arrest the Revolutionary Military Committee and take over Petrograd. Detailed orders were issued and a declaration to the citizens and garrison of Petrograd was prepared; the country was then to be informed of events by telegrams. Colonel Polkovnikov managed to order his cadets out of their academies, but after marching out as a sign of defiance of the Bolsheviks, they were easily beaten, since the Bolsheviks had foreknowledge of the conspiracy thanks to the betrayal by one of the couriers, Bruderer, whom they had succeeded in arresting. This minor attempt at a revolt proved quite a threat to the Bolsheviks, because it coincided with General Krasnov's advance on Petrograd and the Bolsheviks had to divide their artillery to cope with both challenges.

After the Krasnov-Kerensky advance on the Northern front had failed, the only sanctuary the Social Revolutionary leaders could find was the Stavka (the Supreme HQ of the Russian armies). However, after the abortive operations in Petrograd even the journey there was dangerous: Gots and Avksentiev were arrested trying to leave Petrograd, only Chernov slipped away without being intercepted. On 12 November 1917, when all had been lost in Petrograd, the Stavka issued a proclamation condemning the Bolshevik seizure of power and all politicians, especially the Social Revolutionaries, took this declaration as a show of power. In addition to the generals, quite bewildered by the events in Petrograd and elsewhere, the Stavka contained large Allied missions making 'international' consultations possible. Thus Social Revolutionary leaders intended to proclaim themselves as the government of Russia and launch a drive against the Bolshevik government in Petrograd with the Stavka 'forces' in the vanguard. To their great disappointment both the generals and the Allied representatives proved singularly unreceptive to such proposals; the generals were too worried about a Bolshevik takeover at the Stavka itself and the Allied representatives were uninterested in the scheme, being under instruction from their governments to delay armistice talks for as long as possible, for General Dukhonin, the interim C-in-C, had been ordered by the Bolshevik government to begin armistice negotiations with the Germans. Furthermore the Allied representatives on the spot felt that it would not be in their interest to support 'internationally' a Social Revolutionary government, for which neither the troops nor the generals had shown the slightest inclination to fight. While these hesitations and delays were going on at the Stavka Lenin as Chairman* dismissed Dukhonin and ordered his new appointment, Ensign Krylenko, to set out with a sizeable group of sailors to take over the Supreme HQ, which they shortly afterwards achieved.

Russian politicians had one last hope for salvaging political power: during the October coup and afterwards, the whole country had been involved in a general election. It was the most significant political event the Provisional Government had prepared and organised. Its purpose was to give that form of government a legitimate basis so that Russia's future government and power would be based on election results. Even the Bolsheviks sanctioned it and were looking forward to the convocation of the Constitutional Assembly for which the election was being held. Dissident politicians therefore rushed back to Petrograd, for there was every indication from early results of a decisive victory for the Social Revolutionaries. Lenin and the Bolsheviks had hoped against hope to emerge from the election with the greatest number of seats, so the extent of their electoral defeat caused them to alter their plans as to the use of the Assembly. Moreover their coalition partners, the left wing of the Social Revolutionaries, had also suffered a setback and thus they lost any interest in the

*Then, of course, Chairman of People's Commissars.

Constitutional Assembly. Still, past promises and public opinion forced the Bolsheviks to convoke the Assembly in an inaugural session in Petrograd, but even then Lenin must have hoped that the situation after the coup would intimidate his political opponents so that he could dominate the Assembly. However, it became evident during the very first session of the Assembly that Lenin's opponents would not be intimidated. Instead of a Bolshevik Victor Chernov, the leader of the right wing of the Social Revolutionaries, was elected Speaker and the tone of proceedings became distinctly anti-Bolshevik. Lenin therefore withdrew and ordered the guardsmen-sailors to close down the Assembly. Under their threats the Assembly adjourned, and it was only in July 1918, during the civil war, that it re-assembled, this time without Bolshevik deputies.

Only after all the conventional methods of disputing power with the Bolsheviks had failed them did their opponents have recourse to the ultimate means, civil war. While the right wing Social Revolutionaries continued to hesitate for quite a long time, other non-Bolsheviks, especially the monarchist-oriented ones, had decided on civil war as early as 11 November 1917. General Alexeyev, former CGS and Generalissimo, who was in Petrograd during the coup, had tried to organise opposition there, but after failing he had immediately set out for the Don territory, where his fellow general and elected Ataman of the Don Cossacks, Kaledin, an opponent of the Provisional Government, was openly defying the Bolsheviks in turn. In both political and military terms, Alexeyev's decision to go to the Don was shortsighted, but many other generals and politicians reasoned like Alexeyev: opposition to the Bolsheviks was impossible in the centre; it had to be organised elsewhere, outside the capital. Thus Boris Savinkov, a Social Revolutionary leader, Generals Kornilov, Denikin and other internees at Bykhov (who were detained there on Kerensky's order after the failure of the *coup de force* in September 1917) decided to leave for the Don region and raise the standard of revolt against the Bolsheviks there. Thousands of other less significant political and military figures followed suit. It somehow never occurred to any one of them that they were abandoning central Russia to the Bolsheviks, that it would be extremely difficult to dislodge the Bolsheviks from the centre and finally that the Don Cossack territory might have its own problems. (Cossacks were no longer a majority in their territories!)

From the very start the hold of the Don Cossacks over their own territory was precarious. On 1 December 1917 the 272nd Infantry Regiment stationed at Novocherkassk, the Don Cossacks' capital, refused to recognise Ataman Kaledin's authority, but then mercifully instead of fighting it out with the Cossacks the regiment was peacefully dissolved by its officers and sent home. Still Kaledin had under his command two Cossack divisions which were intended for Persia to fight alongside the

British Expeditionary Force. Since there was now no question of their going to Persia, Kaledin hoped to use them as police forces, to consolidate his position. However, although Kaledin had proclaimed martial law in the Don Cossack area, he had also made it clear that he would not interfere with the Soviets established there; this seemed a remarkably mild measure against the Bolsheviks who were using Soviets all over Russia to seize power and were doing so even in the Don region. Though Rostov-on-the-Don was dangerously near Novocherkassk Kaledin refused to intervene directly when the Bolsheviks seized power there through their Revolutionary Military Committee. Nonetheless, on the arrival of the White generals he advised them to take over the city for themselves and to start recruiting and organising their anti-Bolshevik forces there rather than in the Cossack territory. Thus Kaledin and his Cossacks, who had won the election in the territory, appeared exclusively concerned with Cossack interests and autonomy, rather than with the issues of central power with which the White refugees seemed to be obsessed.

It was the Bolsheviks who forced Ataman Kaledin to become their open enemy. They ordered a loyal regiment at Stavropol to march on Novocherkassk and bring down this puny Don autonomous region and Ataman Kaledin. However, the solution was not as simple: every one concerned was reluctant to start hostilities. Thus when the Bolshevik Regiment met the 35th Cossack Regiment, both sides refused to fight and agreed on an armistice. The anti-Cossack march had taken place, but it did not bring about the results that Lenin expected from it. However, it had forced Kaledin to take positive action against the Bolsheviks at Rostov. He sent in General Alexeyev's officers to take over the city, which they successfully accomplished on 15 December 1917 after some considerable fighting and bloodshed. While saddened by this open conflict, Kaledin was pleased to have got rid of the Whites, who were now streaming in hordes into his capital.

Henceforth Rostov became the centre of Russian anti-Bolshevik activity. In the election for the Constituent Assembly the Bolshevik party gained the largest number of votes in the city, but the various non-Bolshevik groups held the majority; all the same this was a precarious base on which to organise anti-Bolshevik movements. Nonetheless, after their disappointment with Kaledin the Whites decided to make do with Rostov. Generals Lukomsky and Markov, whom Kaledin had sent to Vladikavkaz and Ekaterinodar, were recalled and politicians also began to arrive in greater numbers. It was a miracle that amidst the confusion tinged with disappointment and defeat the quarelling generals and politicians managed to reach a 'constitutional' agreement by which the politicians allowed the generals to take command of the struggle in the civil war: in fact power was split between three generals – Kornilov, who became C-in-C of the nascent Volunteer Russian Army, Alexeyev, who was put in charge of finances and foreign affairs, and Kaledin, who was also put in command of Cossack forces by virtue of his election as Ataman of the Don Cossacks. The politicians agreed to serve on a 'Constitutional Council' which was to advise the generals, and which consisted mainly of Russian liberals (Kadets): P.M. Miliukov, M.M. Fedorov, P.B. Struve, A.S. Beletsky, Prince G.N. Trubetskoy, M.P. Bogayevsky and N. Parnov. On 30 January 1918 all these agreements and measures were made public with great pomp and circumstance, but within a month they had all beeome meaningless.

Perhaps it boded ill for the Russian political struggle that power had passed exclusively into the hands of the defeated and demoralised generals, who however personally courageous had proved themselves incapable of dealing successfully even with military problems. Immediately they began to demonstrate their incapability: several generals attempted to organise recruitment for the Volunteer Army, but met with little success. General Markov completely failed at Ekaterinodar; at Taganrog only 50 men signed up; at Rostov General Cherepov recruited a mere 200 men of whom only a third left with the Volunteers when they evacuated the city late in February 1918. Filled with a sense of military urgency by this lack of enthusiasm General Kornilov took sole responsiblity for mobilisation orders, which he had somewhat incongruously issued, and which the Don Cossacks opposed. However, conscription did not improve the numbers of the Volunteer Army either. Undaunted by this fact General Kornilov set up at least his HQ with General Lukomsky as Chief of Staff, and General Romanovsky as Quartermaster-General.

Whilst the White politicians and generals were trying in vain to set up an efficient organisation at Rostov, Ataman Kaledin was trying to solve his own regional problems. He put proposals before the Krug, the elective Cossack regional assembly, which would give representation and voice to the non-Cossack population. This, undoubtedly, would have strengthened politically the Don Krug, but his proposals were never enacted. Kaledin also tried to tighten discipline in his armed forces, but he met with total defeat. Thanks to his involvement with the Volunteers Kaledin drew the full weight of the Bolsheviks onto himself and the Don Cossacks. The Bolsheviks had succeeded in putting together enough armed units to launch a full-scale campaign against the Don. At this point Kaledin's forces mutinied and on 28 January 1918 the northern Don Cossacks deposed him and replaced him by two left wing Social Revolutionary Cossacks, Podtelkov and Krivoshtykov. Thus divided and demoralised the Don Cossacks faced the Bolsheviks who were coming from the north (Voronezh) under the overall command of the politician-soldier Antonov-Ovseyenko, apparently the only Bolshevik capable of commanding an army. Antonov-Ovseyenko divided his forces into two: one group, under Sivers, attacked Taganrog and Rostov with the main purpose of destroying the Volunteers, while the other group, under Sablin, advanced against the main body of the Don Cossacks. These could only field partisan units under the dissident Podtelkov and Kaledin's commander Chernetsov. The prospect of Don and Volunteer collapse was evident and the Bolsheviks would obviously score an easy victory which would undoubtedly strengthen them politically and militarily.

At first Chernetsov's partisans checked Sablin's forces, but then by a lucky chance Sablin caught the unit unawares and destroyed it, killing Chernetsov. Sivers at first also met with a reverse, prepared by Colonel Kutepov near Taganrog; but then the Bolsheviks in Taganrog organised an uprising, cut off Kutepov's supply lines and retreat, and the hapless colonel and his units had to fight their way through to Rostov. On 12 February 1918 at Novocherkassk Ataman Kaledin recognised the hopelessness of the situation and rather than surrender or escape committed suicide. The Krug immediately elected a successor, Ataman A.M. Nazarov. He persuaded the 6th Don Cossack Regiment to move up against the invading Bolshevik forces, but when they actually met the enemy the Cossacks refused to fight and negotiated an armistice. This enabled both Sablin and Sivers to take over Novocherkassk and Rostov unhindered, although they also arrived too late and could only survey the ruin of both the Don and the Volunteers. In a surprise drive on Novocherkassk a Cossack unit under V.S. Golubov seized the town, executed Voloshinov, Speaker of the Krug, as well as the newly elected Ataman Nazarov, and installed itself in power. Despite this the Krug charged the military Ataman, General Popov, to lead some 1,500 Cossacks into the steppes to continue the fight for an autonomous Don. On 23 March 1918 the Soviet Don Republic was finally proclaimed with Podtelkov as President, although power was actually exercised by the Bolshevik military commanders, Sivers and Voytsekhovsky.

After the defeat at Taganrog the Volunteers decided to evacuate Rostov peacefully without a fight. Though the generals had some 1,000 politicians to advise them on how and where to continue the fight against the Bolsheviks, they alone made the inadequate decision to leave European Russia and withdraw into the steppes and wilderness of the Kuban region. In addition to this political blunder the generals also failed to prepare the Volunteers for this type of warfare. General Elsner even forgot radio equipment and henceforth the Volunteer Army fought in absolute political and military isolation. Among the Volunteers who left Rostov for the first Ice March there were three army generals, eight lieutenant-generals, 25 major-generals, 199 colonels and some 215 captains. Only Lieutenant-Colonel Nezhintsov was in charge of his own Kornilov regiment; Generals Markov (1st Officer Regiment) and Borovsky (Cadet Battalion) were in command of no more than weak battalions, while General Bogayevsky was in charge of a small guerilla Don unit and Captain Němeček of the Czechoslovak Engineers Battalion. The Volunteer Army further contained four two-gun batteries and three cavalry detachments. Antonov-Ovseyenko did try to nip the Volunteer problem in the bud when he sent the 112th Regiment to occupy Olginskaya, thus cutting off the line of retreat from Russia. However, instead of blocking the retreat of the Volunteers the 112th Regiment dispersed and went home to Stavropol in the Kuban region, whence the soldiers hailed. Thus the Volunteers were able to leave Russia unmolested, though they immediately quarrelled with General Popov's Don Cossacks, and consequently left on the long journey to the Kuban Cossack area in a huff.

In this way they were forced into a decision, for they found it very hard to make any plausible ones. On 21 February 1918 the Volunteer units concentrated at Olginskaya and for a whole week hesitated. Despite his bad reputation General Kornilov favoured a politically motivated march through the Salsk steppes to the Volga, whence the Volunteers could have retreated to Siberia which was solidly non-Bolshevik. However, this time he was overruled by General Alexeyev and others who felt that the Kuban region would be a more useful base for future action against Russia proper and was under control of a non-Bolshevik Cossack government. This march was perhaps militarily more feasible, but was based on wrong political assumptions. When the Volunteers finally reached the Kuban, after a month of exhausting fighting, they discovered that no Kuban Cossack government existed. The Bolsheviks 'infiltrated' the region in the most unexpected and remarkable way. The 39th Division from the Caucasian front, which had melted away during the confusion of November 1917, had set up Soviets on the route from the front to Russia: there were Soviets at Tikhoretskaya, Torgovaya, Stavropol, Armavir, Kavkazkaya and even at Novorosiisk. On 13 March 1918 the forces of the Kuban Cossack government were defeated by the itinerant troops of the Soviets and the capital Ekaterinodar was abandoned. In fact the Kuban politicians and soldiers were already on their way to meet the Volunteers. On 27 March 1918 Colonel Pokrovsky and his Kuban Cossacks together with General Erdeli's cavalry detachment joined the Volunteer Army. The Russian Volunteers not only failed to find a secure base, but now found themselves condemned to regaining the Kuban region for their new-found allies.

It seems curious that the Volunteers had learnt nothing from their experience in the Don Cossack territory. Yet it looked remarkably clear that the whole Don episode was going to be repeated and prove even more wasteful in bloodshed. Thus the Volunteers spent most of April 1918 taking and fighting for Kuban villages and investing the abandoned capital Ekaterinodar. The Officer Regiment was decimated fighting for regional interests; Colonel Nezhintsov was killed in action, and finally on 13 April 1918 a stray bullet killed the Commander-in-Chief, Kornilov. Operations were at last suspended, the Volunteers regrouped and the dying General

Alexeyev appointed the most senior general, Denikin, as Kornilov's successor. Although the cream of the Volunteers was killed, the army was bigger than when it set out on the first march for it was now swelled by Kuban Cossacks, Cirkassian horsemen and a motley of dependents and camp followers. It now started off on the second march, back to the Don.

In the Don region the Soviet regime had become increasingly unpopular, especially after Golubov, who had led the partisan forces, was passed over and became disaffected. Sivers and the Bolsheviks in the region did not seem to have courted popularity with the Cossacks. They began to persecute the families of the runaway Cossacks and Volunteers and executed several generals, among them General Rennenkampf, so notorious for his defeat in August 1914. On 10 April 1918 a general uprising broke out in the Don region against the Bolsheviks and Esaul Fetisov was elected its leader. Ataman Popov was recalled from the steppes and Fetisov's forces made a dash for Novocherkassk and took it. The Soviet Cossacks, Podtelkov and Krivoshtykov, were caught and subsequently hanged; G.P. Yanov quickly formed a council, which on 21 April 1918 proclaimed itself the Provisional Government of the Don. On his return from the steppes General Popov divided the Don forces into three groups and confirmed the partisan commanders as commanding officers in the South (Colonel Denisov), in the North (Colonel Semiletov) and in the Trans Don territory (Colonel Semenov). However, even this reasonable reorganisation proved insufficient, recruitment for the new standing armies failed and the region was open to Bolshevik attacks.

In this uncertain situation the Don Cossack Krug met again in Novocherkassk in order to elect new leaders and safeguard the security of the territory. The Krug also learned no lessons from the past: it failed again to implement Kaledin's proposal for the representation of the non-Cossack population, who formed a slender majority in the Don region. The Volunteer Army, which had caused so much dissension in the past, was also ignored. On 16 May 1918 the Krug elected the sad General Krasnov of Pulkovo Heights as Ataman of the Don. The election signified a radical change in Cossack policies which would become more reactionary and separatist. Krasnov immediately retired General Popov whose reputation was tainted by collaboration with the Volunteers and defeats at the hands of the Bolsheviks. Above all Krasnov initiated negotiations with the neighbouring Germans in the Ukraine, from whom he wanted the recognition of an independent Don and arms and ammunition to defend the region against the Bolsheviks. His first request was never granted, even after Krasnov had proposed a federal union with the German-dominated Caucasian republics. The second request was satisfied immediately: up to July 1918 Krasnov received some 12,000 rifles, 89 machine guns and 46 heavy guns with 11,500,000 rounds of ammunition. With this equipment the Don Cossacks immediately launched operations against the 3rd and

5th Red Armies.

However, Krasnov had also to come to terms with the Volunteers, who early in May suddenly emerged from the steppes, excited by the windfall of the Don Cossack uprising and independence. At a crucial stage, when the Cossack uprising was in the balance, Colonel Drozdovsky unexpectedly arrived from the Rumanian front with some 2,500 men in his detachment. This arrival tipped the balance in the Cossack's favour and meant defeat for the Bolsheviks. But Colonel Drozdovsky was a Russian who wanted to join the Russian Volunteer Army and not fight for separatist Cossacks who moreover collaborated with the Germans. Drozdovsky obviously strengthened the Volunteers' hand *vis-à-vis* the Don Cossacks, but did not change the basic fact, namely that the Volunteers desparately needed Don Cossack help. On 28 May 1918 Ataman Krasnov and his Foreign Minister, General Bogayevsky (until recently a Volunteer commander) met Generals Alexeyev, Denikin, Romanovsky and the Kuban Ataman, Filimonov, to iron out an agreement on cooperation. The Volunteer generals behaved rather clumsily trying to impress the Don Cossacks with their rank and seniority and claims that they were in fact the real inheritors of Russian power. Of course, they not only wanted to impress the Cossacks, but also 'help them' against the Bolsheviks. They proposed to combine their armed forces, concentrate on the right wing and break through to Tsaritsyn and the central Volga region. This breakthrough would have been mutually beneficial and sound both tactically and politically. However, the Cossacks would have nothing to do with it; the Volunteers wanted too much for little benefit. Thus, in a sense, they forced the Volunteers back to the Kuban region, from where they had only just arrived. There would be no fusion of armies and the Volunteers' task would be more modest; they would clear the Kuban from the Bolsheviks and make it secure for the Kuban Ataman and his Cossacks. Thus the Volunteers were once again sent away from Central Russia into the borderlands. In return they were given arms and ammunition by the Don Cossacks and allowed to stake their claim in Russian affairs by detailing General Kazanovich to Moscow to prepare an uprising in Central Russia. The Volunteers, however, felt most keenly that they were forced into this subordinate role in the civil war by Germany, the Don Cossacks' protectors. The German factor began to complicate the situation at this early stage and would disrupt White unity in the future.

Though the Bolsheviks concluded an armistice with the Germans as soon as they took over the control of the Supreme HQ at Mogilev, peace negotiations dragged on mainly because German conditions for a peace settlement were excessive. It also became clear that the Germans wanted the armistice more than peace: on 17 December 1917 they began to transfer whole divisions from the eastern to the western front. The Bolsheviks, on the other hand, hoped that peace negotiations would damage German morale and could somehow be turned into propaganda battles which would spark off a world revolution. But they were soon undeceived. The Germans refused to accept the Bolshevik peace decree — no annexations and return to the *status quo ante* — as a basis of the peace settlement and General Hoffman spelled out Germany's terms to I.I. Joffe, the chief Bolshevik negotiator: there would be no German withdrawal from any occupied territory and some 18 provinces of imperial Russia would be given the choice of independence or the status of a German protectorate.

After the Christmas recess the wrangling and delays continued, until the Germans impatiently concluded a separate peace with the Ukrainian Rada. On 8 February 1918 Kiev fell to the Bolsheviks, but on that very day the defeated Rada signed a peace treaty with the Germans, who demanded Russian withdrawal from the Ukraine. The Bolsheviks were faced with a power confrontation with Germany, which they had tried so hard to avoid. In response to this pressure on 10 February 1918 Trotsky proclaimed his 'no war, no peace' doctrine, but it solved nothing. On 16 February 1918 the Germans resumed hostilities all along the Eastern front, and two days later moved swiftly into the Ukraine. Lenin, seeing the rapid advance of the German armies, sent off immediately an unconditional acceptance of German terms, but they answered in much harsher tones. Though this time Lenin had a vocal revolt at hand, he nevertheless succeeded in persuading the Bolshevik party to accept the German *Diktat* and sent another delegation to Brest-Litovsk, where on 3 March 1918 it signed peace with Germany.

The terms of the peace treaty were terrible indeed: Russia lost to Germany some 26 per cent of its population (60,000,000), 27 per cent of its arable land and 33 per cent of manufacturing industry. Estonia, Latvia and Lithuania were detached from Russia and Finland was confirmed as independent. Byelorussia was practically all occupied, the Ukraine reduced to the status of a protectorate, while the Caucasian republics, Georgia, Armenia and Adzerbeijan obtained temporary independence. Germany advanced its own frontiers deep into Russia itself and became an important power factor in the internal Russian struggle itself. The Don Cossacks immediately benefited by asking and obtaining German aid, while the Russian anti-Bolshevik movement split into two factions, the pro-Allied and the pro-German. But the problem whether to rest in peace with Germany began to haunt the Bolsheviks and the anti-Bolsheviks alike: it was impossible to forget the terrible losses inflicted on Russia in the war and at Brest-Litovsk. Moreover, Germany appeared such an unpredictable power, ready in its struggle against the Allies to abandon or destroy either or both Russian sides.

However, for the time being the Germans appeared to favour the border, non-Russian nations, though of course not for their own sake but for German power purposes. As soon as they succeeded in occupying the Ukraine the Germans installed in power their own regime, cynically abandoning the one with which they concluded the peace treaty. The weakness of the Ukrainian Rada became evident during the Bolshevik invasion of the Ukraine, just before the peace treaty was signed. The Rada's forces, the *haydamaks*, were irregular units which suffered from an annoying custom of disbanding themselves before military engagements, and they were totally defeated. The Germans (and the Austrians, who had a small occupation zone in the Ukraine) refused to ally themselves with such a tottering regime, and took it on themselves to organise military forces of the new Ukraine. They appointed as Hetman of the Ukraine General Skoropadsky, who wielded dictatorial powers but was clearly under German tutelage. He and his future forces served a dual purpose after the Germans had transferred to the West all German troops they could spare: they opposed the dissolved Rada and its irregulars under Ataman Petlyura and protected the Ukraine against the Bolsheviks, who had retired to Russia proper before the advancing Germans.

While the Germans were present in the Ukraine both the Rada and the Bolsheviks were kept in check and did not dare to challenge the Skoropadsky regime. It would be a different matter if the Germans had to depart, and the latter seemed unconcerned about this possibility and Skoropadsky's fate. The Germans did make an effort at organising a regular Ukraine army, but in the end Skoropadsky was left with only a few irregular units to rely on. The Germans broached several schemes with the Hetman, the most important one in June 1918. They wanted to form, officer and equip the 1st Ukrainian Cossack Rifle Division (Schützen-division), but almost nothing came from this scheme. Similarly, in the Caucasian republics the German military missions made attempts at re-organising local units, but never completed the task. However, where the Germans did not intervene directly and only aided the existing forces, as was the case of the Don Cossacks, they left behind a force capable at least of defending itself.

Where the extension of German power and influence proved most disastrous was among the Russian underground groups. When in May 1918 General Kazanovich arrived in Moscow to survey and report on the various anti-Bolshevik movements he found them utterly demoralised and split: the Right Centre, strongly monarchist, was completely pro-Germany, while the National Centre remained pro-Allies. The Union of Revival, which was socialist dominated, contained both elements, and all three refused to cooperate with each other. Thus they existed side by side quite uncoordinated in complete political and military isolation. The National Centre, which was composed mainly of right wing elements, was supposed to have great financial resources, as all the industrialists and wealthy Russians allegedly belonged to it. But when the Volunteer military section asked for money it was told that the Centre had none and moral support was offered instead. The Union of Revival had no money either, but apparently consisted of many enthusiastic followers, who were ready to rise against the Bolsheviks in the cities or the country, and drive them out of power. All these groups were preparing for uprisings with Allied or German aid, but no one knew when, where or how these rebellions were to be carried out. Thus, for example, local organisations of officers went on quietly meeting and preparing armed uprisings without informing the Centres, usually apparently for security reasons. However, despite these 'precautions' the Bolsheviks inevitably knew full well about the existence of the groups and their plans. It is true that the Russians were not particularly good conspirators, but the Bolshevik counter-espionage seems to have worked extremely well; of course, Allied and German participation in these conspiracies made them more complicated and vulnerable to discovery. In addition the anti-Bolshevik underground movements suffered from another weakness, freebooting conspiracies. Thus the former Deputy Minister of War, Boris Savinkov, a leading social revolutionary, returned from the Don after it had collapsed and posing as General Alexeyev's emissary formed his own underground group, the Union for the Protection of the Motherland and Freedom. For his Union he recruited both monarchist officers as well as fellow social revolutionaries in the central regions of Russia (Vladimir, Yaroslavl, Rybinsk etc.). He also collected large sums of money from Allied (mainly French) sources and, without the slightest knowledge of the Centres, had some 5,000 members ready to rise against the Bolsheviks at any moment. A similar conspiracy was organised by left wing Social Revolutionaries, who at the time were Bolshevik coalition partners and wanted to exploit their positions of power in the Cheka and the Red Army to overthrow the Bolsheviks. Both Savinkov and the Left Social Revolutionaries were hatching their plots in 'absolute' secrecy, independent of each other. When finally their coups erupted, in the confusion they more or less cancelled each other out.

Thus the burden of the initial struggle against the Bolsheviks rested almost exclusively on the various Cossacks' *voyskas* (regions). Apart from the Don *voysko*, the Urals Cossacks were also fighting the 4th Red Army and were proving a serious nuisance to the Bolsheviks. However, all these Cossacks, the Terek and Dagestan *voyskas* included, fought in isolation, alone in their distant regions. The Terek Cossacks were deprived of capable leadership when shortly after their victory in Petrograd the Bolsheviks succeeded in assassinating their Ataman Karaulov. Ataman Dutov found it hard to control his Urals Cossack detachment who were bent on partisan operations and to their cost refused to act in ordinary military fashion. They continued to raid haphazardly Bolshevik-held territory in search of arms, and were really of pure nuisance value. The Siberian and Far Eastern Cossacks were in a similar predicament. However, perhaps isolation and remoteness were also their salvation. The Urals Cossacks speedily lost their capital to the Bolsheviks when the latter struck against them; the Don had to fight for its life all the time. In the Far East Ataman Semenov after his expulsion from Chita simply re-grouped on the Chinese border and went on with raiding Bolshevik-held towns, thus seriously undermining the Bolshevik hold on the Far Eastern province. Similarly General Horvat, who was chairman of the Russo-Chinese Railways and resided outside Russia, at Kharbin in Mandjuria, also organised a small army and waited for a more propitious moment to put it to use against the Bolsheviks. Both Semenov and Horvat were just two of the many local warlords with great potential but no immediate impact on the huge military and power vacuum of Siberia.

However, the Bolsheviks did not sit by idly; as soon as they were reasonably sure that the Russian armies in the field were neutralised and ceased to constitute a danger to their regime they found it necessary to re-form armed forces under their own control. They had two basic reasons for doing so: 1. the great war continued and another German invasion seemed possible; 2. anti-Bolshevik forces began to get organised and the Bolsheviks felt compelled to defend their revolution. At first, after Krylenko had taken over the Stavka in November 1917, the Bolsheviks thought that they could salvage the old imperial army and make good use of it. Colonel Daller proposed to split the army into the border guards and internal 'militia' forces. However, Bolshevik politicians had other ideas: thus Kedrov wanted to form 'Socialist Guards' based on industrial districts from which peasants would be excluded. On 16 December 1917 Krylenko, the Generalissimo, produced his own ideas on the subject in a memorandum to the Bolshevik leaders and they became the basis of Bolshevik military policies.

On 28 December 1917 Lenin attended the congress of demobilisation to clear up his own mind, but while various plans were discussed and a complete demobilisation urged, mass desertions from the fronts made the discussions superfluous. In the end the demobilisation congress voted overwhelmingly for the dissolution of the old army and Lenin requested 'revolutionary' units and the sailors to hold the front lines, while complete demobilisation was accomplished. On 29 December 1917 all the ranks of the old army were abolished and a decision in principle was made to organise a new Red Army through the Stavka and the All-Russian College for the Formation of the Red Army. At the same time Lenin set up the Supreme Military Soviet which helped with the organisation of the Red Army in the rear while the Stavka organised units on the fronts. The Soviet also took over some of the functions of the old War Ministry; thus early in 1918 the Bolsheviks had all the machinery ready for the re-formation of their armed forces.

Early in January 1918 various city soviets, such as Petrograd, Moscow,

Ivanovo, Kazan and Saratov, discussed the problem of the new armed forces and urged Lenin and the Bolshevik leadership to re-establish them. Lenin could see their point and the need, but still continued to discuss the new army, especially at the congress of soldiers' soviets on 28 January 1918. These discussions probably finally helped him to make up his mind and immediately after the congress he personally drafted a decree establishing the Red Army. On 14 February 1918 it was approved by the by the Soviet Executive Committee and became immediately effective.

As if in anticipation of the decree, on 1 February 1918, K.S. Yeremeyev, member of the College of the Red Army*, began to organise its 1st Army Corps in Petrograd. Some 10,000 men of this Corps were subsequently sent to the front: after the decree had become law army corps were organised all over the territory controlled by the Bolsheviks. Many old units were incorporated in the Red Army *en masse* as, for example, the 5th Zaamur Division, 12th Finnish Rifle Division, the Latvian Rifle Division and the 45th Infantry Division. The organisation of the Red Army proceeded most energetically, although the recruitment for it was on a voluntary basis. Another member of the Military College, T.I. Ulyantsov, began to reorganise the fleet.

It is obvious that the organisation of the Red Army was not sufficiently advanced when, on 20 February 1918, the Germans renewed their offensive on the Eastern front in retaliation for the Bolshevik refusal to sign the peace treaty. The young Red Army completely collapsed in face of the disciplined enemy armies and Red units imitated the irregulars and dissolved themselves. On 21 February Lenin asked Sverdlov to form yet another military organ, the Committee of Revolutionary Defence, to speed up the formation of efficient army units capable of resistance to the advancing Germans. But this supplementary call up, stiffened with party members, proved disappointing and with all the enthusiasm in the world it failed even to slow down German advance.

The Bolsheviks certainly learned from this experience. On 28 March 1918 Lenin personally made sure that the Red Army came under central command without elective officers: former tsarist officers were recruited and employed as military specialists. To make sure of their loyalty and also in order to keep political control Lenin imposed on the Red Army dual command; military specialists were checked by and could do nothing without the *politruks,* their political counterparts. Political control was applied at all levels in the Red Army from the Stavka to the smallest unit in the field, and at the top was exercised by Lenin, Sverdlov, Trotsky, Stalin or Ordjonikidze, on the battlefield by the local company political comissar *(politruk).* Bolshevik political leadership reserved for itself all the important decisions, especially during the frequent crises, remained in effective control of the Red Armies throughout the civil war, and became,

* A specialized body for the organization of the Red Army.

therefore, in contradistinction to the Whites, the real organiser of victory in the civil war.

After the conclusion of the Brest-Litovsk Peace many military organisations, including Sverdlov's committee, were dissolved and on 8 May 1918 Soviet Russia had once again the Army General Staff, though at this stage it only had partisan units under its command. In the Ukraine these units were led by Kikvidze, Voroshilov, Rudnak, Sivers, Kotovsky and Primakov. Reorganisation of the Red Armies only started after the German advance had stopped. Trotsky became War Minister (People's Commissar of War Affairs), Major-General Bonch-Bruyevich, Lenin's friend, was the new COS and General Suleyma QMG. Five fronts were established, the Northern, Western, Ukrainian, Southern (Don) and Eastern, and front HQs were set up. Although some armies had only 3,000 men the organisational machine was ready and the Bolsheviks were able to fight a civil war when it broke out in earnest late in May 1918.

Paradoxically for Russia the final impulse for a nationwide civil war came from outside Russia. The wartime allies of Russia had influenced internal struggles throughout the war and continued to do so even after the March and November revolutions in 1917. It is probable that Allied influence in and pressure on Russia would have remained – as previously – indirect but for an Allied army in Russia, the Czechoslovak Legion. This foreign army consisting of some 50,000 Czechs and Slovaks got itself inextricably mixed up in internal struggles in Russia, so that its revolt against the Bolsheviks became the signal for a full-scale civil war.

After the Bolshevik coup the Western Allies were most embarrassed by the Bolshevik victory: they always considered the Bolsheviks at best as pro-German, possibly even as German agents. These suspicions were seemingly confirmed on 21 November 1917, when the new Soviet government officially requested the belligerents to stop fighting and initiate peace negotiations. The Allies were unwilling even to consider such a request and refused to release the Soviet government from the obligations of the Pact of London signed in 1914, which stipulated that none of the Allies would seek and conclude a separate peace. However, since the war continued in the West, the Allies found it impossible to enforce the moral and legal obligations on the Bolsheviks who were the new government. The enforcement of obligations would have meant a direct military intervention in Russia, the removal of the Bolshevik government from power and the replacement of it with a pro-Allied one. But the Allies had to content themselves with solemn warnings, contingency plans and the preservation of the *status quo* in Russia, which meant maintaining the Eastern front in existence as long as possible and keeping as many German troops there as they could.

The Bolshevik problem for the Allies became acute after they had actually made contact with the Germans, concluded an armistice and started peace negotiations. However, even then only very few Allied leaders thought of a direct intervention in Russia with the aim of overthrowing the Bolshevik government; at least while the war lasted this seemed impossible. In the end the Allies, after much hesitation, were forced to settle for a dual policy *vis-à-vis* Russia and the Bolsheviks: they decided to 'keep in touch' both with the Bolsheviks and with the opposition and to aid the latter actively. This policy while extremely confusing was not surprising, for an open rupture with the Bolsheviks seemed impossible: after all there existed always the chance of their changing their minds and not signing the peace about whose conditions at least the Allies had no illusions. Furthermore the Allies had important military, financial, economic and personal interests in Russia and they would all be jeopardised if a rupture occurred. After all the Bolsheviks looked like the inheritors of imperial Russia and would have to be counted on when it finally came to a real peace. But keeping in touch also meant a 'wait and see' policy; after the battles had been fought the Allies would treat with the victor whoever he was which was painfully obvious to both sides.

Lenin and the Bolsheviks always believed that the Allies were organising a military crusade against them and initially saw the only way of checking these efforts in a peace with Germany. However, the Allies were far from such practical considerations and the best they could do was to sign an agreement on 23 December 1917. In this 'convention' the faraway French and British allies attempted to sort out in purely theoretical terms their policy problems in Russia; they also tried to allot each other future tasks. The agreement is a curious document which does not even reflect the *status quo* in Russia in December 1917. Thus the allocation of zones of influence is hypothetical: the Don region was allocated to the British, but it was the French who had a small mission there. In the Caucasus where Anglo-French interests were about equal Britain again predominated, though the French mission in Tiflis seemed very powerful. The proximity of Persia and the presence of British troops there probably decided the allocation of this territory. As for the Ukraine its allocation to the French did not mean that the British would be excluded: in fact the British political agent, Bagge, arrived there at this time and helped the French, especially in financing pro-Allied forces in that country. Neither was the convention meant as a long-term policy: most probably it was the result of Allied anxiety to organise some kind of resistance in the East against the Germans and the Turks, and to support the suddenly deserted Rumanians. Simultaneously with this agreement the two Allied governments upheld their 'dual policy'.

Allied representatives on the spot naturally were not informed of this agreement. They were sufficiently confused by the subtleties of the dual policy. They all tended to interpret problems in black-and-white fashion and when they were ordered to support the anti-Bolshevik opposition almost all thought that a massive Allied military intervention was on the way. If the Allies on the spot were confused the Czechs were completely lost and began to interpret both Bolshevik and Allied actions as traps. The most convincing example of Allied confusion was General Berthelot who was in charge of the French Military Mission in Rumania. On receiving information about Allied support of the Whites he rushed Captain Bordes with 7,000,000 francs to Novocherkassk to support Ataman Kaledin's South Eastern Union. But Bordes with all that money arrived too late: Kaledin was dead, Popov's Cossack unit was in the steppes and the small French mission, which had reached Kaledin in time, but without money, was in the local jail.

Events were moving too fast for policies thought out in Paris and London. In the Ukraine and Rumania the Allies fared no better and in both these countries the Allies had substantial power interests in the form of large military missions and even troops. Here local initiatives and more realistic plans were ruined by ignorance and suspicion. General Tabouis and Bagge tried to use Allied Polish and Czechoslovak legions (their strength amounted to four army corps) to keep the Ukrainian Rada and Rumania on the Allied side. They planned to re-constitute the Eastern front and deploy the 1st Polish Corps on the northern wing, followed by the Czechoslovak Corps, Ukrainian units and the 2nd Polish Corps southwards with the Rumanian army on the southern wing. These plans remained on the paper: the Ukraine pulled out of the war and sued for peace at Brest-Litovsk; both the Polish and Czechoslovak forces refused to move westward against the Germans into a line which they considered a trap. Once again the *dénouement* was swift and tragic for the Allied cause: in the North the Polish Corps came under pressure from the Bolsheviks. It tried to fight, but was defeated and forced to join the Germans who disarmed it. Without the Czechs and Poles the Rada was easily defeated by the Bolsheviks who took Kiev. In March 1918 when the Germans poured into the Ukraine and Russia there was no Polish Corps, the Czechoslovaks were retreating disorganised, the Don and the Volunteer forces were in the steppes and Rumania had just concluded a separate peace with Germany. Now that only the Bolsheviks were left opposing the Germans the Allies were ready to apply the dual policy in their favour.

It is true that among Allied politicians and soldiers the Bolsheviks had but few friends. However even their enemies, such as the French ambassador in Russia, Noulens, were impressed by their enthusiasm and energy and wanted a *rapprochement* and even aid for them. At this stage the most consistent advocate of a *rapprochement* with the Bolsheviks was the British agent in Russia, (later Sir Robert) Bruce Lockhart. On 16 February 1918 even General Poole thought that if the Allies recognised the Bolsheviks they would turn anti-German and re-join the Allies in the war. Indeed when peace negotiations at Brest were broken off Allied representatives in Russia became convinced that the Bolsheviks would turn to the Allies and with their aid re-start the war. General Niessel, the head of the French Military Mission, worked out a defence plan and had it approved by Allied governments. However, the 'belligerent' Bolshevik Trotsky received the French general only after the Bolsheviks had signed a peace with the Germans, and the German advance was halted without the defence plan ever being put into effect.

Another Allied move had failed and the situation in Russia had become even more confused than before. The Allies were now scattered all over Russia, largely isolated from each other. The centres of Allied influence disappeared altogether in the south and were now established in the extreme North. Siberia suddenly became very important for the Japanese, another ally, so far passive had landed troops at Vladivostok. With these developments the question of a direct Allied intervention arose and even became acute.

3

Allied Intervention

Lenin always tried to simplify Allied intervention in Russia, because he was more concerned with political tactics and success rather than with historical analysis and truth. He did not accuse the Allies of trying to smother the Bolshevik revolution because he believed it (in any case he could not have known about it at this point), but because he could claim to be fighting alien interlopers in Russia, and thus exploit the xenophobia of the Russians, even of those he had defeated, for his own purposes. Therefore Lenin analysed the Allied intervention in the following manner: in order to 'smother' Soviet power the Allies plotted against Russia and then intervened directly at Murmansk, Turkestan, Baku, Astrakhan, and the Far East, with the help of the Czechoslovak Corps. However, when these direct efforts were repulsed by the Bolshevik armies, they decided to intervene indirectly by arming Bolshevik opponents and organised four 'marches' led by Admiral Kolchak, General Denikin, General Yudenich and Marshal Pilsudski, the imperialist Pole, against the Soviets. However, these marches were also defeated by the Bolsheviks, because during the civil war they were able to command the support of a majority of the workers and the peasants and to organise a more efficient economy and rear.

However plausible this analysis seemed at the time, historically it was quite inaccurate. It is a fact that after the Bolshevik coup in November 1917 although the Allies were unsympathetic towards the Bolsheviks they had no plans to 'smother' the Bolshevik revolution, but had adopted the dual policy which caused so much confusion among their own ranks. Allied considerations of the situation in Russia were not dictated by class hatred or imperialist plots but by the war. It is, of course, true that many an Allied politician indulged in wishful thinking *vis-à-vis* Bolshevik Russia which they wanted to destroy because it had betrayed the Allied cause in the great war against Germany. This wishful thinking was, if anything, a real weakness in Allied policy, which in any case was irrelevant, since local forces determined the outcome of events.

The most important local force, the Czechoslovak Legion, which produced the least expected challenge to Bolshevik power, is also probably the best example of inefficient Allied planning and the insufficiency of the Allied concept of intervention. On 14 June 1918, in his speech to the executive committee of the Moscow Soviet, Lenin stated that the Czechoslovaks (who had been actively fighting the Soviets for over a month) had been bought by Franco-British imperialism for 15,000,000 roubles and induced to rebel against the Soviets. In computing this sum Lenin quoted Czech communist sources, which were remarkably well informed. The Czech communists knew that the British in the Ukraine gave the Czechoslovak Legion £80,000. They did not know that General Tabouis only gave 400,000 roubles when the Allied representatives had to leave Kiev in February 1918. On the other hand, they had details of sums of money paid by the French consul in Moscow to the Czech representatives Šip and Čermák, which were accurate, but the sum of 1,100,000 roubles, which Lenin quoted, was allocated by the French War Ministry for Czech recruitment and organisation in Russia as far back as July 1917. All this did amount to a substantial commitment, as Lenin would have us believe.

Further illustrations of Allied attitudes are provided in official French documents, dealing with relations with the Czechoslovak army. From the onset of their struggle against Habsburg rule over Czechs and Slovaks, it was obvious to both Professor T.G. Masaryk and his younger colleague Dr Beneš that without an armed force at their disposal they would never achieve their aim, the independence of Czech and Slovak lands, and that as long as the war lasted they would have to work with the Allied governments. Thus as early as 1916 Major Štefánik, another Czechoslovak patriot, set out on missions in Russia and Rumania on behalf of the French government. Štefánik was charged with the task of organising Czechoslovak prisoners of war in those two countries into units for eventual use against the central powers. In 1917 Masaryk was sent by the British War Office to Russia, also to organise Czechs but on behalf of the British government. In this way the Czech leaders active in Russia were of necessity 'paid agents' of the Allied governments. However, this did not mean they were pliable tools, without their own objectives and aims.

Beneš and Štefánik remained in France when Masaryk left for Russia, and continued to press for the recognition of an autonomous Czechoslovak army by the Allied governments, whilst Masaryk did the actual organising. In June and July 1917 Masaryk reached several agreements with the French and Russian High Commands on the recruitment of Czech and Slovak prisoners of war in Russia. It was at this point that the French advanced to the Czechs their first credit of 1,100,000 roubles. While Masaryk concerned himself with the Czechs in Russia, Štefánik went to the United States and tried to organise the Czechs there. Some 20,000 or so actually volunteered but only 235 ever reached France. Beneš went to

Italy on a similar mission. There were some 15,000 Czech prisoners of war in that country, but the Italian government was not by any means eager to see them organised and thus his mission failed.

In the meantime, the Russians formed the 1st Czechoslovak Army Corps. On 7 November the Bolsheviks seized power in Petrograd and their coup accelerated French recognition of an autonomous Czech Corps as part of the Czechoslovak army. On 11 November the French Premier informed the Quai d'Orsay that the recruitment of Czechs was under way and requested it to draft a decree regulating their position. On 4 December 1917 S. Pichon, the new foreign minister, signed the decree which established an autonomous Czech army fighting alongside the French army, and, an *instruction générale* translating this law into practice was finally issued on 7 February 1918. Even at this late stage the French government was slow to finance the Czech army, which was considered to include units from France, Russia, the United States and Italy, because it was still waiting for parliament to vote the proposed credit.

It is well known that until March 1918 the Czechs in the Ukraine subsisted on Russian and Ukrainian credits. It was only after the Germans invaded these territories that Allied representatives on the spot gave them any money. By the end of March 1918 the French consul in Moscow, Grenard, received instructions to pay out credits in Russian roubles. He immediately complied, as Lenin rightly claimed. In the meantime the Czech Army Corps (or Legion, as it was subsequently called,) was in the Kursk province making its way to Siberia. It is obvious that despite Grenard's action the Legion still had to depend on Soviet provisioning and finance, since it took some time for money to filter down to *échelon* level. In fact the Czech soldiers received hardly any pay whilst *en route*, a point that was fittingly exploited by Czech communist propagandists, who tried to demoralise the Legion and force it to join the Soviets rather than go to France and continue the fighting there.

It is still a mystery how the funds which were paid out to the Czech representatives in Moscow ever reached the Legion on its way to Vladivostok. It is established that Šip, the principal Czech representative, who cashed most of the money paid out by the French, dealt with Siberian cooperative representatives in Moscow from whom he bought large quantities of wheat and foodstuffs. Before the revolt Šip made his way from Moscow to Siberia, presumably with money, but it is far from clear how the financial arrangements worked. On 19 April 1918 the American consul in Vladivostok, Caldwell, claimed that the French consul there had been told some three weeks earlier by Professor Masaryk (when he had passed through there), that some 40-50,000 Czechs would arrive within ten days. The consul had no official instructions, supplies or billets and asked for Allied assistance. For a short while Caldwell was able to help on a day-to-day basis. After a fortnight he reported that some 6,000

Czechs had in fact arrived, and that the local Soviet was looking after them. By 1 May 1918 Major Pichon had reached Vladivostok, where he began to take steps to billet and provision the Czechs. Even then the whole undertaking was precarious, for it was still uncertain whether all the Czechs would indeed go there. Some were apparently destined for Archangel. Consequently Major Pichon encountered great difficulties, and the Czechs were left almost entirely without provisions or money. Perhaps the most conclusive proof that the French 'purchased' the Czechs can be found in Clemenceau's telegram to General Lavergne, the chief French military representative in Moscow, on 22 May 1918, a day or two before the Czechoslovak Legion decided to revolt. In this message Clemenceau told Lavergne of a report from the French military attaché in Tokyo that the Czechs in Vladivostok had enough money to keep the units in the city paid and provisioned for two months. Clemenceau then asked Lavergne about the units still in European Russia and authorised him to grant them credits, if this should prove necessary. It is obvious that Allied represent-atives on the spot could not provide information about the Czechs or help them because they were too far from the territory through which the Legion was advancing.

It is therefore clear that far from being 'bought' by the Allies, the Czechs received less support from them than from the Soviets. The small credits paid were those threatened by the 'enemy' (i.e. by the Germans or Bolsheviks). On the whole the Czechs depended on the Soviets for supplies and food, and consequently were reluctant, especially in Vladivostok, to undertake any moves against them. It is also clear that the Allies had little control over the money paid to the Czechs; in fact they had little control over the Czechs and their movements at all. Thus when the Allies finally informed the Czechs that they were to proceed to Archangel instead of continuing to Siberia and Vladivostok, they were first disbelieved and then defied. The French were short of troops for the Western front, which in their eyes was of paramount importance, and they sincerely wanted the Czechoslovaks in France.

Nevertheless the French attitude was more complicated than they cared to admit. Between March and May 1918, during the German offensive on the Western front, the French could undoubtedly have used the Czechs in France. But they were equally preoccupied with Russia's position in the war and still hoped that some sort of Eastern front could be re-established. In their opinion the Japanese were in the most suitable position to launch this venture, but the French were willing to support anyone who would undertake it, even the Bolsheviks. This plan was never realised, and ironically it was the Czechs who were responsible; thanks to the delays and vacilations of the Allies. On 15 March 1918, while the Czechoslovak Legion was slowly making its way to Vladivostok, the French, British and Italians met in London to discuss the possibility of a Japanese intervention in Russia directed against the Germans, for it was thought that there were no Russians, Red or White, capable of re-establishing an Eastern front. The Americans, also potential candidates for such an intervention, ruined this plan by objecting to the Japanese but doing nothing themselves.

Discussions continued, especially in military circles, about intervention by the Japanese (and eventually by the other Allies) in Russia against the Germans. Thus when Lieutenant-Colonel Lavergne, who had become the most senior Allied officer after General Niessel's departure, reported to the War Ministry in Paris that the Czechs were on their way to Vladivostok, and urged it to warn French consuls along the route and to provide shipping for them, he was answered by General Foch. Foch was preoccupied, as were the British, with the Bolshevik moves which indicated that the Bolsheviks might ask the Allies to help them against the Germans. Consequently Foch agreed to an earlier suggestion, that of retaining the Czechs in Russia as a nucleus for a new Russian army, and he suggested that the transportation problem might not be so urgent, since the Czechs could be used on the spot. The real reason for his anxiety to keep the Czechs in Russia for as long as possible emerges from a memorandum prepared by his staff on the following day. It seems the French were negotiating with the Japanese about ships to take the Czechs from Vladivostok and the evacuation of the unreliable Russian troops in Salonika in those same Japanese ships. These negotiations would take some time, so it was thought inopportune to concentrate all the Czechs in the Far East.

Lavergne was in due course informed of these negotiations and suggestions, but he himself was full of initiative. His readiness to take independent action undoubtedly sprang from his equivocal position in Russia. He knew that he would be given charge of military matters, since his ambassador was in Vologda and the military mission was withdrawn, but before he was given official sanction, he entered negotiations without reference to his ambassador. Thus he conducted political negotiations with the Czechoslovak Council in Moscow. When Trotsky asked him indirectly whether he would be capable of stopping the movement of Czechs to the Far East if the Germans launched another offensive against the Bolsheviks, Lavergne looked into the situation. His report made two important points: firstly, that the Czechs could be used to protect Allied embassies in the North even against the Bolsheviks; and, secondly, that the Czechs could not be relied on to fight the Bolsheviks.

This last point was emphasised a day later by the chief of the French military missions at Murmansk, who was asked by Paris whether it would be possible to have the Czechs re-routed and shipped via Murmansk and Archangel (obviously the negotiations with Japan were not progressing). He was against this plan, pointing out that even if the Bolsheviks allowed the Corps to be re-routed, which was improbable, it could not be used successfully against the Germans if they decided to attack the northern ports in strength. If the Czechs were not shipped west, the Bolsheviks would certainly undermine their morale. The Corps could not be considered as absolutely reliable in these circumstances. Parisian officials took this seriously and on 7 April 1918 an order was sent to French military personnel in Russia to screen all the Czechs (and those few Poles) before embarkation and notify Paris of all unreliable elements.

But the situation was further complicated by an unexpected British initiative. So far only the French had worried about the Czechs. They wanted to have the Czechs in the West, but were not sure whether they could not be better used on the spot. If they could not be thus used and would have to be transported to France, were they sufficiently reliable to fight there? Britain had no such reservation *vis-à-vis* the Czech Corps. The Foreign Office had throughout March 1918 been bombarded by Lockhart's telegrams indicating that the Bolsheviks were about to turn against the Germans and fight them with Allied aid. On 21 March 1918 Lockhart told Balfour, the Foreign Secretary, that Trotsky had asked for British instructors for his new army, and on 28 March 1918 Lockhart spoke of a dramatic *volte face*: the Bolsheviks were ready to start fighting the Germans alongside the Allies.

Under the impact of Lockhart's representations, and doubtless for other reasons that have yet to be clarified, on 21 March 1918 the Foreign Office prepared a memorandum for the War Office on the rôle and usefulness of the Czech Corps in Russia. A reply from the War Office was at last forthcoming on 1 April and its first point was to check certain inaccuracies in the Foreign Office memorandum. It was very doubtful whether there were 70,000 Czechs organised in the Legion in Russia (there had been some 42,000 in Kiev before the Bolsheviks took the city). At this stage an attempt had been made to send them under French officer-instructors to the Rumanian front, but this move had failed. The War Office pointed out that the Legion had refused to form the nucleus of the Russian Army, as Trotsky had suggested. So it was now making its way to Vladivostok, probably without artillery and ammunition because of transport difficulties. At Vladivostok it was to be shipped out to France but it was impossible to find the shipping and the troops' morale was uncertain; for these reasons they would have to be kept in Russia for some time. The War Office suggested that, while they were waiting, the Czechs could be used in one of three different ways: firstly, they could be concentrated round Omsk; secondly, they could be re-routed to Archangel; or, finally, they could be concentrated in the Trans-Baykal region for possible aid to Semyonov. General MacDonnough, Director of Operations at the War Office, felt the first proposition was the most attractive as the Legion could then block any action by German prisoners of war in Siberia.

If the motives for the Foreign Office initiative still remain rather obscure, the attitude of the War Office towards the Czechs was one of guarded suspicion. The Czechs were not forgiven for their 'disobedience' of Allied orders to move to Rumania while that country was still a partner in the war. On the whole they seemed to have little military value and it was thought that if they were to be used in Russia at all it would be in a passive way — to prevent any moves by German prisoners of war. The alternative plan, that of assisting Semyonov, was not even argued out. From the Foreign Office memorandum and the War Office reply it is clear that the British were far from 'scheming' imperialists bent on destroying the Soviets by every means at their disposal, as some communist historians have maintained. In this case, the evidence indicates that they were most reluctant to use this 'unreliable' Czech force against the Bolsheviks.

Nonetheless the British initiative did, ultimately, result in the revolt of the Czechs against the Bolsheviks. The extent to which this was intentional will become apparent from a consideration of the various Anglo-French deals concerning the Czechs which followed, after the Foreign Office memorandum had been circulated and discussed in authoritative Allied circles. To all appearances the British government was much less preoccupied with the Western front than the French. It believed in fighting the central powers anywhere, and especially in the East, where the British empire had vital interests. The British like the French were ready to use any forces available for that purpose. But in contrast to the French the British wanted to keep the Japanese out of the Russian Far East if it was at all possible, since they distrusted them. This distrust was based on very practical considerations: it was hoped that the threat of Japanese intervention would force the Bolsheviks to turn against the Germans themselves and invite direct Allied intervention. From Moscow, Lockhart continued to deluge the Foreign Office with telegrams in which he demanded that the Japanese intervention be delayed. His advice was obviously heeded, while no attention was paid in London to the views of Major-General Knox, who advocated immediate action in the East without Bolshevik consent. On 17 March 1918 Knox told Panouse, the French military attaché in London, that he would shortly be leaving for the Far East — intervention was imminent — but on 21 March he complained to Panouse that President Wilson was responsible for the failure of his Far East plans. Yet on 2 April Panouse was informed of plans for the Far East worked out by the Deputy Director of Military Intelligence; evidently the Foreign Office was at least taking Knox seriously. But before these plans could even be discussed the Japanese landed a small force at Vladivostok on 4 April. The British immediately followed suit.

This landing must have been an unexpected unilateral act of the Japanese. In Moscow, Trotsky expressed himself very strongly to Lockhart about the British 'perfidy' in allowing the Japanese landing. Lockhart may even have sympathised with this view, but the move had clearly not been sanctioned by the British. Knox was still in London, and he was to stay there until July 1918, which was a sure sign that the British were not considering any further military action. Only 50 marines had been sent to Vladivostok. The French were informed of these developments in some detail. By 12 April even Moscow came to regard the landing in a different light. Trotsky thought the British had landed so promptly in order to paralyse the Japanese, and in this he was probably correct. In any event the British stock went up in Moscow and Lockhart soon had Trotsky's ear again. A fortnight later there were no British troops in Vladivostok, and shortly afterwards the Japanese also withdrew under pressure from the Allies.

It is plain that by then, all the other Allies had come round to the British point of view, namely that it was more convenient to be invited to intervene by the Bolsheviks than to do so against their will. However, since the Japanese had been so rudely checked and no other ally could provide and land troops in Russia within a reasonable period of time, the unfortunate Czechs came into the discussion again. There followed a sort of seesaw contest between the British and the French whether the Czechs should or should not be withdrawn from Russia.

On 1 April Panouse sent to Paris the first indications of this new British approach, and on the following day he enclosed a translation of the War Office reply to the Foreign Office memorandum. The French, however, were in no mood to consider any reasonable proposal that the Czechs be used in Siberia for they themselves badly needed fresh troops and encouraging reports were received from Russia that the Czechs were indeed on the move and that their morale was excellent. Consul André even asked for instructions how he should deal with the Czechs when they arrived. On 7 April 1918, three days after the surprise Japanese landing, the French General Staff had a reply ready for the British, which Panouse handed to the War Office. This was very cautious in tone, as one might expect in view of the fact that the French depended completely on British shipping. It did not reject outright the British suggestions but contained a compromise proposal. The French still insisted that the Czechs be shipped to France and not used in Russia, but conceded that they might possibly help Semyonov while waiting for British ships to arrive for them. The final decision would only be taken when the Czechs actually arrived in Vladivostok.

This French 'softness' only complicated the situation. The British became convinced that the French would yield and employ the Czechs in Russia if a reasonable pretext could be found. On 8 April, at a meeting of the permanent military representatives of the Supreme War Council at Versailles, the French were imprudent enough to vote for the use of the Czechs in the future Allied force in Siberia if this force should come into being. This vote for a hypothetical contingency did not signify a change in the French attitude. Lockhart reported from Moscow that Lavergne vehemently opposed an intervention by force in Russia, and his views still commanded much sympathy in Paris. On 9 April however, Lavergne unwittingly complicated the Czechs' position still further by suggesting that since their movement to Vladivostok had in any case been stopped by Trotsky on account of the Japanese landing, the Czechs should be re-routed to Archangel.

This was indeed a dangerous suggestion, but Lavergne probably never realised that he had played into the hands of the British. By now the Japanese had refused to ship the Czechs, and if his suggestions were acted upon, the ships could only be provided by the British. On 16 April, the French General Staff once again took the matter up with the British and suggested another compromise. If the British would consent to evacuate the Czechs to France by way of Archangel and Murmansk, the Czechs could in the meantime be used to guard the northern ports. This was possibly what the British were waiting for. Their direct commitment to ship the Czechs to France would in any case give them much more power to decide the fate of the Czechs in Russia.

On 20 April 1918 Lockhart received instructions from the cabinet regarding the Czech Corps. The British government saw the Czechs as the only force in Russia willing to fight the Germans. They were to be re-routed from Siberia to Archangel and Murmansk and then transported to France. To help Lockhart in his negotiations with the Bolsheviks on this matter he was given ideological guidance: the Czechs were said to have declared themselves in sympathy for the Russian peasants. This instruction was certainly sent with the French government's approval, for on the same day Clemenceau instructed Lavergne in a similar vein, although using slightly more sophisticated terms.

It is difficult to discover how serious the British were about bringing the Czechs from Russia to France, but there can be no doubt concerning the position of the French, who were very anxious to have these good fighting men on the Western front. They immediately entered into talks with the British about the details of their transportation. One week after the policy declaration Lavergne received another telegram from the French War Ministry to say that the French were having difficulties with his idea of routing the Czechoslovaks via Archangel. Thereupon the French cabinet took firm steps to remove the Czechs from Russia. At Versailles the military representatives had approved their move north and requested the British government to negotiate the re-routing with the Bolsheviks. On 2 May 1918 the Czechoslovaks figured prominently on the agenda when the Supreme War Council's political and military representatives met at Abbeville. Both the French and British cabinet ministers solemnly agreed to implement a formal resolution, which the conference passed, to remove the Czechoslovak Legion from Russia to France.

It is not clear who, if any, of the French liaison officers with the Legion in Russia was ever consulted about the re-routing idea. Ultimately it was decided that only the 2nd Division, which was still west of Omsk, should be re-routed north. In any case Bolshevik agreement to the plan was not negotiated until 5 May, and even then their approval was only given 'in principle'. Immediately afterwards Lavergne had doubts whether the re-routing project could be carried out; he also urged his government to keep the negotiations secret. The reason for this secrecy was that he did not wish to embarrass the Bolsheviks by revealing that Trotsky had consented to hand over to the Legion, when it arrived at Archangel, some of the Allied stores in the city.

On 11 May 1918 Premier Clemenceau put further pressure on the British by reiterating his position: the French were responsible for removing the Czechoslovaks to the point of embarkation, while the British were to provide the transport. Whether this forceful statement by Clemenceau was realistic or not remains problematic. There are many indications that he was genuinely concerned to bring the Czechs to France. He was under pressure for more troops in France itself and from local French representatives abroad, who were clamouring for ships. To all appearances therefore he did not want the Czechoslovaks in Russia. However, the situation was complicated by the fact that in the meantime Franco-British discussions had started on a large-scale intervention in Russia. On 18 May Lord Cecil wrote to Clemenceau very frankly that, since no ships were available for the Legion, the latter should be used in Vladivostok. He argued that both governments wanted to force the United States and Japan to intervene as well, and the Czechoslovaks could serve as an excellent pretext to bring this about. Four days later Clemenceau, still unaware that the Czechoslovak Legion had finally decided to revolt against the Bolsheviks and fight its way to Vladivostok, protested to Cecil that his propositions violated the Abbeville agreement: the British could not deprive France of Czech troops which were badly needed. At the same time Clemenceau sent a long telegram to Lavergne instructing him to start re-routing the Czechoslovaks to Archangel even against Bolshevik wishes. Negotiations with them were useless and there was no need for a written statement by Trotsky. He added that the British and French cabinets were actively studying the question of the northern ports and their protection.

These were the last instructions by the French prime minister to the local representative in Russia before the outbreak of the Czechoslovak revolt. It is not quite certain what instructions the British government sent to Lockhart, but they were probably very similar. For Lockhart left Moscow for Vologda to see the Allied ambassadors there, and thereupon changed his mind about the merits of Allied intervention. On his return to Moscow he found the Czechoslovak Legion in full revolt, whether he or Lavergne wished it or not. The revolt may have been a godsend to them, but it was certainly not their work.

Thus contrary to Lenin's allegations the revolt of the Czechoslovak Legion was not the work of the imperialist Allies. It was 'organised' by the Czechoslovaks on the spot, and even then it was the revolt by resolute young officers against their timid political leaders, who can also be absolved of responsibility for its preparation. Some of the emerging and eclipsed leaders in Russia did spread rumours of an impending allied intervention, discussed this eventuality and even expressed approval of it. But they took no active steps to promote it. The revolt was a sudden and spontaneous affair which surprised everybody, foe and friend alike. It caught the Allies unprepared, and although it provided them with the pretext they had been seeking for so long they were very slow to exploit it.

Whatever plans France, Britain, the Supreme Allied Council, the French High Command or the Japanese General Staff had prepared for Russia, they had to be scrapped or completely altered after the unexpected revolt of the Czechoslovak Legion. Up to June 1918 all planning was hinged to the Legion and the northern bases at Murmansk and Archangel, which contained plentiful supplies and were considered the best positions for its use in Russia. The Legion was to form the nucleus of the Allied intervention force and when Allied reinforcements strengthened it, it would strike out into Russia against both the Germans and the Bolsheviks. But the revolt brought the Czechoslovaks to the Central Volga region instead, so the northern plan had to be abandoned. Only one feature of it was retained: Allied reinforcements which were already on the way would try and break out of Murmansk and Archangel to Kotlas to link up with the Legion. This was really a hopeless objective, but in Paris, London and Washington, not to mention Versailles, it seemed reasonable that Allied units could march over some 500 miles of desolate tundra without proper supplies and reach the more powerful Legion on the Volga without Bolshevik opposition. Allied forces under General Poole landed in Archangel on 2 August 1918 and though they subsequently tried hard to break out, they never succeeded in getting anywhere near the Volga region. After being literally frozen in during the winter of 1918-19, they were finally evacuated in the autumn of 1919. This northern venture was another example of the haphazard planning of the intervention and a further denial of Lenin's thesis that the imperialist Allies strove to destroy the Bolsheviks. Moreover it was not the Red Army which killed this particular 'plot' of the Allies but bad planning, climate and above all distances.

Still this northern link-up, after the Czechoslovak revolt, was relatively unimportant. Neither the Legion nor the Allies in the north could have benefited from it decisively; it simply caused tactical difficulties. However, the Volga-Vladivostok link-up was of vital importance and here the Japanese might have helped. In a sense they did, when on 3 August 1918 their 12th Infantry Division began to disembark at Vladivostok. By 21 August 1918 an additional 12,000 soldiers had passed through Vladivostok on their way to Manchuria and the Far Eastern province. On 26 August 10,000 more Japanese troops arrived and by November 1918 the Japanese had more than 70,000 troops in Siberia. This then was a massive indication of Allied intervention in the Far East. But in fact the Japanese were in Siberia not as an intervening force against the Central Powers, but as self-declared helpers of the Czechoslovak Legion, that is on their own terms for their own purposes. In reality the Japanese did very little to help the Legion; they occupied territories which they considered within their sphere of influence and apart from giving some aid to their client, Ataman Semenov, they manifested no interest in any Allied undertaking and project.

The saving of the Czechoslovak Legion from the Bolsheviks was in fact supposed to be the first all-Allied undertaking, in which the armies of Britain, France, the USA and Japan (as well as some elements of Italians in China) were to take part. However, Japan rather abruptly chose to act on its own and ruined the Allied action from the beginning. The Americans were most reluctant to participate in the intervention in Russia, but paradoxically Japanese intervention really forced them to join in. It was only on 19 August 1918 that the Americans responded to the combined Anglo-French pressure and the more discreet influence exercised in Washington by Professor T.G. Masaryk, the political leader of the Czechoslovak Legion. One American division was landed at Vladivostok allegedly to save the three Czechoslovak divisions which were fighting the Bolsheviks. In fact the Americans were sent to Siberia to keep an eye on the Japanese. Soon after the landing Masaryk sent his compatriots in Siberia a solemn warning from Washington not to expect too much from the Americans. On 22 August 1918 President Wilson confirmed publicly Masaryk's warning: the Americans were sent to Vladivostok to help the Czechs in that area and not to get entangled in the Allied project of re-constituting an Eastern front against Germany. Though Wilson's declaration clearly stated what the Americans would not do, it did not define sufficiently how they would help the Czechs. The Legion, which was ten times as numerous as the American contingent, had by then been sufficiently helped by the Japanese to achieve their primary objective: on 31 August 1918 the junction between the three fighting groups of Czechs had been effected, and the Legion controlled the whole of the Trans Siberian Railway from the Volga to Vladivostok. The Legion was saved and the US-Japanese intervention had achieved its declared purpose. That neither withdrew from Siberia showed that they were there for other purposes than saving the Legion.

August 1918 was a crucial month for the Allies and their plans in Russia. Had the Americans and Japanese been really willing to intervene and push on to Irkutsk and even Chelyabinsk, the Legion thus freed might have made a decisive difference to the operations launched by it and its allies, White Russians in Russia. But the Japanese failed to react to Czech and Allied exhortations to push on. The Americans proved even more disappointing, for they came ashore and remained passively in Vladivostok until further instructions should reach them. Somehow these instructions failed to arrive and the Americans stayed put practically the whole period of the civil war in Siberia at Vladivostok. Only a few small units branched out of the city. When in 1920 the Americans withdrew, their intervention could be summed up as consisting mainly of interference in economic matters in Siberia. On the whole this first attempt at an overall Allied intervention in Russia was an unmitigated disaster which endangered neither the Germans nor the Bolsheviks, but put a tremendous strain on the wartime alliance. Still, at the time of the armistice in the West, in November 1918, when the failure of this overall Allied effort was crystal clear, the Allies seem to have learned nothing. Once again they were busy negotiating among themselves an intervention in Russia which, this time, should sort out Russian problems and end the civil war; excessive hope was put in the Peace Conference which gathered in Paris early in 1919.

However, at this second attempt at an all-Allies' intervention in Russia there were the most elementary difficulties. The Allies could not agree among themselves on who should represent Russia at the conference. In the end it was decided that no-one should speak for her officially, but private individuals should be invited to address the conference on behalf of Russia and be listened to by the Allies who would then deliver their judgments. When the Conference finally met it had for its consideration one 'coordinated' draft proposal only. The Allied War Council, and in particular Marshal Foch, had prepared a military plan for Allied intervention in Russia only, despite the failure of the first project. This second plan for an overall Allied intervention envisaged a coordinated offensive against the Bolsheviks by multi-national armies under Foch's supreme command. The nucleus of these intervention forces would be formed by the Rumanians, Polish and Baltic armies, while the Czechs (presumably the Legion in Siberia) and the non-Bolshevik Russians (Whites) would play only a subordinate rôle. The Allies would equip these forces and with French officers firmly in command the plan, Marshal Foch thought, would have a good chance of succeeding. However, the Foch plan was narrowly military in design and though some aspects were open to severe criticism (would the Rumanians, or mysterious Balts, or Poles fight?) it seemed on the whole plausible. Its chief weakness was political: why should this purely military operation deliver Russia from bolshevism, and who should be put in power?

On 12 January 1919 the Council of Five began to discuss the Russian problem. The political weakness of Foch's plan became immediately clear: the Russian individuals objected to it claiming that it was crude interference in internal Russian affairs and their objection seemed justified, though not insuperably. As could have been expected the objection of the other states involved was decisive: they had no interest in an armed struggle which should result in re-constituting Russia by 'delivering her from bolshevism'. In the end even Clemenceau thought that the plan was impracticable and both Lloyd George and President Wilson objected to it. On 22 January 1919 the five Allied powers rejected the plan and thus killed the only proposal for a common policy and action in Russia. However, feverish negotiations continued and many an impulsive effort was made to solve the Russian problem. Since these efforts were not results of common agreement they also failed one after another. One such effort, initiated by the British premier, Lloyd George, highlighted the uninformed impulsiveness and disagreements of the Allies. During preliminary discussions Lloyd George advocated negotiations with the Bolsheviks, as the most significant power factor in Russia, since they could not be eliminated in any other way. President Wilson then came round to Lloyd George's idea and drafted his own proposals for settling the Russian problem by negotiations: he suggested that all the parties engaged in the civil war in Russia were to meet at the Prinkipo Islands, off Istanbul, and negotiate there a peaceful settlement of the dispute. The conference would begin on 15 February 1919 and the only precondition of attendance was the cessation of hostilities.

It is undoubted that if the idea of the conference worked it would have been an excellent way out of the Russian imbroglio for Britain and France. President Wilson, who was hardly involved in Russia, liked to play the role of a peacemaker and was therefore delighted with the idea of a conference. However, the French gave only a grudging consent to the common Allied appeal for the conference realising full well that the warring Russians would reject it. However, this appeal for a peaceful settlement of the civil war was so unrealistic that it confused everyone. At first it seemed that even the Russian Whites would welcome it: the Crimean Government misunderstood the idea of the conference thinking of it as an international tribunal by which the Bolsheviks would be tried and outvoted. But when it became clear that the purpose of the conference was not to judge but to arrange a peaceful settlement even the Crimeans rejected the appeal. Both Admiral Kolchak and General Denikin also rejected it, because it arrived at the wrong moment. They were both preparing a large scale offensive against the Bolsheviks, and neither of them was yet decisively beaten. Thus only Lenin and the Bolsheviks saw a direct benefit in accepting the invitation, but even they were prepared to attend only on their own conditions. They demanded prior withdrawal of Allied troops from Russia, and an immediate halt to Allied military aid to the Whites. These conditions would have wrecked the conference in any case, but Clemenceau then decided to take the onus of failure from the Bolsheviks: when he saw that no practical purpose could be served by such an ill-conceived conference — except international Bolshevik recognition, a halt to offensive preparations and an incalculable blow to White morale — he made it known that he also objected to this harebrained scheme and the Whites unanimously rejected the idea.

The Prinkipo conference was the last 'commonly agreed' idea for the solution of the Russian problem. It failed as hopelessly as the first common ideas, plans and common actions. All the Allies had no other option but to return to the old, individual defence of interests in Russia, and as before un-coordinated, often contradictory policies were launched, until a stage was reached when they cancelled each other. During the year of 1919 even the limited agreements between Britain and France became inoperative and led to conflicts and the resulting free for all policy led to the inevitable decline of Allied influence in Russia.

The first of these limited agreements, which Lenin described as the imperialist conspiracy against the Russian revolution, was the Franco-British Convention signed in Paris on 23 December 1917. This convention, which was a clumsy effort at rationalisation of a wholly irrational situation in Russia, ever since it was divulged in the 1930s was a target of abuse for the Bolsheviks, the Whites, and even the Americans, who were naturally not informed. For the two former it was an imperialist plan for the dismemberment of Russia; for the latter a rather cynical division of spheres of interests with which they disagreed. More recently some historians have argued that the convention was in fact a purely military one, in which purely military tasks were dealt with. Others have claimed that it was the expression of the economic interests of the two allies. There is probably some truth in all these arguments, except perhaps in the Bolshevik and White one, for the British and French had never considered dismembering Russia, however desirable it might have seemed at the time. In the light of subsequent events, the convention appears a purely theoretical attempt by the far-away allies to sort out policy problems and to allot each other tasks for future eventualities. There are many factors which support this view of the convention. First of all the convention did not embody the *status quo* in Russia. The allocation of territories was done on a purely hypothetical basis. Thus the Don region was allocated to the British, but it was the French who had a small mission there, while there was no Briton anywhere near the Don territory, or at best a lonely representativee still *en route*. As for the Caucasus, the forces and interests of the two allies there were about equal, though the French mission at Tiflis probably exercised more influence than the British. The allocation of the Ukraine to the French did not mean that the British were excluded from it. In fact the British agent, Bagge, arrived there at about this time, and helped out the French, especially in financing pro-Allied forces, the Czechoslovak Legion among them. Neither was the convention meant as a long-term policy, for though it was renewed a year later, the two allies continued in their own, separate policies *vis-à-vis* Russia regardless. The most plausible explanation of the convention is that it was the result of Allied anxiety to organise some kind of resistance in the East against the Germans and the Turks, and to support the suddenly deserted Rumanians as soon as practicable. However, apart from the abuse which it attracted from friend and foe, the convention solved absolutely nothing.

At the time when the convention was signed the French were still looking for a policy, while the British had already formulated one. In fact two days before the convention was signed, the British cabinet re-affirmed this policy: it was decided to continue to follow the dual policy, namely maintain unofficial contacts both with the Bolsheviks and with the opposition forces in the south, the Caucasus, Siberia, and with the Cossack Voyska, especially the South Eastern Union. This policy remained in force until the revolt of the Czechoslovak Legion in May 1918 and caused a lot of confusion. France insisted on vigorous pursuit of Allied war aims in Russia and this meant roughly the same as the British dual policy. Both governments, on their own, sent missions to all sorts of centres of opposition to the Bolsheviks and tried to aid them at least financially. However, neither hesitated to come to terms with the Bolsheviks whenever they did show signs of turning against the Germans.

Initially it was the success and energy of the Bolsheviks that prompted some Allied representatives in Russia and outside to advocate *rapprochement* with them. The French Ambassador Noulens commented on their energy shortly after the *coup d'état*; however, this very energy made him ultimately a determined supporter of a direct intervention. General Niessel's attitude was more complicated; he could not fail to recognise Bolshevik enthusiasm and energy and at times favoured *rapprochement*. With him much depended on immediate circumstances. The British agent in Russia, R. Bruce Lockhart, advocated an alliance with the Bolsheviks almost without reservation. However, when on 11 February 1918 peace negotiations at Brest-Litovsk were broken off, Allied speculations about the Bolsheviks became wild. Many British and French representatives on the spot performed a daring *volte face* and began to see an advantage in the peace negotiations which they had found so catastrophic, when they were opened. Now it appeared that 'Colonel' Robins, US Red Cross representative in Russia, benefiting from the negotiations, was able to send a subversive mission of Russian Bolsheviks to Germany to start a revolution there. It seemed that the Bolsheviks – especially Trotsky – were coming round to the Allied point of view, namely that it would be impossible to satisfy German imperialism. All the same the Bolsheviks made it clear that they were turning anti-German, because they thought that German militarism was the more dangerous of the two imperialisms and that it had to be defeated first.

On 18 February 1918, when the Germans denounced the armistice and launched an attack against the Bolsheviks, Noulens and Lindley, the British *chargé d'affaires* in Russia, let it be known to the Bolshevik Foreign Ministry, which they did not officially recognise, that Allied aid would be forthcoming if requested. Still it was with evident relish that Allied military observers reported that the German Army was dispersing 'Bolshevik bands'. Indeed the collapse of the Bolshevik forces was so complete that even Trotsky began to entertain the idea of Allied aid seriously. His intermediary, Captain Sadoul, asked Noulens what exactly France would do for Russia and the Ambassador went out of his way to telephone the answer to Trotsky. While he asked General Niessel to get a defence plan ready he radioed Paris, and through Paris all the other allies, urging them to support the Bolsheviks at this juncture. In the meantime Trotsky told Lockhart that the Bolsheviks were ready to retreat to the Urals, but would not stop fighting. This was obviously an exaggeration to test Allied intentions, for by then the Bolsheviks were waiting for German consent to sign the peace treaty negotiated at Brest-Litovsk. Bolshevik bluff worked wonders and all the Allies, with the exception of the United States, approved aid to the Bolsheviks. Immediately all over Russia Allied officers (mainly French) joined the retreating Bolshevik 'bands' as demolition experts and began to blow up railway communications to delay the German advance.

On 22 February 1918 General Niessel had his defence plan ready and approved by the Allied governments. But it took him two more days to see the belligerent Trotsky. When he finally saw him and explained the plan to him, Trotsky, who by then knew that the Germans had just accepted the Bolshevik request to sign the peace and consequently halted their advance, told the General that the plan was good, but of no use. He did not enlarge on his reasons, but it became quickly obvious that France and Britain were taken for a ride, and that the Bolsheviks had not the slightest intention of re-joining the war. However, even this embarrassing experience did not prevent the British and French from trying again to gain the favour of the Bolsheviks.

Shortly after the signature of the peace treaty with Germany the Bolsheviks decided to organise an army, the Red Army, and Trotsky became the Commissar of War. Though the peace treaty forbade him any traffic with the Allies, he nevertheless immediately approached Lockhart asking him for aid in organising the new army. It seemed reasonable that Trotsky should seek British and French instructors to help him with the organisation of the Red Army, for against whom should the new army be used but Germany? The Allies were full of anticipation that the request for instructors should be followed by the Bolshevik invitation for intervention and Britain was ready to send a large number of officer-instructors to Russia. The French had a large military contingent in Russia and all of them were alerted to keep themselves ready for the new jobs. However nothing came of this mission; the Allies were not invited to intervene and the officers had hardly a chance to reach the future Red Army units when the Czechoslovak Legion, an autonomous part of the French army, launched its revolt against the Bolsheviks and ruined this particular project as well as the dual policy so unsuccessfully pursued by France and Britain. Henceforth it was open hostility, but again each ally on its own.

It was natural that France should feel that it should assume the leadership of the armed struggle against the Bolsheviks started by the Legion, which in a sense was its own. On 24 August 1918, after some hesitation, General Janin was appointed by Clemenceau C-in-C Allied forces in Russia, which in practice meant that he was in command of the Czechoslovak Legion. However, many months would elapse before Janin, who was at that moment in France, would actually take up his command in Siberia. Despite the convention the British government also appointed Major-General A. Knox to head a British Military Mission to Siberia, and while it was not clear whom he would command, Knox was in Siberia long before Janin. In Siberia Knox concerned himself with the Legion, on whom he reported to the Allied governments, as well as with the Russians whom he tried to help and organise. When Knox ascertained that the French would not permit him to deal with the Legion he concentrated almost entirely on the Whites, especially since his government, had begun to think of re-establishing the Whites there. After all the Czechoslovaks would have to go home at some stage leaving behind a power vacuum which would have to be filled by the Whites. All these British moves were done without consultation with the French and caused conflict and tension between the two allies in Siberia and elsewhere.

On 5 October 1918 Sir Charles Eliot, the newly appointed British High Commissioner, arrived at Omsk, the seat of one of the White governments, with a set of instructions from the Foreign Secretary, Lord Balfour, but without any knowledge of the French plans and intention: they had not appointed their own political representative. Sir Charles also concerned himself with Russian politics and left the Legion alone. First of all he conveyed to the Russians the shock the Allies felt at seeing them so disunited. Then he tried to investigate the possibility of a stronger Russian government – perhaps a temporary dictatorship. But there was no strong candidate for dictator in Russia and the British candidate, General Alexeyev, was not in Siberia. Thus the British had to make do with weak governments and wait for an opportunity to install a strong one in the future. In any case Sir Charles was much more impressed by the Legion and would have preferred to base himself and British policies in Siberia on that body rather than on the Whites.

The French plans for Siberia were quite different. When General Janin finally arrived he was to implement a plan which envisaged the Legion and Allied (?) troops doing the fighting against the Red Army and destroying it in the end. The Whites hardly figured in French plans; they were there only to carry out auxiliary tasks. According to French reports from Siberia the Whites were not worth anything else. On 12 October 1918 General Janin received a report from Siberia which urged him to speed up his arrival; his presence at the fronts was of the utmost importance; the fronts were in a chaotic state mainly thanks to the refusal of the Russians to obey Czech officers. Only Janin's prestige would impress these recalcitrant Russians, who in any case were quite incapable of planning military operations.

The French must have confided their plans to General Knox at least, for on 21 October 1918 he arrived from Vladivostok at Omsk to sort out Russian problems before Janin could get there. He negotiated with the Russian Commander-in-Chief, General Boldyrev, an agreement which made it clear that the Czechoslovak Legion and Janin were the basis of any settlement in Siberia. Boldyrev quickly signed off his supreme title to General Janin, who accordingly became the Commander-in-Chief of all Allied and Russian forces. In exchange for the title the two Allied countries promised the Whites material and technical aid, and advice with the formation of a new Russian army without committees and with good discipline. This agreement at first sight appeared as a great political and military achievement. But it seems that Boldyrev concluded it only because he was fully aware of his own and White weakness: utter disunity prevented the Russians from achieving anything except quarrel among themselves and question each other's and everybody else's authority. Thus he threw away responsibility rather lightly and in turn Britain and France were saddled with a paper agreement and empty titles, for the Russian Army was not yet in existence. Moreover, the future C-in-C was not yet in Russia and unified command brought neither Russian obedience nor Allied reinforcements. In addition to these negotiations General Knox also became involved in the Kolchak coup d'état, thus cancelling any benefit which the agreement with Boldyrev might have brought to the two allies.

At Omsk the All-Russian Directory which had retreated there from Samara could not come to an agreement with the West Siberian Government, whose capital it was. The Czechoslovak Legion supported the former and as long as the Czechs were in command the Directory seemed secure in power. In November 1918 though, the Legion left the front and refused to fight, and the Directory's position became precarious. General Knox joked with Boldyrev, who was the Directory's C-in-C, about a coup d'état at Omsk if the Directory and the Siberians failed to agree among themselves. As if to demonstrate this point Colonel Ward, M.P., and a battalion of the Middlesex Regiment arrived at Omsk together with

Admiral Kolchak, who had strayed so far inland after joining the Royal Navy as a volunteer. All these persons and forces combined and on 18 November 1918 Admiral Kolchak emerged as the Supreme Ruler of Russia. Thanks to Colonel Ward's Battalion and two small detachments of Cossacks commanded by Atamans Volkov and Krasilnikov the Directory was dissolved, its leading members exiled and Kolchak, after reaching an agreement with the Siberians, was offered the supreme post.

While the circumstances of Kolchak's coup d'état are even now obscure, the coup itself had tremendous effect on Franco-British relations in Siberia. Both the French and British governments, faced with a *fait accompli,* decided to acquiesce, and the coup passed without official protests. But the two allies told the Whites that despite the coup General Janin was still C-in-C of all Allied and Russian forces west of Lake Baykal, while General Knox was in charge of the rear (east of Lake Baykal), of training and supplies. The British seemed to have benefited somehow from this revised agreement and the French became convinced that the whole affair at Omsk was staged by the British. Henceforth suspicions, quarrels and recriminations between the British and French followed.

On 16 December 1918 General Janin reached Omsk and had his first interview with Admiral Kolchak. Despite the existing paper agreements they personally could agree on nothing, and soon Kolchak sent Janin out to the front to take charge of operations, or get out altogether. Janin then saw the extent of the Legion's collapse and quite reasonably assumed that his mission as C-in-C had come to an end. Gradually he handed over his functions to Russian generals and by February 1919 he even stopped attending meetings at Kolchak's GHQ. All his attention was centered on the Czechoslovak Legion and how to get it out of Siberia as soon as practicable. The Whites, and Kolchak in particular, demanded his attention when their front against the Red Army collapsed in November 1919 and they were in dire trouble. The French general attempted half-heartedly to help, but he was no longer in charge of the situation. In the end he did nothing, Kolchak was handed over to the Bolsheviks by the Czechs and the whole of White Siberia lay in ruin. However, he did manage to extricate the Legion, so his mission was at least a partial success; for the overall failure he blamed the British ally (cf. pp. 111 ff).

Acting on their own the British did not achieve anything constructive in Siberia either. After the withdrawal of the two battalions which they had sent to Siberia to help the Legion out, General Knox concentrated on supplies and training, and with both was equally unsuccessful. He supervised the distribution of British equipment to Kolchak's armies and saw many of the soldiers desert to the enemy with their new uniforms. In any case British equipment was very badly distributed and invariably ended in Bolshevik hands after the Whites had collapsed. His personal task, training the new Russian army, also ended in a failure: the trainees refused to be loyal to Kolchak and even before his fall they mutinied against his authority and had to be repressed. In December 1919 the British government decided to pull out of Siberia and accept no further commitments; only the High Commissioner should remain, but only for the purpose of watching the Americans and the Japanese. However, even that proved impossible, for the Commissioner was forced out of Siberia by the Red Army and Lord Curzon then abolished the post and dissolved the British Mission. British policy lay in ruin and Curzon summed up the British policy as 'a totally discredited affair and complete failure'.

After the armistice in the West it seemed for a time that the convention between France and Britain would finally come to life and become operative — at least in the new Russian territories which came under Allied influence. On 13 November 1918 the two allies re-affirmed their zonal arrangements in Russia, although they now made no sense whatsoever. However, once the declaration was made it was forgotten, and each ally continued its own separate way. In the South the French, seeing the rapid collapse of the Germans and their allies in the Balkans, decided to intervene directly with their own troops. Clemenceau disregarded the opinion of his C-in-C in the Black Sea area, the future Marshal Franchet d'Esperey, and asked General Berthelot, who was still in Rumania, to organise a conference of Russian Whites to invite the French to intervene.

On arrival in Bucharest Berthelot immediately got in touch with General Shcherbatchov, the former Russian C-in-C on the Rumanian front. Shcherbatchov was in contact with General Denikin's HQ, and though he had previously flirted with Hetman Skoropadsky and the Ukrainians, he was now considered Denikin's representative. He telegraphed Denikin Allied plans: the Allies were going to land 12 infantry divisions (mainly French and Greek) at Odessa, where Allied HQ would be established. Allied forces would then push on to occupy Sevastopol, Kiev, Kharkov, the Donets and Krivoy Rog basins, and would probably go as far as the Don, if it proved necessary. These Allied divisions were being sent to Russia to restore order, supervise German withdrawal and provide the Volunteer Army with a protective shield so that it could reorganise in peace and prepare to strike out at the Bolsheviks when the right moment came. Berthelot was in charge both of political and of military operations.

All this was almost true, but there were several basic points which were not made clear: the landing and the intervention were purely French affairs, and the British had already made direct contacts with Denikin. Secondly, Berthelot was not as powerful as Shcherbatchov imagined: he had Consul Henno to guide him politically. From the start Shcherbatchov, and through him Denikin, misunderstood a lot of important matters: thus Berthelot's outline of plans and intentions was taken for 'Allied demands and guarantees'. Denikin felt that the Allies were consulting him before launching their intervention: he readily agreed provided the Allies stuck to 'the principles and conditions', which did not exist. As soon as French intervention started the Russian generals were instantly disappointed and later dared to object to 'modifications in Allied plans approved by the Volunteers'.

Politically Berthelot was completely effaced by Allied diplomatic representatives attached to the Rumanian government at Iassi, and they prepared the Russians the greatest disappointment. The Allied spokesman with the Russians, Ukrainians and any other element in southern Russia was Consul Henno, formerly member of General Tabouis's mission in Kiev and Captain of the Dèuxième Bureau. But he was the final interpreter of political instructions from Paris and as such greatly complicated Berthelot's mission. Henno's instructions were 'to check the Bolsheviks (with menaces and without force), to insure that the German Army does not hand over arms to them, and to prepare the way for the French landing in Odessa'. He interpreted this instruction to mean that he was in charge of political matters and decided to consult Russian politicians by convoking an Allied-Russian consultative conference. This was obviously a terrible blunder, but he was supported unanimously by the Allied ministers at Iassi — St Aulaire (France), Barclay (Britain), Vopička (USA) and de Visart (Italy). At this stage Henno ignored the Ukrainians and invited only the pro-Allied Russians. Like Berthelot before him, Henno did not however make it clear to the Russians what they were being consulted about. The 'Russian delegation' misinterpreted its role when they sanctioned the French landing in Odessa and approved Allied intervention as such. These decisions were already made and when it became clear even to them that they were wasting their time they put this consultative conference to good use by working out their own political programme.

Even this programme was to lead to dissension and be subject to misinterpretation, for it was assumed that since it issued from an Allied-sponsored conference the Allies themselves approved it. After long arguments the Russians agreed on two points only: 1. to support the Allies in order to re-constitute Russia in its pre-1914 borders (with the exception of Poland); 2. they further agreed that this struggle would be waged under General Denikin's leadership and he was elected by the assembled Russians Military Dictator. After this molehill achievement the conference dispersed with the false impression that the Allies had accepted to undertake the re-constitution of Russia in her pre-war border and that General Denikin was the supreme commander and leader by the grace of the Allies. Both were misconceptions and the French were going to prove the former one to be such very shortly. Denikin, who was on the way to becoming a British-sponsored general, would be disappointed much later.

The French then proceeded to deal with the situation on the spot. On 14 November 1918 Hetman Skoropadsky, who had headed the pro-German regime in the Ukraine throughout the period of German occupation, tried to change sides and offered to the Allies and to the non-Bolshevik Russians a federal union. Since Denikin and the Iassi delegates considered him a traitor to Russia his offer was rejected. The Allies hesitated, but before Skoropadsky could complicate their plans any further he fell from power and became an unimportant refugee in Berlin. However, on 17 December 1918 Ukrainian nationalists seized power and declared the Ukraine an independent state.

This was an utterly unexpected turn of events for both the Russians and the French. Clemenceau envisaged a peaceful takeover in the Ukraine and failed to take Ukrainian nationalists into consideration. Henno was therefore urgently instructed to deal with the Ukrainian complication and solve all the problems so that the 156th French Colonial Division already en route from Saloniki could land peacefully at Odessa. Henno, instead of negotiating with the Ukrainians, threatened them with the troops *en route* and saw himself ignored, while the nationalists continued their takeover of the Ukraine supported by the withdrawing Germans. It was obvious that Henno could not deal with the situation and that there would be no peaceful takeover by the French in southern Russia.

Nonetheless Henno scored one victory: he kept Odessa as the landing place intact. General S. Petlyura, Ukrainian C-in-C, sent out a small detachment to take the city for the nationalists, but never issued the final order. The Ukrainians deployed round the city which remained under Hetman Skoropadsky's administration with small Polish and Volunteer units as forces of order: thus Odessa represented the future French problems in a nutshell. Just before the French troops landed Henno made his final recommendations to the French government: discouraged by the development in the Ukraine, with the Germans supporting the Ukrainian nationalists, he thought that the French occupation zone should be a narrow coastal strip, a *zone de refuge* – in other words a complete ruin of Clemenceau's plans. On 18 December 1918 the naval units transporting French advanced forces arrived at Odessa. The Volunteer detachment in the city offered to clear it for the landing, and with naval gun support was permitted to do so. The following day General Borius disembarked with some 1,800 men and marched through cheering Odessa with flying colours. However, the very landing of the French intervention forces was already the beginning of an inglorious end of this French effort.

Throughout their stay in southern Russia, between December 1918 and early April 1919, the French had nothing but problems to solve. Even as General Borius appointed the youthful General Grishin-Almazov Governor of Odessa he was heading for trouble. Grishin considered himself Denikin's subordinate and therefore applied to him for approval, which was granted. But Denikin had no jurisdiction in the French zone and was never told that he could only exercise authority in the British zone. However, real trouble started when the French began to negotiate with the Ukrainians, who controlled food supplies. As soon as Colonel Freydenberg promised them some kind of political recognition for foodstuffs, the Volunteers began to talk of French betrayal.

In January 1919 General d'Anselm became the C-in-C in southern Russia and was instructed to hold the *zone de refuge* which stretched from Odessa to Tiraspol, Kherson and Nikolayev. He was further told that there would be no French reinforcements forthcoming, but he would receive Greek and Rumanian troops instead. Soon the Greeks arrived and he wanted to send them to Kherson and Nikolayev, but both these towns were already occupied by Ukrainian nationalist troops. Once again he had to negotiate with the Ukrainians and in return for a peaceful hand-over he promised to restore these towns and territory to them *alone* when his mission was ended in southern Russia. Next the Ukrainians demanded concessions in Odessa, which they considered their city, and when the Russians resisted all the French efforts at change, the French were forced to take the administration of the city as well as that of the *zone de refuge* into their own hands. It was evident that the French hold on southern Russia was precarious indeed, and would collapse as soon as an external danger emerged.

Danger did emerge in the figure of the roving Ukrainian cossack, Ataman Grigoriev, who at that stage operated in conjunction with the Red Army. On 11 March 1919 Grigoriev took advantage of the friendliness of German troops towards him and with their connivance attacked the Greeks at Kherson and Nikolayev and forced them to withdraw. He then began to advance to Odessa and engaged the Allied armies at Berezovka a week after his Kherson-Nikolayev exploit. During this engagement the Volunteer unit refused to fight, while the Greeks followed the bad example of the Zouaves, taking to their heels and abandoning all their equipment, among it two French tanks. After this victory Grigoriev lost any further interest in the fighting and just waited for the Allies to get out of Odessa, which he then wanted to take.

In Odessa itself the French were in a desperate position; the fleet at anchor off Odessa threatened to mutiny. The Volunteers were causing trouble in the city, which they wanted to hold for Denikin, while the French were thinking of pulling out altogether. Denikin however refused to send any Russian units to hold the city for him. Disappointed by the Volunteers and under great pressure from Grigoriev's forces the French Command heard of an open mutiny in the fleet. Its decisions were swift and desperate: despite previous denials the Odessa base had to be evacuated. When on 4 April 1919 the news became known there was panic in the city. The French tired of the Russians, looked after themselves alone and left behind most of the Russians, civilian and military, who wanted to evacuate with them. The following day Grigoriev's partisans took the city on behalf of the Bolsheviks. This unsuccessful French effort at direct intervention left a lot of bitterness between the French and the Volunteers, and indirectly, since the British were responsible for Denikin, put a terrible strain on Anglo-French relations and policies in Russia. Afterwards the French were determined not to aid General Denikin in the slightest but awaited patiently the similar outcome of the British effort at intervention in south eastern Russia.

The British reached the Volunteer-held territory immediately after the armistice in the West. Colonel Blackwood and General Poole inspected the Volunteer Army and administration and recommended to their government recognition of Denikin as Supreme Commander-in-Chief in southern Russia and making him the chief recipient of British military aid. France was not consulted, for the Volunteers operated in what was essentially the British zone. With the first shipment of aid Denikin also received the British Military Mission (some 500 officers and men) headed by General Briggs, whose task it was to control the use of British aid and also advise Denikin on military and political matters. This then was the British attempt at intervention, and indirect one, through the Volunteer Army.

With the Volunteer Army re-forming and re-equipping, Denikin concerned himself mainly with political problems and used the British ally against the French 'bunglers' and 'traitors'. After the fiasco at Odessa the British forced the French to hand all their interests and forces in southern Russia to General Denikin (the Protocol of 4 April 1919) and the French pull-out was so complete that for the first time the British noticed that their indirect intervention was a heavy financial commitment, which began to hurt the economy. Thus after France Britain was also getting ready for a reappraisal of policy, long before the actual catastrophe, Allied conventions and agreements obviously did not work and Britain was shouldering a disproportionate financial burden. But the British proposals for new comprehensive Allied zonal and financial arrangements went unheeded; the French waited with evident *Schadenfreude* for the collapse of the British effort.

Though it took much longer than the French presence in southern Russia, collapse it did and in the end Britain got nothing out of this effort but embarrassment. On 29 July 1919 the British Premier, Lloyd George, summed up what Britain got out of this massive effort at intervention:

> though Churchill had always conceived intervention as a campaign against bolshevism, *he* never thought in such terms: his reasons for intervening were the separate peace with Germany and the eastern front. Although Kolchak and Denikin might fail, they had already served a purpose from his (British) point of view. They prevented Germany from laying its hands on Russian supplies: if things went wrong in the future Britain would not support Denikin for ever.'

This was then the British attitude to the Volunteer movement at the time, when Denikin issued his Moscow directive and his armies were rapidly advancing on the Bolshevik capital. When he was defeated and was falling back as rapidly as he had advanced, the British began to dictate their terms to him.

First, he was forced into internal reforms, which came too late and proved ineffective. Then they forced him to recognise all the various succession states, such as Poland, the Baltic republics, the Georgians and the Armenians. By then, however, nothing could stem the Bolshevik tide, and these reforms proved equally ineffective. For all these concessions the new High Commissioner, Professor Mackinder, promised Denikin that Britain would evacuate all the compromised officers and their families if the situation became untenable. However, when all this failed Britain forced Denikin to negotiate with the Bolsheviks a surrender. Britain took it on itself to act as an intermediary and Denikin was told that if he refused to come to terms with the Bolsheviks, Britain would stop its aid forthwith, which meant that he would have to surrender unconditionally.

Denikin tried to delay negotiations as long as he could and then on his arrival in the Crimea, which was the last territory the Volunteers held on to, he rather resigned the leadership and went into exile. The Volunteers then appointed General Wrangel as Denikin's successor and inheritor. Wrangel also tried to delay negotiations, and when this became obvious the British warned him. Then on 1 June 1920 Admiral Sir John de Robeck delivered him a British government ultimatum not to launch an offensive against the Red Army, but by that time Wrangel had managed to divest himself of his British sponsors and disregarded the ultimatum. Ten days later de Robeck was instructed by the British government to withdraw the Military Mission still in the Crimea and sever all relations with the Volunteers. Thus ended the British effort, as embarrassing as the French; only this time Britain could initiate negotiations with the Bolsheviks on its own, without a dependent Russian ally.

It is true that the Volunteers got themselves a replacement ally, France, but even they knew that as an ally France was temporary and above all her reason for supporting them was not they themselves, but Poland. Poland was considered a wartime ally of France, and in June 1920 it was locked in a mortal struggle with the Bolsheviks. France needed the Volunteers to divert some of the strength of the Red Army from Poland, and the Volunteers realised that as soon as the Polish affair was resolved either way it would be their turn and all they could expect from France was aid in evacuation of White combatants and their families. French intervention (if it can be called that) in Poland was very indirect and consisted of training and equipping Polish forces during and after the war. France also had a large military mission there, but the Poles preferred to work on their own and French tutelage was not welcome. In any case this particular

French effort against the Bolsheviks ended as an unqualified success thanks to the Polish victory near Warsaw; by August 1920 the Red Army was routed and disintegrated, but inevitably it now turned against the Volunteers and their Crimean base.

The French had a chance of abandoning the sinking ship of the Volunteer movement in October 1920, when Premier Millerand became President of France and a new government was sworn in. Millerand however insisted on supporting the Volunteers to the end. He refused to recall the French Military Mission and instructed them to aid the Volunteers in 'every suitable way'. However, there was not much they could do: on the eve of the decisive battle, on 23 October 1920, the French High Commissioner de Martel, General Brousseau and Amiral de Bon promised Wrangel full French assistance, but this was obviously moral encouragement rather than help. The French navy then cooperated with the Volunteers and prepared an effective evacuation plan which it carried out to perfection. At least this last phase of French intervention in southern Russia did not end as a fiasco, though it was a failure.

If the Japanese intervention is discounted — and it lasted until 1924 and with it the Far Eastern. Republic, a non-Bolshevik buffer formation — all the Allied efforts in Russia, whether concerted or individual, ended badly. Ultimately no one benefited from them, either politically or economically. German influence and German puppets (the Bolsheviks) were not only not eradicated, but in many ways were forced to unite and fight well. Economically both France and Britain lost their investments in Russia and commercial relations were resumed only slowly, after long delays. Needless to say Russia did not derive any benefit from the intervention either; in fact it stimulated and just about kept going the civil war, while a decisive effort was never even contemplated. On the other hand it never vitally threatened the Bolsheviks, but rather helped them to divert the attention of the Russian people from domestic disasters and put the blame for them on interventionist forces, the foreigners and the Whites. It was a disorganised, wasteful effort, but certainly not a conspiracy against the Russian revolution, neither was it organised marches against the Soviet republic.

4

Civil War in Siberia

In the Central Volga regions and Siberia the civil war was ignited by the revolt of the Czechoslovak Legion against the Bolsheviks. In contrast to the South these vast regions of Russia had no organised White movement, albeit a number of anti-Bolshevik groups operated there. Thus practically all the Cossack *voyska* mustered bands of armed men in the Urals, West Siberia, Ussuri and East Siberia and tried to seize power from the Bolshevik-dominated Soviets. Officer organisations did also exist, but they had to lie low: they consisted mainly of refugees from the Bolsheviks, had no central leadership and locally were extremely weak.

Politically Siberia and the Central Volga were absolutely dominated by the Social Revolutionaries. All the same after November 1917, the Bolsheviks succeeded in ousting the Social Revolutionaries and establishing Soviets controlled by them. The Derber Social Revolutionary government was chased out of Tomsk; Irkutsk submitted after a little fighting, while the various Far Eastern governments could only continue at Kharbin in Mandjuria outside the reach of the Bolsheviks.

Both Germany and the Western Allies were interested in Siberia and its fate. The Germans had most of their PoWs interned there and in addition wanted to lay their hands on the grain stores, while the Allies had large military stores at Vladivostok and obviously wanted to prevent the Germans evacuating their prisoners of war and seizing the immense grain stores in the region. Each side did its utmost to realise its objectives, and the western Allies were prepared even to intervene directly through the eastern ally, Japan. However, it was to be the 'forgotten' and 'independent' ally, the Czechoslovak Legion, which was to prove the decisive power factor in the region, but that only after its quarrel with the Bolsheviks in May 1918.

The revolt of the Czechoslovak Legion against the Bolsheviks, which was to set Siberia ablaze, was an improvised affair, just like the Legion's projected withdrawal from the Ukraine to Vladivostok and France. Professor Masaryk, the leader and organiser of the Legion, departed from European Russia on 7 March 1918 for Washington leaving behind a number of plenipotentiaries and vague instructions: 'the Czechoslovaks were to execute the evacuation agreement which he concluded with the French Military Mission in Russia on 18 February 1918. They were to travel to France *via* Vladivostok and while doing so remain neutral, i.e. avoid interfering in internal Russian affairs'. However, Masaryk was farseeing enough to have ordered the Legion to *defend itself energetically*, if attacked by any *Slavonic force* in Russia or Siberia. He evidently foresaw difficulties, but nevertheless considered his departure more important than staying on with the Legion and extricating it from the quicksands of the Russian revolution.

On its way to Vladivostok the Legion had concluded a number of local armistice agreements with the Bolsheviks. The most important one was signed with Colonel Muravyov, C-in-C of the Soviet forces in the Ukraine. In a personal declaration Colonel Muravyov expressed his and Soviet consent to the evacuation of the Legion to France. Since the Legion withdrew from the Ukraine new agreements had to be negotiated by Czech plenopotentiaries, P. Maxa and J. Klecanda. In Masaryk's absence the talks were badly tackled from the very beginning. To make doubly sure negotiations were started locally with the Southern front C-in-C, Antonov-Ovseyenko, and centrally with the Sovnarkom. Klecanda was in Petrograd and then in Moscow for this purpose with a few other members of the Czechoslovak National Council, which was the political organisation responsible for the Czechoslovak Legion. However, they were all isolated from the Legion soldiers entrained in seemingly endless échelons heading east towards Vladivostok. Surprisingly Klecanda was very successful in Moscow; the central Bolsheviks, anxious to avoid complications with the Germans and also probably· fearing the nearness of this disciplined armed force with its tsarist officers, were more than willing to permit the Czechoslovaks to move from such danger areas as the Ukraine and the Don into the vastness of Siberia. On 15 March 1918, after negotiating with Aralov, a Bolshevik military leader and Stalin, the nationality expert, Klecanda was given Sovnarkom permission to evacuate freely to Siberia. As these negotiations were proceeding in Moscow, Maxa was conducting his own at Kursk. The Kursk Bolsheviks reasoned very differently from the Moscow ones, for they saw a retreating Legion, necessarily suffering from chaotic arrangements and lack of supplies. The Kursk Bolsheviks argued quite differently with the Czechs; they were reproaching them for abandoning the German front and leaving them, badly armed as they were, to· oppose their own national enemy. Maxa proved receptive to these arguments and, unable to consult with his Moscow colleagues, he signed a local agreement on 16 March 1918, one day after the central Bolsheviks had conceded a practically unmolested evacuation of the Czechoslovak Legion. The terms of this local agreement were unfavourable to the Czechs and so vaguely defined as to cause disagreements in the future. In accordance with it, all the 'excessive' artillery, machine guns and also armoured cars were surrendered to the Bolsheviks, who issued a festive proclamation thanking the Czechoslovaks for their 'brotherly gifts'.

In Klecanda's report on his negotiations with Aralov and Stalin there was unbounded optimism. According to it the Bolsheviks trusted the Czechs and would even help them as much as possible with the formation of the second Army Corps, for which the Czechs hoped to recruit Czech and Slovak PoWs in Siberia. What possibly cheered Klecanda most was Stalin's permission for the Czechoslovak National Council of Moscow to remove to Omsk. Perhaps Stalin and the Bolsheviks were feeling quite favourably inclined towards the Czechoslovaks at this stage; but the climate in Russia was rapidly changing. Soon Klecanda became convinced that the Bolsheviks were hatching a secret plot against the Legion. On 21 March 1918 Maxa wrote hopefully: 'For the time being we ride on... It is almost a miracle.' It came to an abrupt end on 22 March, when the chairman of the Penza Soviet, Kurayev, issued an order by which all Czech trains were stopped and the Legion was to be completely disarmed. Klecanda heard of this difficulty in Moscow and had several interviews with Trotsky, who in the meantime had become Peoples' Commissar of War. He found him distrustful of Czech intentions in the Far East, where Essaul Semenov was actively anti-Soviet. Klecanda soon lost his temper and had several quarrels with the new Commissar, but was no match for him: in any case it is doubtful that Trotsky caused this stoppage. As far as Kurayev was concerned the immediate cause was Antonov-Ovseyenko's telegram from Kursk alleging the violation of the local agreement by the Czechs. Kurayev also had several reasons of his own for stopping the Czech trains: the Czechs were behaving provocatively towards Russian civilians and Soviet representatives. The slowness of evacuation irritated the Legion soldiers. On 24 March 1918, with the trains standing still, General Podgayevsky, commanding officer of the 2nd Division and one of the few Russians remaining with the Legion, marched into Kurayev's office with an armed escort to tell him that he would hang him if he did not release the trains.

Thus tension and suspicions increased on both sides, and each side started threatening the other. In Moscow Klecanda dared to threaten Trotsky without an armed escort, while at Penza the political representative Maxa disagreed with General Podgayevsky's tactics. Maxa was backed by another Russian officer, General Dieterichs, but with Czech politicians and soldiers dissenting he proposed to Kurayev the surrender of most of the Legion's arms in return for his permission to let it proceed to Vladivostok. Kurayev telegraphed these proposals to Moscow and Stalin replied with a telegram in which he accepted Maxa's proposals and imposed a few more conditions, such as the dismissal of 'reactionary' officers, which the Czechs at Penza were quite willing to accept. Trotsky then called Klecanda's bluff and the latter in disgust left Moscow to investigate on the spot the incredible news of Czech capitulation. Soon afterwards he died of pneumonia and was thus saved from witnessing the complete collapse of the Czechoslovak political leadership which proved so unsuccessful in the face of the Bolsheviks.

So far it was the various armistice and 'disarmament' agreements which were the cause of the slowing down and stoppages of Czechoslovak trains. In April 1918 another factor began to aggravate the relations between the Legion and the Soviets. On 5 April the official journal of the Czechoslovak Legion in Russia *Ceskoslovenský denník,* announced that a group of Czech communist agitators had arrived at Penza amd Samara to launch a recruitment drive for the Red Army. Since Penza had become the key point for the further movement of the Legion trains a communist party branch was established there, as well as the 1st Czech International Regiment. The communists' activity did not consist of newspaper propaganda only, but also of direct contacts with the Czech and Slovak soldiers. Though the effect of this activity was not remarkable the Czechoslovak National Council felt itself threatened enough to order the Legion's soldiers not to leave their trains at Penza, and the agitators were debarred from trains.

However, the greatest pressure exerted by the Czech communists on the Legion was through the local and central Soviet authorities, especially through the Arms Control Commission, whose members they were, and whose decisions on the spot meant either good speed or delays for the Czech trains. In April 1918 St Štrombach, commanding officer of the 1st Czech International Regiment at Penza, wrote to the Moscow Czechoslovak Communist Centre that he had asked Kurayev to hold up the Czech trains as much as possible and permit agitators to undermine the Legion from within. Though Kurayev disliked the request he acquiesced in it, especially when the Czech communists produced some results. However, these results were dangerously misleading: apart from a few soldiers the most encouraging success was the 'desertion' of two members of the Czechoslovak National Council and four regimental delegates to the projected Czechoslovak Legion congress. After this success at subversion the Penza communists became over-optimistic: they became convinced that by the artificial delays the Legion would be unnerved and ultimately become so disgusted with its journey to France that it would revolt against its 'reactionary' political and military leadership and join the Soviets. Great hopes were centered on the coming congress which, it was thought, would unleash this expected revolt.

However, communist tactics at Penza were soon proved naive and their campaign of subversion misfired psychologically. The Czechoslovak leadership, if it existed in a real sense after Professor Masaryk's departure, was not blamed for the delays. In fact the soldiers were turning against the

Soviets whom they clearly recognised as the cause. While men waited endlessly in towns and villages along the Trans-Siberian railway they were preoccupied by two thoughts: to put between themselves and the Germans as many miles as possible and to reach Vladivostok as well armed as practicable, for the journey through Siberia — whence many had come — meant passing by many PoW camps full of hostile Germans and Hungarians. During the intermittent periods of waiting they also saw local Soviets arming these very same PoWs. The International Units of the Red Army seemed to them the cover for the recruitment of their national enemies and increased their doubts as to the real intentions of the Bolsheviks towards them. The Czech communist propaganda left them sceptical. They saw the Czech and Slovak communists escaping from the Legion, when it was in difficulty, for better conditions in the Red Army. They saw the Arms Control Commission twice dissolved when its members became too friendly with the Legion by accepting bribes and conniving at concealed arms. The men asked themselves what was behind the Soviet demands for arms: Penza asked for the agreed arms; Samara for as many more to defend itself against some Cossacks; Omsk asked for machine guns permitted by Penza, while on arrival at Irkutsk the last remaining rifles were requested as a condition for the trains being let through.

As delays multiplied and tension mounted the Legion's nerves became edgy and discipline was getting out of hand. Incidents were occurring which should have warned the Penza communists as well as the Bolsheviks in Moscow that the Legion might get out of control. On 26 April 1918 Lieutenant Bajer, whose regiment had been immobilised before Penza for some considerable time, marched on the town with a strong escort to 'purge it'. The unfortunate National Council had to exert great efforts to dissuade Bajer from the purge and calm the whole regiment. However, the Czech communists blundered still further: they skilfully released such alarming rumours as that they were now the only recognised representatives of the Czechoslovaks in Russia and that the National Council's credentials had been withdrawn by the Soviets and its identity papers invalidated. Other rumours had it that the complete disarming of the Legion was imminent and its repatriation to Austria-Hungary assured.

The Legion was forced to act in its own defence. The National Council released counter-rumours: the Bolsheviks were labelled as German puppets and there was talk about their dark plans. Many officers began to propagate plans for 'every and any contingency'. But nothing substantial was done, no agreement reached, even though it was becoming increasingly evident that a final showdown with the Soviets was probable. Senior Czech officers agreed with Generals Shokorov and Dieterichs that a peaceful passage to Vladivostok was imperative under any condition the Bolsheviks might impose. Others thought the right moment for shooting one's way to Vladivostok had not come yet. Only 'Captain' Gajda, commanding officer of the 7th Regiment, whose contempt for the Bolsheviks was boundless, was serious about taking action if they tried to block his way to Vladivostok. He ordered his COS, Captain Kadlec, the only Czech officer with staff experience, to prepare plans for such a contingency. In the 1st Division similar plans were prepared by General Kolomensky and Colonel Dorman, but they made them under protest, as they had no faith in armed action against the Soviets. However, tension was rising and something had to be done. At Kirsanov all the officers of the 1st Division, which had been most delayed, tried to do something. They held a conference and passed unanimously a resolution in which they not only refused to surrender any more arms, but on the contrary demanded from the National Council fresh equipment and arms.

This was certainly no right action; the resolution was absurd. The National Council had neither arms nor equipment and in any case favoured negotiations with the Bolsheviks rather than a showdown. This paradoxical demand clearly points to the unreality of the situation in which the Legion found itself. Isolated as it was it began to see in the delays and disarming a Bolshevik plot to hand it over to the Germans. Opinion in the Legion was hardening for strong action. Men egged on their officers who in turn put pressure on the senior officers and the political leadership. In this confusion plans began to be hatched without the slightest regard for their political implications and above all with no thought of the far away Allies, under whose command the Legion was.

Though there were French liaison officers with the Legion, for all practical purposes the Legion was cut off and left to its own devices. Without consulting the Legion the Allies decided that they had not enough shipping to bring them to Europe from Vladivostok. In Moscow General Lavergne was therefore charged with negotiations with Trotsky to re-route the Legion to Archangel. On 21 April, when negotiations were successfully concluded, Chicherin telegraphed to stop the slowly rolling trains again. The Czechs west of Omsk were to go to Archangel. This new order surprised everybody, the Legion as well as the National Council. The Allies acted over the heads of the Czechs thinking that as an Allied army unit they would obey their orders whether they made sense or not. They were soon undeceived. In the prevalent psychosis in the Legion the German name of the Russian adjutant who signed the telegram meant that the order was a German-Bolshevik trap to divide the Legion in order to destroy it. Gajda's idea of shooting one's way to the Pacific became popular.

By now the confusion was inextricable. On 9 May 1918 the hesitant Maxa was rushed to Moscow to get a clarification of Chicherin's telegram, which everybody refused to obey. To his surprise Maxa found out on arrival in Moscow that the re-routing order did come from the Allies and had Trotsky's blessing. But by then he also was cut off from the Legion, as much as the Supreme Allied Council, the various military and diplomatic missions in Russia, and the central Bolsheviks themselves. A series of misunderstandings and incidents, in an atmosphere in which everyone suspected everyone else, led to the final break.

At this time Lieutenant Syrový, the future C-in-C of the Czechoslovak Legion in Russia, wrote a situation report on his regiment which succintly summed up the desperate muddle the Legion was in: '. . . no one wants to go to Archangel . . . as soon as this [change of direction to Vladivostok] became known the soldiers began to grumble . . . [they grumbled] for several reasons . . . [they feared] hunger, danger from the Germans and the sea with the German U-boats . . . intrigues of the Germans and the Russians alike and the stupidity of our leadership . . . they would rather run away and go independently to Vladivostok . . .' Lieutenant-Colonel Voytsekhovsky, the future White C-in-C, similarly summed up the mood of his 3rd Regiment. On 6 May 1918, facing semi-mutiny, theCzechoslovak National Council, or what was left of it with Maxa in Moscow, decided to convoke the military congress, for which the election had already been carried out. Thus it prepared for itself a *coup de grâce* with typical nonchalance. The Czech communists, who also convoked a party conference to Moscow for 20-21 May, were going to be equally surprised by the outcome of the long expected congress.

On 14 May 1918 an incident occured at Chelyabinsk where a pre-congress conference of the 1st Division was taking place. During a stop at the station a Czech soldier was wounded by a piece of iron thrown out of a train repatriating some Hungarian PoWs. The train was stopped and the culprit lynched. But in turn the lynching party was arrested by the Soviet forces guarding the station. Tempers rose, Czech reinforcements marched into the town and freed the imprisoned soldiers. At the same time arms were seized from the town arsenal.

Incidents were taking place all along the Trans-Siberian between the Czechs and the Soviets, but this particular one shocked Moscow into action. It seems obvious that the patience of the Moscow Bolsheviks ran out. While they allowed these extremely suspicious 'Allied' troops to remove to Vladivostok they had nothing but trouble with them. The permission to evacuate them to France via Siberia was in any case given against the wishes of Siberian Soviets. Now there were Japanese troops in Vladivostok, Ataman Semenov was raiding Soviet territory, the Allies were plotting 'something', and the Whites were restless especially in the provinces and above all in Siberia. The Czechs who had reached Vladivostok were accumulating in the town and no ships were in sight. The Chelyabinsk incident was the last straw: while the Czechs were at least partially disarmed the Soviets would have an advantage in a showdown. The Czech politicians Maxa and Čermák, who were still in Moscow, were abruptly arrested and forced to sign an appeal to the Legion to surrender all its arms to the Soviets. At the same time telegrams went out bidding the local Soviets to disarm the Legion forcibly if it refused Maxa's appeal.

In the meantime at Chelyabinsk the pre-congress conference was in session; discussions centred on the re-routing order which was disbelieved, and on continuing the journey to Vladivostok even against the will of the Soviets. There was still some hesitation: above all the junior French officer advised against such an action. But then the Chelaybinsk conference read an intercepted telegram by Aralov ordering the Soviets to disarm the Czechs by force. It was obvious that the Bolsheviks meant business and the Czechs were forced into a decision — if forced they would shoot their way to Vladivostok. Subsequent Trotsky's telegram ordering the Soviets to disarm the Czechs or shoot them if they resisted, was also intercepted and read by various regimental commanders after the conference at Chelyabinsk had dispersed for action. On 25 May 1918 the weak forces of the Maryanovka Soviet actually tried to execute Trotsky's order against Gajda's 7th Regiment. Without much reflection Gajda went into action and started the revolt in his section of the Trans-Siberian; the rest of the commanders and men followed suit.

The revolt automatically deposed the political leadership, the Czechoslovak National Council. Its place was taken by young radical politicians, such as B. Pavlů, who had backed the Legion's resolute action. In the Legion the command, which opposed the revolt, was also deposed and purged. In effect the officer-delegates Čeček, Gajda and Voytsekhovsky were given full command of all the troops in their respective areas. All the hesitant Russian officers were either dismissed or even arrested; some ran away at the inception of the revolt. Young Czech officers took their places. The Bolshevik charge that Russian officers encouraged the revolt sounds most implausible. The Czech officers needed no encouragement from that quarter, once they had the wholehearted consent of their men. Vladivostok was not such a great way and they were confident that they could get there without much trouble, fighting only the Soviet irregulars. If successful the vistas were limitless: there were no Russian generals left and the new radical and youthful National Council controlled promotions.

However, even at Chelyabinsk, while some delegates enjoyed their new powers and others dreamed of future rewards, there was no agreement on united action against the Bolsheviks. Undoubtedly this did not disturb the young, inexperienced officers who in any case preferred improvisation. All the same, by failing to define the purpose and limits of the revolt which they were launching the Czech and Slovak politicians and officers perhaps unwittingly completed the anarchy in the Legion, and this boded ill for the future. In these unfavourable conditions, with the Bolsheviks thundering from afar but impotent on the spot, and with the Allies far away, the young Czechoslovaks sparked a revolt which was to lead them to Vladivostok and France, and which in fact led them into the morass of the civil war.

However much Captain Gajda might have talked tough, the revolt would have been impossible without unanimous backing from the men of the Legion. In fact in many places the men forced their officers to act. They were in a state of high excitement, with a great fear of being divided into smaller groups, disarmed and handed over to the Germans by their 'Bolshevik agents'. Their single purpose was to get to Vladivostok, beside which aim they had not the slightest regard for the political or military implications of the revolt. Gajda became the perfect embodiment of his men: he was animated by a blind hatred of the Germans, hardened by the years of war and heightened by the present condition. He sensed instinctively that his men felt like himself. At Novonikolayevsk he was the least threatened but it was he who took action first. Throughout the initial phase he saw Germans everywhere; they spied on the Legion and he had them mercilessly shot without trial. They officered the Internationalist Units and he told his men that by fighting the Bolsheviks they were fighting the Germans: 'It is the old game, as in the war.' He raided German PoW trains, prevented the evacuees from returning home; his men cleaned up PoW camps, which often meant summary executions of PoWs with or without arms, and kept the camps under Czech control. He liquidated Lavrov's Hungarian Internationalist Unit and wrought vengeance on the Baykal Bolsheviks, for they had captured, tortured and killed his friend, Colonel Ushakov. Throughout the fighting, he proudly remarked later, no prisoners were taken. He was cold about the fate of the Imperial family, for he was told that the Tsar was being taken to sign the Brest-Litovsk Treaty and he believed it. Thus fighting in bands with no special discipline and nevertheless winning easily, he and his men reached Vladivostok; when Gajda and the men turned back to the Urals, it was the beginning of the end of the Czechoslovak Legion.

The momentary cohesion which the Legion achieved by means of fear and the *idée fixe* of Vladivostok collapsed as soon as the Pacific city was reached. There were no other aims, there was no common plan, no anticipation of the next step. The revolt brought about the inevitable: interference in Russian internal affairs and civil war, and with it the complications and divisions and further demoralisation. Military necessity forced the Legion to seek White support and Gajda was again the first Czech commander to become involved. His grandiose plan dispersed his weak forces in the drive East and West and in the effort to secure his flank to the South. As his forces were insufficient for such tasks he sought support from the Novonikolayevsk Officers' Association even before the revolt. But the two sides proved incompatible allies and subsequent enmity showed that they were both interested in short-term advantages. On 4 May 1918 the Novonikolayevsk Soviet arrested Captain Gajda and this obviously discouraged the White officers to commit themselves to such a weak ally. But when the revolt started and the Whites saw Gajda's successes they changed their minds and swiftly joined in: they actually took Tayga and Tomsk, though the cities were abondoned by the panic-stricken Bolsheviks under the impression of Czech victories elsewhere. However, most often the White efforts to take a town or a city came to nothing and Gajda had to send them Czech units to achieve the task. Since he was dispersing his precious Czechs in support of the Russian Whites Gajda thought that he could compensate himself by enrolling Russian volunteers, officers and men, into the Legion. Thus his friends from the battlefield, not the generals from the Officers Associations, Colonels Pepelyayev and Grivin, helped him to organise and command auxiliary units in Central Siberia and Irkutsk. Subsequently it was these Russian auxiliaries who fought the most important and bloody engagements in the Trans-Baykal region.

Captain Gajda's western advance was completed on 9 June 1918 when his units made contact with the Voytsekhovsky group, but his eastern drive reached the Vladivostok forces only on 31 August 1918. The other groups, commanded by Lieutenant Ceček and Colonel Voytsekhovsky, naturally became involved in Russian internal struggle and apart from the revolt also ignited civil war in the Central Volga region, the Urals and western Siberia. Colonel Voytsekhovsky started the revolt very reluctantly: on 19 May he declared that he was taking his forces to Vladivostok and only eight days later did he take the city of Chelyabinsk, which was several miles from the Trans-Siberian railway station. He obviously lacked Gajda's enthusiasm and as a Russian (the name indicates that he was a Russianised Pole) he probably saw more clearly the political implications of the revolt. He developed his operations east and west rather slowly and made contact with Ceček and his group on 6 July 1918.

Though the most exposed, the Ceček group seems to have been the last to revolt, but then almost instantly it became enmeshed in the Russian internal struggle. On 27 May 1918, when Gajda was fighting and the reluctant Voytsekhovsky launched his revolt, the Legion at Penza was addressed by the Bolsheviks Kurayev, Minkin and a Czech communist Rauser at a meeting to which officers were not admitted. But even without their officers the men refused to surrender their arms and remained determined to fight it out. The Penza station was taken over peacefully but the next day when Lieutenant Švec, in Ceček's absence, led his men to take the town he had to fight for it. Some 150 Czech communists were killed in action and 250 taken prisoner. As could be expected from the unnerved Legion many of the captured Czechs were summarily shot or disappeared – the rest were imprisoned. However, the behaviour of the exasperated Czech soldiers was also tough towards the Russian population. The Social Revolutionary Duma which took over the administration of the city begged the officers to discipline their men. Whether they wanted it or not the Legion was restoring the pre-Bolshevik administration and getting involved in the internal struggle of Russia.

As soon as Lieutenant Ceček arrived he took over command and on 31 May 1918 ordered the Legion to evacuate Penza and continue its journey towards Vladivostok. Two days after the Legion's departure the Soviet returned to Penza and took over the administration because the Social Revolutionary Duma ran away after the Legion. Neither the White nor the Red Russians could see the purpose of the Czech revolt and were more mystified than the Czechs themselves. The progress *à la Penza* continued along the railway line to Samara on the Volga. Ceček took the town on 8 June 1918 and drove on to Buguruslan and Ufa where he joined the Voytsekhovsky group. However, Samara was not evacuated by the Legion as Penza and other towns before; Ceček handed the town over to the Russian auxiliaries who had helped him by diversionary attacks in the country around to take the city. Moreover Ceček left a small garrison to help the White auxiliaries to keep the city if the Soviet forces returned. In doing all this Ceček was not only influenced by the Whites, but also by the Allied consuls whom he found in the city and who gave him the latest information and advice.

At Samara the Legion finally found out that there were no ships at Vladivostok to take them to France. The Czechs also found out that the Americans and the French sanctioned the revolt and obviously were going to exploit it for other purposes than that of getting the Legion to France, to fight Germany there. They would do the next best thing: they would fight Germany in Russia on the Volga. On 24 June 1918 the *Ceskoslovenský denník* clarified the situation somewhat: the Allies were launching their intervention and the Czechoslovak Legion was the *avant-garde* of the Allied armies. The Eastern front against Germany would be re-constituted on the Volga and Allied armies would come to the Legion's aid from Vladivostok and Vyatka. Such announcements were taken most seriously by the fighting Czechs and their feasibility was never questioned. So the planless desultory fighting of the Legion continued. However, the line of the Volga was kept and the Vladivostok forces were ordered to return to the Volga: the control over territories taken would be stabilised and when the Allied armies arrived offensives would be launched against Germany via Soviet Russia.

While waiting for these armies the Legion was dragged deeper and deeper into internal Russian conflicts. The Central Volga region was the political bastion of the Russian Social Revolutionaries and they were everywhere putting up their administrations after the defeat of the Soviets by the Legion. In addition at Samara there were large number of members of the dispersed Consitutional Assembly and deputies continued to stream into Samara after it had been put under White Social Revolutionary administrations. The Whites were not at all interested in a front against

Germany, but welcomed most warmly the Legion's help. They formed their own units which immediately began to operate against the Bolsheviks, a sort of pre-offensive against the Germans. The Komuch forces, named after the Constituent Assembly, continued to request Czech aid even for very distant operations and together they took Simbirsk and even Kazan, where the small Czech unit captured the Russian gold reserve. Still nothing was coordinated, not even overall strategy. Lieutenant Ceček (who was no fool) dared to suggest to the Samara Komuch that they should attempt to make contact with other anti-Bolshevik centres such as the Urals Cossacks, Don Cossacks and even the Volunteers in the South. He was told that the Legion could do whatever it wanted, but the Samara Komuch was not interested: such contacts would have opened the floodgates of refugees and with them the influx of right wing politicians and reactionary generals. Thus only the Czech 4th Regiment went south to reach Nikolayevsk which was not far from the Urals and Don Cossack fronts.

If the Whites and the Legion refused to get organised and make meaningful plans the Bolsheviks finally got over the initial shock of the revolt and began to show signs of revival. On 27 August 1918 they reached an agreement with the Germans on freeing the Soviet forces facing each other which they could transfer east. Trotsky ruthlessly restored discipline in the Red Army and while the Legion and Komuch forces continued to roam the countryside he built up his forces and reorganised the front. In the early days of September he launched the most devastating offensive. Kazan fell without much fighting, for the Czechs had to withdraw to avoid encirclement. Nikolayevsk was abandoned one day after it had been taken by the Czechs, who suffered heavy losses. The Komuch and the Legion were withdrawing most swiftly, abandoning Simbirsk, Volsk, Syzran and on 8 October 1918 Samara, the Russian capital of the Komuch.

The chaotic withdrawal and heavy losses began to affect the Legion's morale. On 20 October 1918 the heavily mauled 4th Regiment mutinied and a few days later the 1st Regiment did the same; the 2nd and 3rd Regiments were on the verge of mutiny; the whole 1st Division had collapsed. General Ceček, promoted during the fighting, was relieved of his command and replaced by Colonel Švec, who committed suicide when the men he led early in the revolt refused to obey his orders. In the 2nd Division, which had returned from the Far East under General Gajda, morale was not much higher. Exhaustion, heavy casualties, lack of supplies, the Siberian winter, the Bolshevik offensive, the lack of Allied armies to relieve them — all combined to destroy the Czechoslovak Legion as a fighting body. It had started the revolt to get out of Russia; not only did it not get out but it also sparked off the civil war and now had to disengage and try and get out of the conflict. It was the turn of the Whites to take over and fight, and they did it only reluctantly.

It was seen how inextricably were the Czechs involved in the civil war in the Central Volga region and Siberia. As soon as they collapsed recriminations followed: the Legion started the civil war prematurely, did not allow the Whites real scope for organising themselves nor to take over the direction of the struggle. Much is true in the criticism of the Legion and its revolt, but it is equally true that from the beginning Russian politicians proved extremely reluctant to assume their responsibilities once the Legion toppled the Soviets. Even when they came forward their administrations and armed forces proved most unstable and helpless without the Legion's support.

In many towns of the Central Volga the Russians treated the revolt as a foreign affair which did not concern them. At Simbirsk the Whites succeeded in raising only a minute unit, while at Kazan they were more interested in organising horse races, which the Bolsheviks had forbidden, than in the organisation of armed forces. Only at Samara, under substantial Czech protection, were the Whites able to organise a government and armed forces. General Galkin recruited many officers from the local officers' associations, but the men were mainly collected by Colonel, later General and Commander-in-Chief, V. Kappel, who spent this initial period of the civil war fighting with the Legion. The Social Revolutionary leader, Avksentiev, formed a sort of administration which claimed jurisdiction over all Russia, since politically it was based on the majority faction of the Constituent Assembly. Similar administrations were formed in Siberia, at Omsk, Tomsk and Chita as well as in the Urals. Cossacks of Orenburg, Urals and other Siberian regions formed their own separate governments in which the leaders were politicians; the Cossacks were imitated by various national minorities such as Bashkirs, Mongols and Tartars. Under pressure from the Czechs all these governments, administrations, movements and armies decided to meet at Chelyabinsk to form from its midst an All-Russian government, an anti-government to the Bolshevik one in Moscow.

The very idea of forming a Russian government opened the floodgates of disunity and unleashed the most undignified scramble for 'power'. Most of these White governments were not secure even in their localities and depended heavily on the Czech Legion. Now they launched hysterical accusations against the Bolshevik government as if this anti-Bolshevism was going to procure for them positions of power in the future government. A little more meaningfully they also began a feverish build-up of their mini armed forces. Thus the Minister of War of the Komuch government at Samara, General (initially Captain) Galkin, 26 years old, succeeded in organising the HQ of the future National Army of Russia. As a result he began to consider himself the Minister of War of Russia and failed to see the irreality of this claim. His chief of staff, an old and wily general, P.P. Petrov, cut the ground under his superior's feet by confirming in the command of the units they themselves raised and organised the two youthful Colonels Kappel and Makhin. Neither Galkin nor Petrov played subsequently important roles in the civil war, but the Colonels did, especially Kappel who became the Commander-in-Chief just before the collapse of the Siberian movement and his death. The Colonels, however, considered the units under their command as their personal troops, owing allegiance to the anti-Bolshevik cause rather than to any government or administration. Still the political soldiers and politicians seemed to ignore this power dichotomy and continued to press for an All-Russian government.

While the All-Russian conference at Chelyabinsk, scheduled for 15 July 1918, had to be abandoned altogether because the Siberian and Far Eastern representatives were unable to arrive in time, the other conference convoked to Ufa for 1 September 1918 had to be delayed. The Siberians were still late in arriving but more importantly, Blücher's Bolshevik partisans broke through the White lines and threatened to capture the whole representative assembly gathering at Ufa. The Ufa conference was conceived even more broadly than the Chelyabinsk one, and apart from the White governments and Cossack armies, various national minorities of Siberia and Turkestan were invited to and were represented at the conference. They were joined by the representatives of the Czechoslovak Legion, Russian political parties (Social Revolutionaries, Mensheviks, Trudoviks, National Freedom, and Unity (Yedinstvo) parties) as well as local government representatives. Some 200 delegates gathered at Ufa to thrash out the future of non-Bolshevik Russia. It was a unique gathering at least in one respect: never before nor since has such a large and heterogeneous assembly of anti-Bolshevik Russians and others met and reached an agreement.

However, the agreement that the Assembly did reach did not stem from it, but was largely forced on it by pressures and events outside it. While the conference was still in session the Czechoslovak Legion began to collapse under the impact of the Bolshevik offensive, so that in the end the All-Russian government, only just created, had hardly any Russian territory left under its control. On the spot political pressure was exercised by B. Pavlů, the political representative of the Czechoslovak Legion and Major Guinet, a French liaison officer who considered himself as the chief Allied representative. Forced by these two foreigners the assembled Russians agreed to set up an All-Russian Directorate and even suffered the indignity of having the candidates for the Directorate approved by them. The conference also passed a special vote of thanks to the Czechoslovak Legion and dispersed.

Apart from the Directorate and a week's discussions the results were disproportionately small. Much time was wasted in discussions of constitutional niceties: what was to be the competence of the All-Russian

Directorate *vis-à-vis* all the other governments? In reality this question was solved by the Bolshevik advance and occupation of territories in Russia; still the constitutional claims of the Directorate did cause a lot of confusion subsequently. On the other hand the Cossacks refused to recognise any authority except their own autonomous *voyska* (armies), while the national minorities failed to be recognised as autonomous. A little paradoxically only the Russian liberals wanted a military dictator to lead the All-Russian Directorate; in the end the Directorate was a sort of electoral coalition capable of winning the next election but quite unsuited for wielding power. The Russian Socialist Revolutionary, Avksentiev, the Siberian Social Revolutionary leader, Vologodsky, the Northern (independent) Social Revolutionary, Chaykovsky, (represented by Zenzinov since Chaykovsky was at Archangel) and the liberal leader, Astrov (represented by Vinogradov since he was in the South with General Alexeyev's Volunteers) became the chief ministers and theoretically remained the All-Russian government until November 1918 when a *coup d'état* at Omsk removed them from this theoretical body.

The Directorate not only had no territory but also lacked a power basis. As its first appointment was that of Minister of War it was hoped that he would provide the power basis; however, General Boldyrev though he had experience had no armies. He hoped that gradually he would bring together under his overall command the motley of forces, private and foreign armies, then fighting in what was now the Russian civil war. But it proved to be an impossible task and he mistakenly thought that it would be possible if he could impose his command on the foreign Czechoslovak Legion, which, however mutinous, did continue the fight against the Bolsheviks. Exploiting the bad morale of the Legion Boldyrev approached Allied representatives who began to arrive in Siberia and the Urals and ultimately achieved the impossible: the Legion was subordinated to him a few days before he was swept from power in the same coup as the Directors.

Boldyrev's error is quite easy to explain: he saw how much all the White governments and armies depended on the Legion and therefore assumed that through it, by commanding it, he would be able to wield real power. The Legion was involved in the internal Russian political struggle all the time, at Samara, at Ufa and all over Siberia. Thus at Omsk, the seat of the West Siberian Government under one of the Directors, Vologodsky, the Legion intervened against the right wing elements (Minister Mikhailov) when it wanted to purge the left wing elements with the Cossack troops at its disposal. The Cossacks had assassinated Novoselov, but did not dare, after Czech warnings, to liquidate them all, and above all the West Siberian government remained a right-left coalition. At Yekaterinburg, the Social Revolutionary leader, Chernov, stayed alive thanks to Czech protection, while at Samara the Komuch regime lasted as long as the Czech garrison.

Thus the command of the Legion would give Boldyrev power to act decisively in Russian affairs as well. However, this assumption presupposed the Legion's willingness to act on Boldyrev's behalf and above all the Legion's ability to continue to act as it did.

However, in early November 1918 as a result of general demoralisation and the armistice in the West the Czechoslovak Legion ceased to be a military body. It no longer obeyed the orders of its officers and quite arbitrarily began to abandon the fronts. It was most fortunate for the Directorate and the Whites in general that military operations had to be suspended in any case because of the winter conditions and that gradually other military forces arrived to take over the front line. Before he actually fell Boldyrev had under his nominal command quite considerable forces: in the north he had General Gajda's 2nd Division (the rest of the Legion was unlocatable), General Pepelyayev's Tomsk Corps, General Grivin's Irkutsk Corps, General Verzhbitsky's special unit and a few Cossack formations. They althogether amounted to some 19,600 men and 2,300 horsemen. In the west General Lyupov commanded a motley of units of some 9,000 men and General Voytsekhovsky 14,500 men on foot and 5,000 men on horse. The south was held by Ataman Dutov's Cossacks of whom little was known, but who apparently wielded 10,500 rifles and 5,000 sabres. On the spot Boldyrev controlled no one, not even Cossack detachments (not to mention security units).

After the fall of Samara the All-Russian Directorate transferred to Omsk, which seemed safer than the industrial Yekaterinburg. Omsk also contained Allied political representatives who could be used to strengthen Boldyrev's control of the Czechoslovak Legion, as well as the West Siberian government. Immediately disputes broke out: they could not agree on the appointment of the Minister of Police, and rather more fundamentally the Siberian government wanted the Directorate to transform itself into a purely representative organ and pass on to it all its powers. The Directorate vehemently opposed this solution, but the West Siberian government began to ignore it and act quite independently. In October 1918 on his arrival at Omsk Admiral Kolchak was appointed War Minister and within a month a *coup d'état* made him supreme ruler of Russia and *de facto* leader in Siberia.

The coup at Omsk which put Admiral Kolchak into power resolved the conflict between the Directorate and Siberian government and demonstrated the weakness of the White movement; political institutions were volatile and brute force exercised by minute groups of men invariably resolved political conflicts. Admiral Kolchak tried to be humane: instead of massacring the Directory as the Cossack units of Atamans Volkov and Krasilnikov, carrying out the coup, wanted, he exiled them. His person only supplanted this moribund body, but otherwise he left everything undisturbed: the Siberian government continued to function as before, while he concentrated on the conduct of the war. He took over overall command of the fronts and established the supreme headquarters (Stavka) at Omsk. Next he tried to exercise real command and launch an offensive with his forces. In fact it was the beginning of his end.

Like his predecessors Kolchak very quickly found out that the fate of the White movement in Siberia was tied most uncomfortably to the fate of the Czechoslovak Legion. He also tried to unravel this mysterious link and also failed. First of all, he tried to seduce the Legion, especially its officers, into his service. They invariably received the best equipment, were allocated the best billets, were paid French army rates and officers were promoted clearly beyond their capacity and experience. However, even Gajda's division was demoralised and eventually left Kolchak's service though Gajda and some Czech officers stayed to command the newly raised Siberian soldiers. When he finally saw his failure with the Legion Kolchak turned unnecessarily nasty, and using his influence with the Allies under whose nominal charge the Legion was, he forced the Legion to withdraw and serve him in an auxiliary capacity as guardians of his rear.

All this was achieved in the most parsimonious manner after a whole series of conflicts. Not everything was Kolchak's fault either. The Allied Commander-in-Chief, General Janin, and the youthful Minister of War of Czechoslovakia, General Štefánik, arrived at Omsk only in December 1918, and were both men with whom negotiations could prove useful. Instead Kolchak antagonised them from the start. On 16 December 1918 Janin and Kolchak had their first tempestuous interview and could agree on nothing. Štefánik had to employ all his Slovak charm to calm down the irascible supreme ruler of Russia who refused to recognise any previous agreements on command or the joint Allied declaration of 26 November 1918 which defined concretely Russo-Allied relations. Kolchak insisted that Janin take over the supreme command of the fronts which after Boldyrev's departure fell to the Legion's commander, the youthful General Syrový, as Kolchak's plenipotentiary. This was Kolchak's new agreement with the Allies and they had no choice but accept it. On 20 December 1918 Janin left Omsk for Chelyabinsk to implement this new arrangement.

From the beginning the implementation proved difficult and soon it became clear that it was impossible. Although Kolchak desperately needed the Legion and Allied aid he obstinately insisted on cutting off his nose by putting the Legion and the Allied representatives on the spot into impossible positions. After Janin had taken over from Syrový he was advised by the Russian Chief-of-Staff, General Dieterichs, that he should withdraw the Legion from the front, for it was hopelessly demoralised. Janin readily agreed to the withdrawal, but immediately noticed that with it the *raison d'être* of his command evaporated: Russian units simply did not obey his orders and he left the front for Omsk full of forebodings. On 4 January 1919 he was told rather forcefully by Kolchak to withdraw the

Legion as it was demoralising Russian troops, and shortly afterwards Kolchak issued a nonsensical ultimatum to Syrový — either withdraw the Legion or be disarmed.

Everyone was angry, but no one saw the full implications of this order-ultimatum. Janin and Syrový knew that the 1st division had withdrawn in any case and the 2nd was waiting for an opportunity to leave; while they were both more than willing to order withdrawal they were understandably annoyed by the ultimatum, which in any case Kolchak had no power to implement. Kolchak must have hoped that some Czechs would stay with his armies, but at this junction he wanted to get rid of Czech and Allied officers, cost what it may. Consequently, on 13 January 1919 Janin and Štefánik officially ordered Czech withdrawal from the fronts and two days later General Syrový handed over to the Russians the command of the Urals front. Immediately the 2nd Division, which was part of the Siberian army under its former commander, General Gajda, began to exhibit signs of mutiny. Syrový was rushed to inspect the division and was presented with an unanimous request for withdrawal. Thus Kolchak was left with no fighting men, but a factious general and a few officers who could not even command their Russian soldiers. But he got rid of the meddling Allied officers and the Legion, and now tried to recoup his losses by forcing the Legion to guard the Trans-Siberian railway in his rear.

As the Czech trains began to move out of the war area Janin finally realised that he would never hold effective command in Siberia; although he returned to Omsk to be near the Admiral he became incurably pessimistic. Kolchak in the meantime lavished all his care on the creation of the Stavka, which he organised on a massive scale and staffed with all the Russian officers available in Siberia. For his Chief-of-Staff, who actually ran this impressive organisation on Kolchak's behalf, he chose the young Colonel Lebedev, who before joining Kolchak had been politically active in the Officers Association, but lacked general staff experience. Kolchak tried not to interfere with the command at the front, but he firmly subordinated the armies to the Stavka which he thought he could control on the spot. Although these arrangements were not the most efficient, in the conditions of Siberia they seemed to him the best; almost immediately after his assumption of power he decided to put them to a test.

Early in December 1918 the Stavka and the Northern front were ordered to prepare active operations against the Red Army despite the winter. Kolchak wanted to test not only his military setup but also his fighting men, who were going to fight for the first time without the disciplined Czech battalions. General Gajda, who had so far been a successful battalion commander, worked out the operation with Colonel Lebedev and the result was both a great victory and a fiasco. Gajda in fact did not wish the operation to be launched on his front, but in the South. However, he was overruled by Lebedev, who, according to Gajda, opposed the southern drive because it would have opened the way to the Volunteer Army and as a consequence he would have lost his job to a more senior general from the South.

It appears that both southern and northern offensives were over-ambitious and wasteful. In the end General Pepelyayev's Siberian Corps, only just assembled and still insufficiently equipped, attacked and rather surprisingly routed the 1st Red Army. On 24 December 1918 Pepelyayev's armies took Perm, the provincial capital, and captured extensive stores in the town. Although for Kolchak this was a great triumph, which proved to him that he had no need of the Legion, Pepelyayev's casualties were terrible: some 5,000 of his men were killed in action or froze to death, among them 494 officers. Kolchak benefited politically too and the Western Allies henceforth began to consider him as a real supreme ruler.

However, the success of this one operation in reality proved nothing, except to enable Kolchak to cherish illusions of grandeur. The Bolsheviks investigated the Perm catastrophe thoroughly and reorganised their armies as a result. Kolchak did nothing; he did not make good even Siberian losses. Although he proclaimed mobilisation all over Siberia, only a trickle of men actually joined his armies. His recruits were never properly trained, equipped, nor lodged in barracks, but eternally in railway coaches. Nonetheless, encouraged by the success at Perm Kolchak now ordered feverish preparations for a general spring offensive, which would ulti-mately take him to Moscow itself.

Kolchak divided his armies into three groups: in the north he retained General Gajda in command of the Siberians. In the west he had a motley of Russian and national minority units under General Khandzhin, while in the south the 'armies' were under Ataman Dutov's command. With the exception of the Cossack troops Kolchak's men were raw recruits, insufficiently trained, hardly equipped, some without boots. In these circumstances Kolchak should have thought of consolidation rather than of offensives, and he was solemnly warned by Allied officers on the spot. General Janin was most discouraging and pessimistic: in February 1919 he illustrated his pessimism in a report to Paris: with the Czech withdrawal and the fall of Orenburg Kolchak's armies were not in a fit state to launch an offensive. A *coup de force* at Omsk and troubles at Krasnoyarsk did not divert Kolchak's attention from offensives to possible weakness in his rear; he simply blamed these internal troubles on Allied muddle-headedness. He could cope with these troubles and suppressed them ruthlessly. Janin then summed up his conclusions: politically the regime was a disaster; both the reactionaries and progressives suffered from inertia and were capable of enthusiasm and spirit only when fighting each other. The military situation was equally depressing: he no longer attended conferences at the Stavka which were purely ceremonial — elementary ignorance and muddle reigned everywhere. The Stavka officers were incapable of reorganising military units and did not know how to form a regiment. Only General Dieterichs had experience, but lacked the strength of character and failed to oppose the muddlers. Military incompetence and indiscipline extended from the top to the bottom: frontline troops were uncontrollable and both officers and men acted like a rabble – the city of Perm was to all purposes sacked. 'Admiral Kolchak does not even try to improve the working of the Stavka nor the discipline on the fronts. He has complete confidence in his officers and on their advice issues nonsensical military orders from Omsk which will soon have disastrous effect on his personal prestige. The regime as a whole is blind: it does not have even the most elementary intelligence service.'

This prophetic report only prepared the Allies for defeats, but otherwise helped no-one. Kolchak absolutely refused any Allied advice and ignored all warning signs. Shortly before his offensive the Bashkir troops in his western army deserted *en masse* to the Red Army and Janin prophesied similar disaster on the southern front if Dutov's HQ were not re-organised. Nothing could make Kolchak change his mind and the offensive was fixed for the first days of March 1919. It was quite rightly assumed that the Red Army would be taken unawares, and this element of surprise would more than counterbalance the fact that Kolchak's offensive would not be a concentrated thrust in the centre, but would be launched on all three fronts.

In the North, where Gajda had some 34,000 men with 2,465 cavalry, the White Siberian army advanced immediately without much resistance. Its objectives were Vyatka, Kotlas and the eventual link-up with the Allied armies locked up at Archangel. In the South Dutov's Cossacks attacked only for the offensive's sake; they were quite incapable of offensive actions and should have remained on the defensive. In the overall plan of this spring offensive their rôle was only a minor one, so their lack of progress caused no disquiet at Omsk. However, the armies of the West (centre) under General Khanzhin were to perform the most important task of this offensive – defeat the Red Army in the foothills of the Urals, break through the lines to the Volga and then to Central Russia and Moscow. In the actual offensive the 100,000-strong armies of Admiral Kolchak initially advanced on a front of some 700 miles, which meant that they were physically overextended. Gajda's 1st Army penetrated some 150 miles into the Bolshevik-held territory between Perm and Vyatka. No battles were fought and the Red Army withdrew in reasonable order. Then the Siberians slowed down and without ammunition and supplies came to an abrupt halt. In the South Ataman Dutov's forces surprisingly wiped out all the Red Army advance early in the year and re-took a huge chunk of territory between Orsk-Orenburg and Uralsk. General Khanzhin, who within a month penetrated some 250 miles into Bolshevik territory, was approaching Samara on the Volga. Although these initial successes were most encouraging it became clear as the offensive developed that the Red Armies were withdrawing according to a plan: the number of prisoners captured by the Whites was disproportionately small to the territorial gains and there were hardly any deserters. The Red Army was obviously undefeated and its counter-offensive plans were causing the Whites great worries, for in their offensive enthusiasm the Whites disregarded the most elementary principles of war: they committed their reserves to the battle at its commencement, paid no attention to such vital matters as safeguarding their communication lines and their intelligence proved quite blind. When in June 1919 the Red Army finally counter-attacked Kolchak's armies collapsed.

At the crucial stage in the battle in the West Khanzhin's troops proved quite unequal to their task and mutinied. Ukrainian units fighting on this front quite unexpectedly assassinated their Russian officers and, dressed in their British battledress uniforms, crossed the line to join the Red Army. Bashkir calvary also went over to the Bolsheviks who as a result managed to cut off the lines of communication of Khanzhin's armies. The front rapidly collapsed, the Whites retreated in panic and by the end of June 1919 the Red Army reoccupied all the territory lost previously. With the collapse in the centre the Northern Army had to beat a hasty retreat not to be cut off from Siberia: the retreat quickly changed into a rout with the Siberians running home without guns and abandoning without a shot the cities of Perm and Ekaterinburg with all their stores. In the South the Red Army rapidly re-took Orenburg and Uralsk and got ready to strike deep into Turkestan. Admiral Kolchak had to reorganise both the command and his armies if he was to stem the Red Army advance.

At first Kolchak thought that if he reshuffled his commanders he would save the situation, but instead only increased panic and confusion. Gajda was called to Omsk and took over the command of the dismissed Khanzhin. The incompetent Lebedev, about whom front commanders unceasingly complained and who had demonstrated his strategic inability in the spring offensive, still remained as Chief of Staff. However, Gajda's successor as commander of the Siberians was not the Siberian General, Peplyayev, but the Russian Bogoslavsky. Perhaps fortunately for the South no reorganisation was carried out there, for Omsk and Kolchak had lost all effective contact with Dutov's Cossacks. Before the reshuffled commanders could apply themselves to the task of reorganising their forces they had to resolve their quarrels: Gajda objected to the Stavka and its interference and was dismissed. Ironically Lebedev also went and his place was finally taken by General Dieterichs – possibly the only experienced staff officer capable of reorganising the defeated armies.

By July 1919 demoralisation began to affect not only the command and the armies at the fronts, but also the rear. In January 1919, after the

Czechoslovak Legion had disengaged in the West, it was gradually transferred to duties in the rear, especially to guard the security of Siberia's lifeline, the Trans-Siberian railway. Although Kolchak disliked the Czechs he raised no objection to their propping up his rear, especially after it became evident that the troops that he had detailed for these duties could not control the situation. In fact these Kolchak detachments instead of pacifying the rear created new problems for Kolchak and the Czechs. It was said that the behaviour of Ataman Annenkov's cossacks at Omsk and Western Siberia created more Bolsheviks than the unit succeeded in killing. Similarly Ataman Krasilnikov's cossacks and General Rozanov's brigade behaved so atrociously at Kansk and Krasnoyarsk and in the country round that they had soon widespread peasant rebellions to deal with. As they could not cope with the problems they themselves created, the Czechoslovak Legion was called in, especially after the peasant rebel-partisans began to raid the towns garrisoned by the Legion. Much to the dislike of both Kolchak and the Legion the Czechs were again drawn into the civil war in Siberia.

Although the Legion did take part in punitive expeditions against the peasant partisans it acted mainly in response to partisan attacks against the Czech soldiers or against the Trans-Siberian. The Legion was most anxious to preserve it intact, for it expected at any time Allied orders of evacuation. However, the Allies were in no undue hurry, claiming the shortage of shipping; thus the Legion was stuck in Siberia with the Kolchak Whites whom it increasingly detested. It was demoralised by this obvious abandonment by the Allies and even more by the nature of its duties in Siberia. As its demoralisation became known publicly, both the Allies and Kolchak rediscovered it and wanted it to start fighting once again on their behalf.

When General Syrový ordered the Czechoslovak Legion to withdraw from the Urals front to Central Siberia it was to prevent its final collapse and preserve it as a fighting force. However the withdrawal seems to have completed the decomposition of the Legion, for it was sabotaged by the Whites and quite unprepared. The Legion was sent to the wilderness of central Siberia without any billets being prepared, with no supplies and with impossible tasks to perform: thus the 1st and 2nd Divisions were to guard some 150 versts of the Trans-Siberian each, while the 3rd Division, still being formed, was to be responsible for some 450 versts. The withdrawal of the Legion from the West was spread over three months and coincided with peasant insurrections in the East. The arriving units were often thrown into fighting as reinforcements despite their small numbers and lack of equipment; moreover many units understood the withdrawal as evacuation home and this new fighting was a terrible surprise for them. Soldiers began to clamour for regimental committees, only just abolished. Discipline began to crack and mutinies made their appearance. Thus, for example, in March 1919 the Legion was expected to relieve the town of Tayshet besieged by the partisans. When the trains of the 4th Regiment finally arrived the soldiers refused to leave them, held a meeting and unanimously voted to continue the journey to Vladivostok rather than fight the partisans. After the most undignified and unmilitary scenes at Tayshet station the officers succeeded in persuading their men that without a fight the journey could not be continued.

At this early stage officers could still use the argument that without clearing its way through Siberia the Legion could not be evacuated. The men, however, became more than suspicious after the delay during the summer; the officers proved more than willing to carry out orders. Thus Colonel Žák, Commanding Officer of the 1st Division, refused any deal with the partisans, who offered him and his division a troublefree passage to Vladivostok, and cleared his way with arms. Many Czech officers went even further and Major Beránek even offended the Whites. He insisted on public proclamations of the death penalty for rebellion, spying and 'agitation'. Though the Whites widely practised this law of war they never admitted it publicly, and above all hated to have it proclaimed by foreigners. Despite the warlike noises and actual fighting when forced into it, the Legion was really on the verge of collapse.

By June 1919, when even Kolchak came to the conclusion that it would have to be used to 'save Siberia', the Legion lapsed into complete chaos. As a volunteer body the Czechoslovak Legion had always had the privilege of being consulted about (and voted on) any important decision affecting its fate in Russia. In the past it had voted almost unanimously to revolt against the Bolsheviks in May 1918. In June 1919 it wanted to vote for the evacuation from Siberia and for this purpose it convoked an army congress for which the elections were carried out during the withdrawal from the Urals despite official prohibition. Delegates from all Czechoslovak units in Siberia began to arrive at Irkutsk, the Legion's HQ, to discuss at the congress evacuation, guard duties and partisan fighting. It became obvious that the congress would be used by certain elements as a springboard for a general mutiny. However the men of the 1st Regiment, garrisoned at Irkutsk and composed of war veterans, were puzzled by these 'unofficial' delegates, 'unofficial' congress and indecisive talking. Above all they were prepared to obey orders, for they doubted that the congress and the delegates could get them out of Siberia any sooner than their actual leaders. The command and the political leaders were equally puzzled, but then suddenly General Syrový acted: he ordered the ejection of the delegates from the barracks and the 1st Regiment rid itself of these uninvited guests. But the delegates appealed to the units which elected them for protection and their reaction was equally prompt. The garrison at Innokentskaya, not far west from Irkutsk, mutinied, locked up its officers and left for Irkutsk. At Kansk the 4th Regiment was also in full mutiny, but remained at Kansk. On arrival at Irkutsk the Innokentskaya mutineers took over the editorial offices of the *Ceskoslovenský denník*, issued public demands for the resignation of B. Pavlů and R. Medek, the political leaders, and the arrest of all officers. By now the men of the 1st Regiment became convinced that the congress and the munities were 'senseless adventures', went into action against the delegates and their 'protectors', and threatened to use their artillery if they did not surrender. Though the problems at Irkutsk were resolved without a bloodshed the events were the deathblow to both Czechoslovak political and military leadership. However, this was not understood outside the Legion either by the Whites, or the Allies, or the Czechoslovak political leaders at home. White counter-espionage confused the complete anarchy in the Legion with a temporary malaise: new recruits in the Legion had no discipline; old soldiers were tired and the committees which still ran the Legion's affairs were infiltrated by left wing elements. However, the Whites were soon going to be undeceived about the Legion.

Kolchak's 'purges' of July 1919 did bring some relief to the White armies and a measure of consolidation. The Red Army still continued its victorious advance, but gradually it slowed as General Dieterichs regrouped his forces and by the end of August 1919 reached a line a few miles west of the Ishim River, having retreated over 600 miles since the beginning of May. However, the Red Army was also over-extended, by now badly led and fairly exhausted. It was remarkable that after this unparalleled retreat Dieterichs should have been able not only to check the Red Army's advance, but regain the initiative. Early in September 1919 Dieterichs' armies took the offensive and advanced on the northern front to an average depth of 100 miles, driving the Red Army back to the line of the Tobol River.

In the meantime the Red Army had scored an overwhelming victory in the Orenburg-Uralsk area on the southern flank. It secured complete control over the Tashkent Railway and drove the Dutov Cossacks deep into Turkestan. This success in the South and the Red Army's reorganisation in the North finally reversed the military situation on the Tobol: by the end of September Dieterichs' forces far from continuing their advance were unable to maintain themselves on the line of the Tobol. In the middle of October 1919 the Red Army counter-attacked and completely turned the tables, though the success was not due to superior numbers but to better discipline, This time the blow proved fatal not only to the White armies, which retreated in panic, but also to Kolchak's government.

Admiral Kolchak ruled Siberia most inefficiently. With his attention concentrated on his armies he caused havoc with its operations, acting on bad advice given to him by ill-chosen advisers. In administration he proved equally inept: enormous frauds were perpetrated by his Minister of

Supplies, Zefirov, with army supplies. Politically he was also a disaster: he appointed as his military governors unintelligent, or at least politically simple, soldiers who systematically confused legitimate political demands with Bolshevik intrigue, and everyone, except the monarchists, with Bolsheviks themselves. Generals Ivanov-Rinov, Romanovsky and Rozanov instituted the system of hostages and as late as November 1919 Rozanov executed 27 non-Bolsheviks at Krasnoyarsk for political crimes. On the whole Siberian Social Revolutionaries and officials of the Siberian Cooperative Movement rather than actual Bolsheviks or their sympathisers had been systematically persecuted and executed.

In particular Kolchak's disregard of the *zemstva* (self-government) led to the greatest estrangement of political opinion. Although he had promised government on democratic lines and no limitation of public rights his centralisation immediately brought him into conflict with the zemstva, which were dominated by socialist revolutionaries and social democrats who resented this centralisation as the manifestation of the excessive influence of the extreme right. Zemstva discontent reached its climax in February 1919, when several members of the executive committee of the Maritime province *zemstvo* were arrested and without trial removed from Vladivostok. Though they were subsequently released others were not so lucky. The harm was done, and the action of the Kolchak government, combined with indiscriminate punitive measures against the peasants, had merely the effect of manufacturing Bolshevism right and left and weakening Kolchak's authority where it was most needed to ensure his military success. Recruiting fell off steadily and peasants resisted conscription altogether; desertions at the front became numerous while the Red Army troops were reluctant to come over to the Siberian Whites as they were fairly sure of being shot.

In addition the financial and economic situation was as bad as it could have possibly been. Throughout Kolchak's rule Siberia had over 30 forms of currency, from a Romanov rouble to the picture on a cigarette box, and in many places the latter token was more valuable than the former. The financial confusion was increased by extensive forgeries and the Minister of Finance's refusal to reform the currency. The depreciation of money led to an enormous increase in prices — far higher than they were under the Bolsheviks. No improvements were possible until the transport problem had been solved, but that was never to be (partly because of the dishonesty of the officials at Vladivostok who for speculative purposes of their own prevented the removal of supplies from the city). The wholesale requisitioning of stocks by the Kolchak government brought imports automatically to a stop, while after the loss of the Urals the productive capacity was paralysed and even the railway became dependent on supplies from abroad. The influx of refugees, for whom neither accommodation nor occupation could be found, increased the chaos and there was practically a complete absence of clothing and other articles of necessity. Although even Kolchak was aware of these weaknesses he did nothing about them: he convoked an economic congress of the principal districts and economic institutions in Siberia too late and even then failed to implement its recommendations. Thus the Kolchak regime was shaken by military failure, was politically bankrupt, economically corrupt and exhausted.

Late in October 1919 the reorganised 5th Red Army had broken through Dieterichs' lines and threatened to cut off the 3rd (Siberian) Army. Dieterichs had to disengage and withdraw his three armies, or what was left of them, to the defences beyond the river Irtysh. This tactical military move entailed the evacuation of Omsk, the political capital of Siberia. Admiral Kolchak, who was now engaged in frantic negotiations with the Allies and the Legion, tried to persuade his general to make his stand before Omsk, pointing out the political importance of such a stand. He also hoped that the Allies would oblige the Legion to fight its way home via Omsk and Denikin, and he was offering the Legion the pay in gold. However the old general, who knew the Allies and the Legion better than Kolchak, failed to be convinced by his supreme commander; instead he pointed out to him that a stand before Omsk would be in danger from Petropavlovsk and such an encircling movement by the Red Army would lose Kolchak not only the battle but also his remaining armies. In desperation Kolchak listened to the discredited Lebedev, who had found another youthful and incapable General, Zakharov, to save Omsk. Dieterichs resigned, Zakharov took over the command and within 48 hours came to the same conclusion: withdrawal was absolutely necessary. This change of commanders, plans and orders opened the floodgates of chaos and virtually meant the end of White Siberia.

On 10 November 1919 the Irtysh River finally froze up and Kolchak's armies were able to cross it and establish defensive positions on the other bank outside Omsk. Four days later Admiral Kolchak and his command left the city in seven trains, taking with them the gold reserve captured by the Czechs at Kazan. Twenty-four hours later Red Army units from Petropavlovsk made a dash for Omsk, capturing enormous stores, artillery and transport. Nothing was saved and when the Red Army broke through the Irtysh lines the chaos was indescribable. All White Siberia was on the move along the Trans-Siberian — the White armies on foot or in trains, refugees also on foot or, if lucky, in trains and the command and political leaders still in trains. The railway was gravely overloaded, for on 28 September 1919 the Czechoslovak Legion had also commenced its own evacuation. All this inextricably mixed up stream tried desparately to reach the Pacific Ocean.

The Czechoslovak Legion, which was once again a decisive military factor, felt extremely frustrated: it was 'betrayed' by the Allies whom it blamed for the delays in repatriation. Its political leaders were just dismissed and sent home, but the unpopular officers were trapped with their men in the White mire of Siberia. Everything was dissolving into chaos and the Czechs now vented their frustration openly, accelerating the process of dissolution. Before leaving for Czechoslovakia Pavlů proclaimed the Legion's political views publicly: he called the Kolchak regime, created by Czechoslovak bayonettes, a cruel anachronism in Siberia, and Admiral Kolchak and his men butchers and political assassins. However damaging these public declarations might have been they were much less dangerous than the conspiracies other Czechs were engaged in.

Long before Kolchak's departure numerous Czechs — soldiers and officers as well as politicians — were involved in political intrigues which began to bear fruit. Kolchak knew nothing about these intrigues and as late as October 1919 he wanted to recall General Gajda. However, as soon as Gajda, who had been dismissed so abruptly in July, reached Vladivostok he set to work. He remained in his armoured train in Vladivostok station and turned it into the HQ of the Siberian Social Revolutionary movement. With his encouragement the central bureau of the Social Revolutionary military organisation was formed in September 1919. Kolosov was put in charge of Krasnoyarsk; Kalashnikov, one of the staff officers who served under Gajda, became the military leader at Irkutsk; Gajda himself assumed leadership at Vladivostok. The talkative Gajda soon betrayed the SR plans to the Allies, principally to the acting British high commissioner, with the result that the British ambassador lodged a strong protest with President Masaryk. Gajda had involved too many people in this conspiracy; General Boldyrev was consulted and enlisted and even local Bolsheviks voted to join in an uprising. However General Rozanov was also informed of what was afoot, and it is said that he provoked the final crisis. The uprising started on 17 November and by the next day Rozanov suppressed it ruthlessly with Japanese help. Gajda was captured, maltreated and handed over to Girsa, the Czech representative, in whose care he survived. The American mission also saved the lives of many local Bolsheviks and SRs.

Although the uprising misfired in Vladivostok, at Krasnoyarsk and Irkutsk SR insurgents with Czech connivance and help won the day. As a result of these disorders, General Syrový ordered the seizure of the railway west of Krasnoyarsk, so that Czech evacuation could proceed. This meant that the remainder of Kolchak's forces, the three army corps beating their retreat along the Trans-Siberian, could not intervene against the rebels at Krasnoyarsk. Kolosov began to negotiate with the garrison and General Zinevich: Krasnoyarsk finally went over to the SRs in December, only to fall to the advancing Red Army.

If on the whole the Krasnoyarsk conspiracy was encouraged by the Czechs in a passive way, the Irkutsk rebellion had their active support. Long before the actual rebellion Czech left wing elements were in contact with the SR underground. J. David, a socialist member of the Czech parliament, even introduced the SR representatives to the Czech Parliamentary Mission which arrived from Prague. The HQ also knew of the arms traffic in the town, but it failed to inform the Kolchak authorities. On 12 November 1919 the city duma and the Irkutsk zemstvo met at a conference to discuss future political action. Since the Omsk government was still on its way in trains to Irkutsk, General Syrový thought it propitious to make a public declaration of Czech neutrality and the principle of self-interest. When the Omsk government finally arrived on 19 November, the Czechs began to implement their declared policy: promising their support to any White group which would best assure Czech evacuation.

On the very day of its arrival at Irkutsk, the Omsk government received a *démarche* from the Czechoslovak HQ. Responding to Czech pressure, Guins (chief administrator of Kolchak's government) sent a telegram in the name of the government to the Supreme Ruler, asking him to appoint a new government. Kolchak, who was held up on the Trans-Siberian, consented and the politicians at Irkutsk began to negotiate amongst themselves as to who should form the next government. On 23 November V. Pepelyayev, the former Minister of the Interior and brother of the C-in-C of the Siberian Army, became the Prime Minister and quickly took steps to conciliate the Czechs. At Irkutsk the atmosphere was so hostile to the Kolchak government that Pepelyayev saw clearly that he could not survive without Czech support. He promptly concluded an agreement with Dr Girsa after he had placed a 15,000,000 rouble loan at the disposal of the Czechs and left for Taiga to meet his brother and the Supreme Ruler. Unfortunately for Pepelyayev and Kolchak they had bribed the wrong Czechs; even if they had wanted to, Dr Girsa and the Czech Command would have been unable to help them effectively. In any case Kolchak immediately made sure they would not even want to: when the notorious Memorandum by Pavlů reached him, Kolchak sent a telegram to Pepelyayev to protest to Sazonov, his Paris representative about it, stop all dealings with the Czechs and demand their recall. Since Kolchak's own train depended on the Czechs these measures were hardly wise and Pepelyayev did not hesitate to say so. Then the Czechs timidly withdrew the memorandum and a few days later Kolchak asked Pepelyayev to drop the protests. He also expressed the hope that some measure of cooperation would be achieved.

This eminently reasonable settlement of the Russo-Czech quarrel seemed promising. However Kolchak's retreating armies began to quarrel with the Czechs and also to disintegrate, and this was the last nail in the Supreme Ruler's coffin. When the Czechs seized the Trans-Siberian railway the three White armies, which in fact split up into smaller units loyal to Generals Pepelyayev, Voytsekhovsky and Kappel, were retreating along the Trans-Siberian tract. The strain of the retreat played on the generals' nerves. General Voytsekhovsky shot General Grivin for insubordination; Polish officers 'suppressed' Colonel Ivakin at Novonikolaevsk for obstruction. On 7 December the Pepelyayevs arrested General Zakharov and forced his resignation as C-in-C. When on 11 December Kappel assumed supreme command, the White Army was already in ruins.

The new *entente cordiale* between Omsk and the Czechs lasted only a few days. On 8 December the Czechs acted on Kolchak's behalf and suppressed an insurrection in the Irkutsk gaol. All this confusion caused by the disorderly retreat of Kolchak's armies left the Red Army free to pursue its offensive at the greatest speed it could muster. Although the advance seemed smooth and leisurely, the Reds' irregular allies, the Siberian partisans, were playing havoc with the transport. The Czech evacuation continued painfully slowly; on 10 December a huge bottleneck developed at Mariinsk and Kolchak's train was only allowed through after humiliating requests and protests. On the 12th the Czechs had further difficulties at Krasnoyarsk and this time Kolchak had to wait for a week. Whatever political arrangements might have been made at Irkutsk by Dr Girsa and V. Pepelyayev, they were becoming superfluous, for the Czechoslovak Legion and the Czech politicians would soon be unable to honour any agreements. It was generally considered that General Janin no longer exercised any influence over the Czechs and it also became evident that General Syrový exercised no command in practice. On 10 December 1919 he was forced to announce the evacuation of the Czechs as top priority and henceforth only Czech trains were allocated fuel.

As Kolchak's situation became more isolated and precarious, the measures he thought of were even more desperate. While his armies were on the run, deserting, mutinying and surrendering to the Red Army, he thought of nothing better than issuing paper promotions and appeals. By now the Czechs controlled everything — even the telegraph lines. Nevertheless, he sent off the fateful telegram appointing Ataman Semenov, his erstwhile enemy, as C-in-C of the White forces, bidding him at the same time to stop the Czech evacuation in retaliation for his personal 'detention'. It was a stupid order, but the Supreme Ruler was approaching insanity. The Czechs let through the order to Semenov, but Kolchak was definitely lost. He reached Nizhne Udinsk, when Krasnoyarsk rebelled, and he was cut off from Kappel and his 'army'. Further east Cheremkhovo was in the insurgents' hands and on 24 December the Irkutsk uprising began. Nizhne Udinsk itself was also in insurgents' hands but the station was held by the Czechs. Kolchak continued to ignore the fact of his deteriorating condition and since his entourage thought of leaving the train and of making their way to Mongolia, he had them dismissed. He maintained his faith in the Allied representative and the Czech Command.

Yet again he was relying on the wrong people. In the circumstances resolute action was needed and Kolchak had several chances of making good an escape, since the road to Irkutsk led to a certain death. Though Nizhne Udinsk was hostile to him, the Czech garrison, Major Hásek's assault battalion, which was a crack unit in the Legion, was favourably inclined to Kolchak. Major Hásek was far from being a left-winger and would undoubtedly have listened to proposals or plans had Kolchak or his men approached him. No-one did anything and Hásek's battalion in the absence of any other orders obeyed those of General Syrový and departed. Kolchak's last chance to escape from a trap of his own making thus passed. Possibly his faith in the Allies was even more illusory; the Allied representatives had no troops and had to rely on General Janin for the execution of any order concerning Kolchak. Since, however, Janin's orders were no longer obeyed by the Czechs, Allied appeals were empty gestures. Syrový's orders were obeyed and disobeyed as circumstances allowed and although Kolchak could see it, he passively waited for the inevitable to occur. General Syrový received a shock at Irkutsk when the Czech garrison almost joined in the insurrection because it apparently offered the best means of getting out of Siberia. He realised that he would never complete the evacuation without the help of the Russian insurgents, so he decided to negotiate. He needed coal from Cheremkhovo and mediation with the Red Army, and they could help with both. In return he was prepared to help the insurgents by forbidding the Kolchak garrison to use its artilllery under the pretext that its bombardment of the insurgents would destroy the railway line and station. The garrison gave up fighting and withdrew, and on 5 January 1920 the insurgents were the undisputed masters of Irkutsk. All other towns west were in their hands and Cheremkhovo continued to supply much needed coal to the Czech trains. Moreover on 11 January 1920 a delegation of the new regime, the Political Centre, left Irkutsk under Czech protection to conduct armistice talks with the Red Army.

Smooth evacuation now seemed certain, and there remained only three other problems to be solved — those of Kolchak, the gold reserve and the White forces. The first problem was easily dealt with. The hapless Kolchak was under Czech protection in a coach flying Allied flags. On 7 January his coach left Nizhne Udinsk at long last, but it was only for a very short journey. While there was no love lost between Syrový and Kolchak the handing over of Kolchak to the Political Centre* was not an act of free will. Syrový was under pressure from the Allied representatives, who were still at Irkutsk, to save Kolchak. Syrovy was not the heartless man some historians tried to make of him: Prague and Beneš from Paris were also pressing him to save Kolchak, however disagreeable it was for the Legion. He personally saved many a White general and politician who applied to him in time by putting them on the Czech train to Vladivostok. Time was running out to save Kolchak: Syrový could not be sure of his own troops, so he tried to shift the final decision onto General Janin, his nominal

*An anti-Kolchak coalition dominated by Social Revolutionaries, but with Bolshevik members.

superior and Allied representative. On 14 January he explained to him the situation on the telephone and made it quite clear that not one Czech soldier would lift a finger to 'protect' Kolchak from his own people. However, Janin refused to give a clear directive and gave Syrový a free hand. If circumstances demanded it, he was to hand over Kolchak: *'fais de ton mieux en sauvegardant le nom tcheque. Je t'approuve.'*

On 15 January 1920 Allied representatives were at Kharbin, Janin was at Verkhne Udinsk. General Skipetrov's detachment was on the other side of the Baykal and the SRs were outraged by the execution of the 31 hostages whom the retreating Kolchak forces took with them from Irkutsk. General Syrový's counter-espionnage reported restlessness among his own men: they had contacts not only with the SR forces but also with the partisans. Some were scouting for the latter, all were conducting a vigorous campaign for an armistice, quick withdrawal and the abandonment of Kolchak and his likes to the Russians in power. From Syrový's point of view the situation was hopeless: his rearguard was under Bolshevik attack and on the run. He also knew of the fate of the Polish officers, murdered by their own men when the trapped Polish Legion surrendered to the Red Army at Kamacharga on the 7 January. If he gave orders to let Kolchak through Irkutsk and the Political Centre objected to or even opposed with arms the passage of Kolchak, his soldiers would desert and disobey the order, thus putting at risk his own life and those of his officers. He finally decided to hand Kolchak over to the Political Centre, and at the same time gave the Japanese ample opportunity to save Kolchak if they so wished, for while all the other Allied units had left Irkutsk, there was still a Japanese unit at the station. Negotiations on the actual handing over were conducted by Dr Blahož, the political representative. On 15 January Dr Blahož told B.A. Kozminsky of the arrival of train No. 52. At 7 p.m. a special commission consisting of N.S. Feldman, Captain Nesterov and V.N. Merkhalov arrived at the station in full view of the lounging Japanese soldiers and took into custody Admiral Kolchak and V. Pepelyayev after giving Lieutenant Borovička a written receipt. 112 other persons, including G. Zhukovsky, formerly the Russian consul in Prague, Klafton, the journalist, and professor Boldyrev, the organiser of the St George Cross units, were also arrested and taken to the Irkutsk gaol.

The easiest task had been accomplished to everyone's satisfaction, although it was mixed with horror. The Czechs avoided a strike on the railway and at Cheremkhovo in the mines by handing over Kolchak. They also convinced the Allied representatives that they could not save Kolchak, who in any case was abandoned by everyone, including his own supporters in the Trans-Baykal region. At the same time mutiny was avoided in the Legion. But to save themselves the Czechs really needed an immediate armistice, since the Red Army was hard on their heels. In this context the handing over of Kolchak was the final proof of Czech sincerity and goodwill to negotiate with the Bolsheviks. The Bolsheviks, however, asked for more: they wanted them to surrender the gold reserve which they had taken from Kolchak at Nizhne Udinsk.

Political morality apart, much greater pressure was put on General Syrový in the case of the gold reserves than in Kolchak's case. Though Dr Beneš had also intervened in Kolchak's favour, he intervened in much stronger terms in connection with the gold. But all outside attempts at solving the problem on the spot were doomed to failure. The reserve was the only bargaining point the Czechs held over the Red Army. When the Czech representatives finally reached the Red Army to start the negotiations for an armistice, it was thought that by manoeuvring and delay a settlement could be made when the Legion had left its present dangerous location unharmed, still in possession of the gold reserves. The Bolsheviks saw through the scheme and countered by appealing directly to the Czech troops on the spot to surrender − at the same time they launched a few attacks on them to prove they meant business. On 19 January 1920 the Czechoslovak National Council still favoured delays but the ambushes laid for the Legion by the Red Army at Nizhne Udinsk and Tulun on the 29th convinced it that there would be no evacuation without an armistice and that there was little else to be gained and much to lose in delay. In a last effort orders went out to the rearguard 3rd Division to protect itself, but when the officers reported their doubts as to the feasibility of the order an armistice was signed at Kuytun on the 7 February, the very day Admiral Kolchak and V. Pepelyayev were executed at Irkutsk.

The terms of the armistice were on the whole favourable to the Czechs: their evacuation was guaranteed provided the Legion evacuated its own forces and those of the non-Russian allies (Latvians, Italians etc) only, did not destroy the railway, bridges and other Russian property and returned evacuation trains and the gold reserve, which was to wait under a mixed guard at Irkutsk until the last Czech was evacuated and the Red Army took over the city. There was no real Czech sacrifice involved and in any case the Czechs, at least those in Siberia, were so desperate that they would disregard any Allied pressure. The Czechs, however, could not disregard the remnants of the White Armies which continued to retreat before the Red Army. These erstwhile comrades in arms were in a bad state: their numbers were reduced by mutinies and insurrections all along the Trans-Siberian, but even after Krasnoyarsk they amounted to some 30,000, a considerable force. In December 1919 Colonel Birule reported that the White retreat was a terrifying affair. However, the Czechs soon found that atrocities were committed by both sides: forcible requisitions of food, lodging and transport and the shooting of captured prisoners were commonplace signs of desperation. At the time of the armistice the Whites were under the command of General Voytsekhovsky, the highly acceptable Russian officer, since General Kappel, another acceptable officer, was lying dead in the Czech train *en route* to Chita. Under the new commander, Czechs and Whites had cooperated in destroying a partisan force at Zima.

After the armistice some Czech units continued to help the Whites, but the Legion and the Whites could no longer cooperate officially. When General Voytsekhovsky arrived at Irkutsk, he delivered an ultimatum to the Revkom and prepared an attack on the city, but he was asked by his Czech friends, Colonel Krejčí and Lieutenant Colonel Buřila, to call the attack off. The White Army was now so exhausted that Voytsekhovsky was not sorry to be forced to abandon the attack, despite the insistence of the sacked General Zakharov and several other generals bent on revenge. In return the Czech Legion agreed to take care of some 1,000 Whites who could march no further. The Voytsekhovsky force by-passed Irkutsk, reached the Baykal, crossed it and joined the Semenov forces in the Trans-Baykal Region.

With General Voytsekhovsky's passage beyond the lake of Baykal, the Czech Legion had solved the problem of the Whites. The White Political Centre at Irkutsk collapsed on the 20 January 1920 and the different White groups set out for their respective strongholds: Verkhne Udinsk, Chita, Vladivostok, all on the other side of the Baykal; the diehard Kolchakovites went furthest. The Red Army respected the armistice with the Legion scrupulously, even if this meant the Whites would benefit. Its ranks were depleted by frostbite, typhus and supply problems and the presence of the Japanese army in the Trans-Baykal seemed an insurmountable barrier to its advance. To have reached Irkutsk without much fighting was success enough. On 1 March 1920 the last Czech train left Irkutsk, the gold reserve was handed over to the special commission of the Russian State Bank and the guard to the 7th Company of the Irkutsk Soviet Regiment.

Political intrigues and supply considerations had certainly slowed down the Czechs. The rearguard had had trouble with the Reds but there was also constant friction with the Semenov troops and even with the Japanese army, both of whom feared that the Legion was helping the SRs and even the Bolsheviks to penetrate into their territories. The Czechs were not allowed to leave their trains at Chita, where several incidents almost sparked off armed fighting. In one of the worst incidents Japanese troops surrounded a Czech train at Chita and threatened to machine-gun it unless the officers disclosed where the Bolsheviks were hidden. Since the Bolsheviks turned out to be White troops retreating before the Red Army the dispute was quickly settled. Even General Semenov ultimately proved reasonable and resigned himself to letting the Legion through his region without hindrance, especially after the Czechs had agreed to sell him war material.

At Vladivostok there was a great concentration of soldiers and nationalities and the atmosphere was explosive. The Czechs were quartered in barracks in the town and on the islands, but as sanitary arrangements were not outstanding the threat of typhus hung over the whole population. The political situation in the town itself was also complicated. Girsa and the Czech politicians were actively intriguing against General Rozanov, the White commander, and were aided by General Graves and American diplomats. On 31 January 1920 the local SRs (helped by the Bolsheviks) attempted a coup and were successful. Among the insurgents there fought many Czech deserters from the Legion. This did not deter Dr Girsa from supporting the new regime whilst the Japanese hesitated, allowing the Maritime Provisional Government to be established with a pledge of Czech support. Because of their ambiguous position the Japanese were asked to withdraw but their representative, Matsudayre, rejected the demand on the grounds that the Japanese presence was required to protect the Czech evacuation. This led Dr Girsa to declare that Japanese protection was no longer needed, as he had full confidence in the Maritime Provisional Government. A few days later some Japanese citizens were massacred by local partisans at Nikolayevsk and provided the Japanese with a pretext for action against the Russians at Vladivostok. On 5 April they rounded up all the Vladivostok leaders, including the Bolshevik Lazo and executed them on the spot or handed them over to the Kolchak Whites who finally killed them.

The ruthless action of the Japanese stunned the Czechs and the Americans. They could not retaliate openly because the Japanese were supplying ships for the evacuation, but they continued to sympathise with and sometimes give protection to the SRs and the Russians left in their struggle against the Japanese.

The evacuation dragged on throughout the summer of 1920. The rearguard 10th Regiment reached Vladivostok at the end of May 1920 and was shipped out on U.S.N. *Evelyn* on 1 June 1920. On 30 November the evacuation was declared closed; some 67,750 people had been evacuated, including 56,459 soldiers. The Kappelevtsy, as the remnants of the Whites called themselves, crossed the lake and managed to march in closed order until Chita. Many went to China, Manchuria or Vladivostok; General Voytsekhovsky rejoined the Czechoslovak Legion and was evacuated to Czechoslovakia, where he died in 1935, a general of the Czech army. The Americans left Vladivostok in April 1920 thoroughly disgusted with their experience. The Japanese stayed in Vladivostok until 1922, but the Far Eastern Republic which they had established lasted until 1924, when the last Japanese troops left the Far East of Russia.

General Voytsekhovsky's fate was symptomatic of White Siberia itself. There the civil war was started by an alien element, the Czechoslovak Legion, whose presence was quite fortuitous. Despite this the Legion's fate in Siberia was bound inextricably with that of the White movement, whose revolt against the Bolsheviks it had brought into existence. Because of the international implications and complications the Czechoslovak Legion could only leave Siberia with honour after it had made secure a White Russia; conversely a withdrawal in dishonour had to bring down the White regimes. Both parties vaguely realised this, but neither was able to eschew its prejudices and harmonise their interests. The result was inevitable: the Bolsheviks defeated the Whites and conquered Siberia. The Czech Legion was forced to sneak out of Russia leaving its erstwhile White allies at the mercy of the Bolshevik enemy. It had fought most wasteful battles and the two years of blood and suffering had brought nothing but shame and ruin..

5

Civil War in South Russia

I

In the South the Whites continued their struggle against the Bolsheviks as divided as in the fateful days after the Bolshevik coup. The Don Cossacks kept the Volunteers at a safe distance and maintained vigorous autonomy. Even their campaign against the Red Army took them to the limits of what they considered their autonomous region: in fact the fighting was extremely desultory and brought no significant success to either side. Ataman Krasnov found it impossible to recruit suitable officers among his Cossacks to lead his men who, despite German aid, were miserably clad and armed. General Semenov, who ostensibly commanded Krasnov's Don Cossack armies, never once inspected the front and in the end escaped from the Don with 3,500,000 roubles. Cossack operations against Voronezh, which they considered as their city, petered out rather ignominiously, but the Cossacks scored an unexpected success when their forces penetrated to the Volga and besieged the city of Tsaritsyn (later Stalingrad, then Volgograd) which was not a Cossack town. Krasnov hoped that the fall of Tsaritsyn would restore the morale of his men, but instead the city was relieved by Red Army units from Northern Caucasus. He could not know that these troops marched there after disobeying orders; instead he blamed the Volunteers who undoubtedly had let these troops slip through their lines to embarrass Krasnov and the Don Cossacks.

In Northern Caucasus the Volunteers reached a turning point on 16 August 1918, when they took the Kuban Cossack capital, Ekaterinodar. At long last they managed to control a large chunk of territory and an important city, and therefore decided to get down to planning the political and military future of entire Russia. This was probably easier than solving the difficulties on the spot: the Kuban Cossacks were proving as difficult in their autonomy demands as the Don previously. However, here the rôles were reversed: the Kuban Cossacks depended on the Volunteers and therefore had to acquiesce. To escape from this unpleasant reality

Volunteer leaders took up planning, but before anything significant could be drafted General Alexeyev, the only leader with a certain political acumen, died, and planning was left to his reluctant successors.

General Denikin, who succeeded Alexeyev in command of the Volunteers, encouraged the drafting of a constitution without actually taking part in the work. He was after all a soldier and to his mind it was the politicians' task to plan the future political arrangements in Russia. At first the politicians he put in charge of the drafting were Russian liberals and they might have produced a properly liberal constitution. However, after the fall of Yekaterinodar Northern Caucasus was flooded by refugees from Central Russia, among whom predominated right wing politicians. Thus although the constitution was drafted by liberals (mainly K.N. Sokolov and V.A. Stepanov), it was not entirely liberal in its basic concepts but reflected the right wing pressures. Its most significant failing was that it made the army Commander-in-Chief also the political head with dictatorial powers. While General Denikin was a competent soldier, he was quite inept in politics in general, and inexperienced in foreign affairs and financial matters in particular. To mitigate this obvious weakness the constitution provided the supreme commander with a Special Council which was a sort of government to be used by the C-in-C in the exercise of power. However, General Denikin proved unable even to conceive how he could share power with this body: the Council turned out to be a purely consultative body which, if anything, made the General feel uneasy. Apart from this the constitution contained many more anomalies; its two sections dealing with the inviolability of private property and existing laws made it an absurd political document. In the conditions of civil war property and laws ceased to exist and it was not politic to make them the cornerstone of a programme of action while engaged in such a war. The Volunteer Army while campaigning lived of necessity on the land it conquered. Although it tried to make forcible requisitions look like purchases, auxiliary troops consisting mainly of Caucasian tribesmen were less sophisticated: they sacked the territory they controlled and pillaged that of the enemy. Similarly with the provision that 'existing laws were in force': it was constantly broken by the Volunteer Army and the supreme commander himself. General Wrangel, another Volunteer leader, publicly admitted this state of affairs: after a battle his men lined up captured Red Army officers and NCOs and executed them. All the captured Red Army men then joined the Volunteer Army. Another General, Pokrovsky, was notorious for hanging people right and left without trial, while countless political assassinations, and similar lawlessness were the most striking examples of violation of these basic constitutional articles. In October 1918 General Denikin himself issued an unconstitutional order by which all officers fighting in the Red Army against the Volunteers were punished by death.

Despite these absurdities the constitution was approved and came into effect on 8 October 1918. General Denikin was proclaimed the supreme commander of the armed forces in southern Russia and civil dictator. After all the political commotion connected with the proclamation of the constitution nothing much had really changed: lawlessness necessarily continued and the population in the White territories remained as indifferent to the 'new' regime as it was towards the old one. The Special Council, if treated as a government and given certain powers, might have improved the administrative chaos and legal anarchy which pertained in the White South. However, General Denikin never considered giving any power to this 'peculiar collection of personalities'. To his mind all Russian politicians had proved themselves quite incapable of wielding power during the Provisional Government's tenure, and now it was the Volunteer Army which had shed blood for the White movement which had the exclusive right to wield power. He put General Dragomirov 'in charge' of the Council and thus completely stultified it. The Council contained some capable organisers who might have aided the White movement; its 'minister' of trade and industry was V.A. Lebedev, an aircraft manufacturer, whose organisational ability was generally recognised. But neither he nor the Council were allowed to implement any of the policies discussed. By 31 December 1918 the Council held 21 meetings and resolved nothing. Denikin did not even bother to attend its meetings, although he carefully read the proceedings, and above all vetoed all the practical proposals contained in them.

In addition to government the Volunteer Army proved equally unsuccessful with the administration of territories under its control. By the end of 1918 they at least learned the lesson of autonomous Cossacks and left the Cossacks to administer themselves. Still, to make quite sure, Volunteer officers were appointed as governors to oversee self-government by the Cossacks. Though not ideal this arrangement worked reasonably well in Cossack territories, but in non-Cossack areas the Volunteer administration proved calamitous. The case of General Uvarov at Stavropol became notorious. He simple-mindedly tried to put the clock back to the tsarist days when he had held his last appointment: he handed the confiscated land back to the landlords and even tried to persecute the local national minorities. In the end, and too late, General Denikin found out and dismissed him before he could provoke a rebellion, but Uvarov remained convinced that he was doing his duty according to the constitution which supposedly applied in the Volunteer-held territories. The Volunteer officers who were appointed as civil governors by General Denikin were almost invariably monarchists, and they maintained bitter political hostility towards the existing administration, such as the liberal zemstva, and especially towards city unions dominated by Social Revolutionaries, whom they treated like the Bolsheviks.

Such political troubles and administrative difficulties did not disturb General Denikin unduly; he continued to concentrate his attention on military problems and army reorganisation, especially after the armistice in the West in November 1918. However, with the end of the world war the supreme commander and leader of Southern Russia inevitably became involved in foreign affairs and his inexperience in this field had catastrophic effects on the Volunteer movement and himself. Within a few days of the armistice in the West Russian politicians, encouraged by the Allied military and political representatives in Romania, had made another abortive effort at sorting out political problems and bringing under their control the various warlords and their armies. However, even this conference, held at Iassi between 16 and 21 November 1918, failed to achieve anything. Originally it was convoked to approve the Allied landings in Southern Russia, on which the French Premier Clemenceau decided without consulting even his British ally. Since only pro-Allied Russians were invited to this conference it was no surprise that they unanimously approved the Allied (French) occupation of Southern Russia as replacements of the Austrian and German occupation armies. Then the assembled Russians proceeded to take advantage of the unexpected and unprecented gathering of politicians to work out a political programme for the many anti-Bolshevik groups and movements they represented. Sadly for them they could only agree on one point: Russia should be 'restored' in its pre-1914 frontiers (with the exception of Poland which should remain independent). This precious point of the otherwise unacceptable programme stuck to the White movement all over Russia and shortly afterwards General Denikin and the Volunteers accepted it as one of their basic principles. It invariably had a catastrophic effect on the White movements for it alienated from them all their natural allies – the various nationalist and autonomist movements, such as the Don and Kuban Cossacks, the Finns, Estonians, Georgians and Latvians, Adzerbeijanis as well as the Lithuanians and the Poles, who flatly refused to believe that they were the only exception. In all else the Iassi conference was a comedy of errors and misconceptions as a result of which General Denikin finally became convinced that he was the 'approved' political and military leader in Southern Russia, and the Russians that the western Allies were consulting them before 'intervening' in Russia on their behalf and not to safeguard their own interests.

In consequence General Denikin began to act and asserted himself as the supreme leader. On 23 November 1918 the first Allied ships arrived in Southern Russia and Denikin, feeling supreme, took political advantage of General Poole's arrival to square a few domestic accounts. He used Poole to bring to heel Ataman Krasnov and the Don Cossacks; on 26 December 1918 the Don finally submitted to General Denikin and the Volunteers, and early in January 1919 their armies were fused and General Denikin became commander of all the armed forces in Southern Russia. It was an absurd fusion and the Cossacks never really agreed to it: some 10,000 Volunteers absorbed 100,000 Don and 60,000 Kuban Cossacks. Denikin thought that the soldiers would accept this subordination provided he purged the political leadership: the Don leaders, Krasnov, Denisov and Poliakov were forced to resign and go into exile. The Kuban Premier Bych was replaced by Sushkov and many other politicians were removed from the Cossack areas. However, only Denikin believed in this unification of armies and politics and he seems to have become intoxicated with the success of this political manoeuvre.

General Denikin also came to believe that he could use the Allies, who had made many 'promises to his representatives' to acquire the Crimea and the Ukraine. Early in December 1918 he wrote to General (later Field-Marshal) Franchet d'Esperey treating him as a fellow general and urging him to send in his troops before the Bolsheviks could take advantage of the German withdrawal. General Franchet d'Esperey, who was under orders from Premier Clemenceau, ignored Denikin and the Volunteers, who to his mind were under British protection, and eventually moved his forces to Odessa and Sevastopol. To Denikin's amazement he did nothing else and above all refused to hand over the occupied territory to Denikin's representatives. Moreover, quite inexplicably the French command began negotiations with the Ukrainian nationalists instead. The Volunteers never discovered the significance of what appeared to them as a breach of promises, and when in February 1919 British aid arrived it made Allied policies in Southern Russia utterly incomprehensible to the Russians. Denikin was never told of the zonal agreement between the British and the French; he continued to assume that the Allies were there on his behalf in order to destroy the Bolsheviks. When this was achieved the Allies would hand over to him liberated Russia in its pre-1914 frontiers.

The puzzled and disappointed Denikin was nevertheless quick in taking advantage of British military aid and began to reorganise his armies. Faced with French silence he left the National Russian Army at Odessa and the Crimean White Army to the care of the French command. He divided his forces into three groups: the Volunteer Corps (General Mai-Mayevsky), the United Forces (General Vinogradov) and the United Cavalry Corps (General Shkuro), and immediately wanted to launch offensives. He was dissuaded from it by the British who wanted him to carry out a mobilisation and equip his forces with the arms with which they were supplying him. This necessitated another reorganisation and only the Volunteers remained as before, though they formed an army group. The other army was that of the Don which, as a sop to Don Cossack separatism, was commanded by General Sidorin, an acceptable Don Cossack officer. The Kuban Cossacks, Terek and Caspian units were grouped in the Caucasian Army and placed under General Wrangel. Despite the reorganisation Denikin's efforts were put out of gear by two disasters on his left flank. In April 1919 French and Greek troops, who were supposed to form a protective Allied shield between the Bolsheviks and Denikin's Southern Russia, suddenly and without warning moved out of Southern Russia after they had suffered a series of reversals at the hands of local anarchists and their own troops mutinied. The National Russian and Crimean Armies also panicked, abandoned Odessa and the Crimea and raced to Denikin-held territory, which consisted of the Kuban and Don regions and the country round Rostov. Allied departure left behind political confusion, weakened the Ukrainian nationalists and the Volunteers. The intervention was utterly useless.

By May 1919 General Denikin had only some 64,000 men ready for an offensive. With the arrival of the Crimean and Odessa units he acquired a further 15,000 men, but his armed forces were still modest and he could not contemplate a large-scale offensive against the Red Army. However, the arrival of massive British aid was a turning point: he received not only arms and ammunition but also tanks and aviation and that seems to have compensated him for the trouble that the Allies caused in Southern Russia. He was prepared to fight for the 'lost territory' and even to strike against Moscow itself. Although his armies were not yet properly organised and his rear unpacified, Denikin decided on a grandiose offensive on the broadest front possible, stretching from Astrakhan to Odessa. His armies had to fight not only the Red Army but also the various anarchist armies, among whom Makhno easily mustered 60,000 men. In his HQ at Ekaterinodar Denikin worked out an impressive plan of operations which envisaged in particular a two-pronged drive against the Bolsheviks: 1. the Volunteer Army was to attempt a thrust against central Russia through Kharkov, its first objective, while 2. the Caucasian Army set out for Tsaritsyn and Central Volga in view of establishing contact with Admiral Kolchak's forces in Siberia.

When the offensive finally came, despite some disquieting failures, it was a surprising success. In the far East the Volunteers failed to take Astrakhan, although they got to within 40 miles of the city; this partial failure undoubtedly decided the fate of the Central Volga region. Even then the failure was more political than military. Although Denikin seriously underestimated Bolshevik strength in the region his troops fought well and advanced rapidly. More seriously Denikin failed to exploit his military advantage: the British organised his Caspian flotilla well, but he brought it into battle too late. He was most hampered by unresolved national problems, and the uprisings in Dagestan and the Terek territory tied up much of the forces which he needed to take Astrakhan.

On the Volga front General Wrangel's Caucasian Army had to beat off a Bolshevik offensive before proceeding with its own. The 10th Red Army led by Voroshilov and Stalin threw some 90,000 men into the offensive and failed. Wrangel's counter-offensive brought with it Tsaritsyn (the future Stalingrad and Volgograd), a prize which had eluded the Don Cossacks after a whole year of hard fighting. In the far West the Volunteer Army took the Crimea and reached Odessa without much exertion, but the most surprising success was scored in the industrial Donets region. The Volunteers' tactical use of railways demoralised the Red Army which also had to cope with peasant uprisings in its rear. In late June 1919 Kharkov fell to the Volunteer Army and the first objective of this great offensive was achieved.

Ignoring the failures and encouraged by the success General Denikin made two fatal decisions: 1. politically he placed himself under Admiral Kolchak who headed the All-Russian government in Siberia and was recognised by the Allies: 2. militarily he issued the Moscow directive to his armies (3 July 1919). The first decision appeared sound, especially since the Western Allies had only just recognised Admiral Kolchak as Regent of Russia; Denikin's submission to Kolchak indicated that at long last the Whites had achieved political unity. In fact this manoeuvre was more designed to silence local autonomists, especially the Don and Kuban Cossacks, rather than achieve political unity, which in any case only existed on paper since the South and Siberia were physically separated. The second decision was more disastrous in the short term: while his other military operations continued unabated Denikin concentrated his best armies and cavalry in the centre and launched a win-or-die drive to Moscow via Kursk, Orel and Tula.

The consequences of these decisions became apparent rather rapidly. In the East with the failure at Astrakhan the drive from Tsaritsyn along the Volga hardly got off the ground. The Caucasian Army was stopped before breaking through the Red Army lines and never established contact with Kolchak's armies, who had also been stopped in their advance. In the West the Volunteer advance in the Ukraine also bogged down: unresolved political and nationalistic conflicts resulted in the Whites fighting each other rather than the Bolsheviks. The Ukrainian Directory (a nationalist government) and its forces under General Petlyura had been gradually driven out of the Ukraine proper into Gallicia, where an autonomous West Ukrainian government under E. Petrusherich maintained itself precariously in power. While the Ukrainian Petlyura's enemies were the Bolsheviks, the West Ukrainian government's enemy was the Poles, with whom Petlyura was secretly negotiating an alliance. Suddenly, in June 1919, the Polish army launched an offensive against Gallicia and drove out Petlyura's forces together with the Gallician forces under General Tarnovsky. The combined Ukrainian armies retreated across the Zbruch River back in to the Ukraine, and finding that the Red Army was in full retreat after defeats by the Volunteer Army made a dash for the capital, Kiev. On arrival they found the city besieged by General Bredov's forces: Tarnovsky favoured an agreement with Bredov and the Volunteers, but Petlyura insisted on taking the capital himself and immediately internecine fighting broke out in central Ukraine. Farther south, around Odessa, where the Ukrainian General Omelianovich-Pavlenko was operating, efforts were made to find an agreement, but the results were the same as in Kiev. Both flanks of Denikin's Moscow drive were thus weakened and compromised, and the offensive should have been stopped, if not abandoned.

Moreover, as a result of political mishandling the Don Cossacks began to collapse. Since December 1918 the Don Cossacks were treated by the Volunteers as separatists, which they were; however, to the Volunteers this meant that the Don leaders could not be trusted politically and their armies were inferior to the Russian Volunteers. The Don forces' morale seems to have depended on their political leaders' treatment and as a consequence it slumped low. The Volunteers behaved incredibly clumsily — they vetoed Don appointments, forced resignations of both politicians and army officers and refused to deal with any Don Cossack leader who had shown the slightest hostility towards the Volunteer army or movement in the past. This meant the retirement and exile of some of the most capable Don leaders; in addition a number of Don politicians were inexplicably assassinated or otherwise disposed of. Paradoxically the Volunteers depended most heavily on the Don cavalry and as a concession to Don separatism the high command tolerated Don cavalry raids into the neighbouring Russian provinces whose objective was obviously not military, but pillage and sack. It was probably this 'consession' which ultimately undermined the Don army morale, and when finally popular Cossack commanders were dismissed right and left the Don armies collapsed and sealed the fate of the Moscow offensive. In September 1919 General Mamontov and his cavalry army returned to the Don after a raid deep into the Tambov province. The raid was in military terms a tremendous blow to the Red Army which was re-grouping and preparing for a counter-offensive. The raid disrupted these preparations, cut off supply lines and destroyed military stores in the province; it was also the last belligerent act by the Don Cavalry Army. General Mamontov fell ill with typhus and his Cossacks pratically dissolved, taking home the booty brought from central Russia.

Early in October 1919 General Sidorin's Don Army took Voronezh and General Mai-Mayevsky's Volunteers Orel, two vital cities for the conquest of Moscow. By now General Denikin realised the dangers on his flanks, in the Ukraine and the Volga front; however, after the fall of Voronezh and Orel he could not resist the temptation of taking Moscow and played everything on a last gamble. From Orel General Kutepov immediately engaged his forces to break through to Tula, the last important city before Moscow, but he was advancing slowly and with difficulty. Then on 20

October 1919 his advance came to a halt and rapidly changed into retreat. The Red Army, which had its counter-offensive disrupted in September, had finally recovered and struck, while the White Army was over-extended and its élite cavalry withdrawn. The Red Commander, Colonel Kamenev, concentrated all his cavalry forces under another Don Cossack, S. Budenny, at the point of junction of the Volunteer Army and the Don Army between Orel and Voronezh. Budenny engaged and routed the White Cavalry Army under General Shkuro and made a large breach in the front between the two armies. Colonel Kamenev then launched his counter-offensive which finally forced the Volunteers to abandon their Moscow operation. However, apart from the dangerous breach the fronts were maintained and there was no panic or precipitate retreat.

The military situation in central Russia required all the attention the Volunteers could give it; above all the dangerous gap in the front had to be filled. But instead General Denikin ordered one of the most puzzling operations of his command. Throughout the summer of 1919 General Wrangel had complained that the Kuban Cossacks who formed the bulk of his Caucasian Army failed to send him reinforcements and equipment, and he was therefore unable to pursue his offensive on the Volga front. At first Denikin's GHQ pacified Wrangel with excuses and then with driblets of reinforcements; however, Wrangel remained convinced that his lack of success at Tsaritsyn was due to the sabotage of the separatist Kuban Cossacks. Then in November 1919 General Denikin suddenly changed the tune, proclaimed some Kuban Cossack leaders as traitors and charged Wrangel with purging them. Although Wrangel felt very bitter about the Kuban Cossacks the obvious political short-sightedness of Denikin's order made him hesitate; disclaiming all political responsibility he finally obliged. On 12 November 1919, after some street fighting in the Kuban capital, Ekaterinodar, General Pokrovsky's forces withdrawn from the Volga front surrounded the Kuban Rada and hanged publicly one of its leaders, Kalabukhov. After this show of force the Kuban Cossacks agreed to purging themselves: old leaders resigned and went into exile, new were appointed, but the Kuban region as a base and the support of the Russian White movement ceased to exist.

Thus, after he had cut off his rear, General Denikin decided on reshuffling the front command, as if to cut off his nose as well. Throughout November 1919 the fronts had been under considerable Bolshevik pressure but were withstanding it well, despite the disorganisation of the rear wreaked by GHQ and various anarchist-peasant forces which began to harrass the White armies and cut their lines of communication and supply. Denikin now turned the command reshuffle into his old conflict with Wrangel. He had discredited Wrangel politically by ordering him to sort out the Kuban problem and it seemed that he also wanted to discredit him in military matters. After the defeats at Orel and

Voronezh General Denikin wanted to carry out a limited reshuffle of his commanders, but General Wrangel insisted on a sweeping one, otherwise he would not take command himself. Denikin urgently needed Wrangel in command, for many of his field commanders were on the verge of collapse and the front needed an experienced and tested soldier to hold it steady. However, he was also aware of the fact that even his limited reshuffle of command in the middle of battle would have a harmful effect on the White armies. He must have looked for a scapegoat when he accepted Wrangel's proposals for large scale changes in command: Generals Mai-Mayevsky and Yefimov were mortally insulted when they handed over command to Wrangel; General Mamontov simply faded away and his successor, General Ulagay, failed to find Mamontov's cavalry to fight the Red one. The newly appointed field commanders proved incapable of stemming the Red Army advance, for their men now turned out to be demoralised and beaten. General Pokrovsky with the depleted Caucasian Army at Tsaritsyn had to run when the Red Army attacked; General Dragomirov abandoned Kiev on 2 December 1919 and General Schilling retreated in panic to Odessa, whence he also fled to the Crimea, abandoning soldiers, their families and refugees, like the French Army in April 1919, to the tender mercy of a motley of Red Army and anarchist units, which had routed him so ignominiously. Still General Denikin had confidence in Wrangel's Volunteer Army and Sidorin's Don Army to save the situation, though in case of catastrophe they had orders to retreat onto Novocherkassk and Rostov rather than to the Crimea, which made more sense militarily though not politically. Although in his order of the day on 10 December 1919 Wrangel urged the Volunteer officers and soldiers most eloquently to stand and fight, not even his subordinate commanders had it in them: General Kalnitsky's Reserve Corps containing only some 200 men disintegrated completely under very slight pressure from the enemy. General Yuzefovich's 5th Cavalry Corps (only slightly stronger than the Reserve Corps) disappeared from the front without a fight, leaving General Kutepov and the 1st Volunteer Corps to face the Red armies. Kutepov with his 2,500 men did some skilful rearguard fighting using the railways to his advantage. However, his very dependence on the railways dictated the course of his operations, and he also was forced to withdraw when Budyonny's cavalry threatened to cut him off the line of retreat. In the end even the solid field commander Wrangel had to admit defeat, though he was not going to take it lying down.

General Wrangel's disagreements with General Denikin as political and military leaders were a legend. Both were without any doubt honest soldiers; however their attitudes to civil war problems, which were anyway above their intellectual capacities, were totally different. Denikin was a liberal staff officer, humbled by his experiences in the revolutionary period 1917-18, who concentrated on military affairs which he thought he understood best. But he still continued to behave like an imperial staff officer rather than a civil war commander and his transparent honesty and old-fashioned sense of officers' honour made him quite unsuitable for the post of supreme commander. His operations were brilliant on paper and academically most plausible, but in civil war reality made no sense; his appointments and their timing were invariably ill-judged and aggravated his lack of political sense. As a supreme dictator he was an unmitigated disaster. By November 1919 General Denikin and his GHQ completely lost control over events and for all practical purposes disintegrated, although Denikin lingered on as the supremo until March 1920.

While General Wrangel's honesty and honour could not be doubted either, his revolutionary experience was far from humbling; if anything it made him as determined and aggressive as it had made Denikin hesitant and conciliatory. He was by inclination a field commander who preferred the fronts to GHQ, and in the circumstances of the civil war it undoubtedly made him more realistic. As early as June 1919 he had warned Denikin that his Moscow directive was a strategic error and henceforth never stopped criticising Denikin's military decisions. However, apart from this greater sense of realism there was precious little difference between the two men; above all in politics Wrangel was as shortsighted as and perhaps even more naive than Denikin. He had always believed that a resolute show of force − 'hang a few subversives' − would solve political problems (Kuban Cossacks) or restore civilian morale (Rostov). Basically Wrangel agreed with Denikin that politics were a dirty business and soldiers should keep out of it. Nonetheless, by his criticism of the liberal Denikin he focused on himself the hopes and ambitions of the Russian right wing and monarchist elements, although, perhaps a little paradoxically, just like Denikin he was a sort of liberal. Despite this, in December 1919 when Wrangel's opposition to Denikin became irreconcilable, he became the spokesman of the 'resolute' White officers who formed the basis of the Volunteer armies. At this stage though they were all shortsighted and their resoluteness did not go very far, and after resolutely assassinating White politicians, whom they blamed for failure, they continued to retreat before the Bolsheviks, nevertheless still resolved to assassinate even their erstwhile leaders. Even in foreign affairs Wrangel seemed to attract paradoxes: thus he became the focus of hope for all the disgruntled pro-German elements in the White movement, just because he was critical of Denikin's total dependence on the British. Thus with all these ambiguities, beliefs, hopes and ambitions around him it became inevitable that his clash with Denikin would result in the elimination of one, or another, and ultimately of both.

In November 1919 Wrangel forced on Denikin most of the command changes, and then went on to criticise Denikin's political decision to defend the Don rather than withdraw to the Crimea. But he did not stop there. At the end of December 1919, when he considered all the battles lost and the military situation hopeless, Wrangel did not hesitate to write to the Don commander, General Sidorin, saying so and blaming Denikin's GHQ for it. Then rather belatedly the British Mission voiced its criticism of Denikin's GHQ and Wrangel strengthened its case by telling the British about his doubts and reservations, which surely was not very loyal. Next Wrangel proposed to Denikin to fuse the command of the Don and Volun-teer armies thus depriving himself of command, but also escaping from the responsibility for the final débâcle. Then suddenly, on 19 December 1919, Denikin discovered a conspiracy against himself at GHQ and treated the conspirators who later probably assassinated his Chief of Staff, General Romanovsky, rather roughly. Still Denikin proved hesitant even in the suppression of the conspiracy and failed to decide whether the leader of the conspiracy was General Lukomsky or Wrangel. As it happened neither general hatched this particular plot, but acting on his suspicions Denikin removed Wrangel from his command and appointed the joint commander of the Don and Volunteer armies General Sidorin, who was undoubtedly more hostile towards him than Wrangel. Perhaps a little ironically Wrangel was sent to the Kuban to command the Cossacks whom he so violently repressed only two months previously. Since it proved impossible to assume command in the Kuban Wrangel wandered off to the Crimea, and after another conflict with Denikin he was exiled to Turkey. At long last Denikin triumphed over Wrangel, but the victory was shortlived.

With military failure all round General Denikin finally turned his attention to political problems: their resolution seemed to offer the last chance for survival. The British Military Mission had advocated political reform as a means of reviving morale in White Russia for some time, but succeeded in impressing the generalissimo only when the military situation became desperate. By then General Denikin had no armies left to command, so he turned to the neglected politicians, dissolved his Personal Council and decided to appoint a government of South Russia. Although he had hardly any Russian territory left under his control Denikin nonetheless appointed a federal government, but this Russian government was based on the separatists, and in particular on the Don Cossacks. Politically this was a recognition of the *status quo;* militarily it was hoped that Don Cossack forces would fight for a Russian government dominated by Don leaders, which was a sad miscalculation. On 10 January 1920 General Bogayevsky became Denikin's Prime Minister, while the Don, Kuban and Terek cossack *krugs* (parliaments) were encouraged to assemble and elect new leaders. The military situation was indeed quite desperate to reduce the Russian generalissimo Denikin to such incredible concessions and reversal of policies. But even then Denikin refused to be consistent: on the one hand he magnanimously promised the Cossacks to give up his dictatorship and let them rule themselves in their regions; on the other he still forbade them to form an United Cossack Administration which they needed to run their regions. This was the final paradox: he could not put into practice the best intentions and the most plausible schemes. By then he himself and his Volunteers had absolutely no power to control, not to say to run, the Cossack regions. He could only drag them into ruin.

These desperate political concessions in any case were the result of a sustained British pressure. At first the British Military Mission only supervised the disbursement of British military aid. However, after the military defeat of the Volunteers and Cossacks in Central Russia the British Mission became the instrument of direct pressure by the British government and assumed immense power; in the end it dictated everything, even troop movements, and even assumed the responsibility for the security of the White leaders. Rather belatedly the British government wanted Denikin to come to terms with the Green peasant movement in Southern Russia which was chiefly controlled by the anarchist peasant Makhno. Denikin had good military reasons for such an agreement, but the British wanted much more – they also wanted the cessation of hostilities and even joint actions against the Red Army, but on the basis of a political agreement, which, it was argued, would broaden politically the White movement in Southern Russia. All this came only a few months after General Ulagay had scattered Makhno's forces and in return Makhno assassinated Volunteer negotiators. The British insisted, negotiated with Makhno themselves and reduced Denikin to muted protestations. This initiative came to nothing; after much dangerous talking the rapidly deteriorating situation of the Volunteers precluded an agreement. The Green units continued to harrass Cossack and Volunteer forces and cut their supply lines, also to occupy territory evacuated by the Whites. Denikin simply could not be saved in this way.

By then though the British government was prepared to go to any lengths to resolve what was now its Denikin problem. Since the British Mission actually controlled all remaining military stores and supplies the British could force Denikin into a complete reversal of anything – as the ultimate humiliation he was obliged to accept British mediation between himself and the Bolsheviks. The British government thought that by negotiation they could prevent the Bolsheviks from destroying the Volunteers and Cossacks altogether; an armistice would be negotiated, Denikin would resign and he and his officers (and their families) would be evacuated from Russia. There would be an amnesty for the soldiers, while the officers would be taken to Lemnos Island to shift for themselves as best as they could (the precedent was General Yudenich's North Western Army). The Cossacks would have to come to terms with Georgia. In March 1920 General Denikin finally accepted these proposals, put himself entirely in British hands and ceased to be a White leader.

At first it seemed that Denikin's political concessions and reforms had put a new lease of life into the White armies. General Pavlov succeeded in reorganising the Don Cossack cavalry which managed to catch unawares Dumenko's cavalry, demoralised after the plunder of Rostov, and defeated it. Dumenko's defeat had a galvanising effect on the White armies hampered as they were by the Green detachments. It was hoped that this victory had saved the Kuban region at least; Pavlov even began to prepare for a counter-offensive to re-take the Don region. However, the Red Army speedily sorted out its problems: Dumenko was shot for indiscipline and on 25 February 1920 Pavlov's cavalry was decisively defeated in turn. The Greens and Reds resumed their offensives and henceforth all White opposition collapsed. General Denikin became completely dependent, even for his personal safety, on the British Military Mission, and his ruined armies on the British navy. Decisions were now made by the British and although Denikin favoured retreat to Turkestan he and his soldiers were shipped to the Crimea. The Don forces were no longer army units and escaped from the advancing Red Army as rabble. Don Cossack leaders remained with the Volunteers leadership at Ekaterinodar, hoping that the Kuban Cossacks, whose forces counted some 30,000 men, would defend their capital. Nothing was done, although the Kuban forces had only the Green detachments to face. They followed the Don rabble escaping from the enemy in forced marches along the Black Sea coast to Tuapse. The only military force still in existence, the Volunteer Corps, was also ordered to abandon Ekateridonar, cover the retreat of the leaders and withdraw to Novorossiisk, a port which was the supply base of British aid, still containing large stores of materials and munitions. It now became the evacuation base for the Volunteer armies.

Although the defeat in the Kuban area was on the cards since February 1920 nothing was done to prepare retreat and evacuation from Novorossiisk. This was partly due to the delay in General Denikin's 'decision', but above all due to the general demoralisation of the Whites. All sorts of forces operated in and out of the city, but martial law was only proclaimed on 24 March 1920, three days before the evacuation proper. The British and French had large numbers of ships in the Black Sea, and might have evacuated everybody and everything had the evacuation been properly organised, but General Denikin and his defeated staff became sullenly despondent and left everything to the Allies, who had to cope as best as they could. General Holman reported to London that despite chaos and difficulty Admiral Seymour, who was in charge, was able to save even the extensive British stores. The British government ordered the British Mission to save the families of the following Russian politicians and soldiers: Khomyakov, Guchkov, Rodzianko, Zvegintsov, Lvov, Shulgin, Astrov, Trubetskoy, Dukhonin, Kornilov, Markov, Kaledin, Nazarov and many others. This detailed order was carried out to perfection. Nonetheless, despite Allied efforts some 22,000 White soldiers were captured in the city, and over £1,000,000 worth of stores were left behind. On 27 March 1920 Novorossiisk fell to the Greens and then to the Red Army, while the Volunteers on Allied ships were approaching the uncertain coast of the Crimea.

When one tries to summarise General Denikin's ascendancy in South Russia in the period 1918-20 one is struck by the abyss between intention and action. Denikin inherited the Volunteer Army by accident, after the death of Generals Kornilov and Alexeyev, at an early stage of its development. His declared purpose was to lead this army, strengthen it and build it up so that it would reconquer Russia from the Bolsheviks. For this limited task he was probably the best suited and most capable military leader in South Russia. But to accept his relative ability and understand his predicament must not mean to ignore his failings. In addition to his questionable military strategy he completely failed to transform the political character of the movement, to balance military necessity with popular appeal or adopt a flexible policy *vis-à-vis* the non-Russian nationalities. Considering the nature and situation of the Allied governments these failures were of decisive significance for Allied aid. They were also crucial to the problem of internal unity.

General Denikin was, as he never tired of saying, first of all a soldier, and not a politician. As a soldier he was neither liberal nor reactionary but a simple bureaucrat for whom seniority was of paramount importance. When political decisions were forced on him he tried to take a middle course. He distrusted the extremes on both sides and refused to commit the army to any political programme. Only when his middle course failed did he take more liberal measures, but could not carry them out in practice. Such liberal measures were undoubtedly an expression of his personal views, but neither he nor the army believed that he had any right to allow his personal ideas to prejudice the future of Russia. He personally believed that Russia would be different after the civil war – the people would be free, the peasants would have small farms, the workers would have safeguards against exploitation and the nationalities would have their civil liberties and autonomy. But the civil war had to be won first; things should stay as they were until a Constituent Assembly could change and regulate them.

However, winning the civil war required more than simple soldiers. Denikin himself may have wanted a more liberal course for his movement, but the fact remains that the landowners used the Volunteer Army to seize land back from the peasants. His military administration, which was quite unsuited for putting right such transgressions, never really became a government, and could not become one as long as it was so totally dominated by the army. His intention of instituting land reforms alienated from him army sentiments; on the other hand when the liberals complained, they were told to wait for the Constituent Assembly. Denikin belatedly proved himself capable of evolving a policy, but his reactionary subordinates then carried it out in reverse.

As a consequence General Denikin was considered a reactionary dictator. Except the few who knew his moderate views and aims, everyone else on the outside saw his movement as the most extreme reactionary regime, which it was not. Even as a leader Denikin was misleading: he seemed to be defending his own authority against all others, demanding but refusing to compromise or make any concession to achieve cooperation or get aid. He did not seem to have the full support of the Cossack armies, on whom he so heavily depended. This was not just appearance, and Allied governments, together with many of the Russian and non-Russian peoples, asked themselves such a question: does such a weak and reactionary army and movement stand a chance against the Bolsheviks? Does it really deserve support? The answer was most frequently negative.

Professor Miliukov took the Allies to task for drawing such negative conclusions after he had observed conditions in the Volunteer camp. As he put it, Europeans were 'unhappily too much inclined to brand every attempt to use military force for restoring order in Russia as being counter-revolutionary . . .'. The restoration of order by a strong military hand in Russia did not exclude liberal policy as soon as order was established, but was in fact the precondition for such a policy. This reasoning had some merit, but even assuming that the Allies should have judged the Volunteers on this basis, would their decisions have been different? The Allies were in fact not too hesitant but too prone to accepting the arguments of military necessity as a substitute for political maturity, both in Denikin's case and in the case of their own representatives. In any case, as a result of Denikin's total dependence on British aid, he ceased to be an independent factor and became a puppet.

The Volunteer Army itself was rent with internal cleavages and helped to undermine faith in itself both at home and abroad by its actions. The case of war booty was a clear example. Denikin's Council had tried to channel all booty through the central command in order to prevent plunder and speculation, but it failed. Commanders in the field claimed the right to retain captured material, and the practice of self-equipment soon transgressed all legal limits and became sheer plunder and violence.

There remains finally the failure of the Volunteer forces to attract the support of the non-Russian nationalities. Although under strong pressure from Allied governments, who made tremendous efforts at producing the winning combination of a united military offensive and democratic political backing, Denikin simply refused to resolve the so-called nationality problem in such a way. Even if other shortcomings of Russian leadership are discounted this failure to cooperate with Allied efforts was probably the most decisive for the outcome of the struggle. Denikin could not execute a land reform in chaos, and he could not force the Allies to secure his supply lines, but he might have filled the gap to a considerable extent by adopting a policy of cooperation with all the borderland governments on the basis of federation. The slogan of 'One Russia' was interpreted to mean not only a united Russia but a unitary state, and it remained absolute until the time when its modification ceased to have any practical meaning.

The army had actually worked with the Cossacks on a federal basis all along, and in February 1920 Denikin established the South Russian Authority, which was essentially a federation with a legislative council and a council of ministers responsible to it. But this federal structure was put up with the Volunteers' closest allies at the very end but was never tried with the non-Russian nationalities, where it would have had much greater significance. Volunteer policy persisted in its tendency to view the demands for autonomy as treasonable separatism. Even during the decisive phase of the civil war Denikin insisted that any change in the Russian constitution should come from a Constituent Assembly after the war had been won. Only after his defeat he accepted the idea of reunification through negotiations with the borderland states, and it was too late.

The unity of Russia and federalism need not have come into such conflict, as they were not necessarily contradictory concepts. The complete dismemberment of the country was not accepted by any major Russian party or force. However, in the upheaval of the revolution and civil war the split between the empire and its economically vital borderlands had actually taken place. By refusing to accept that there was no longer a Russia in the old inclusive sense Denikin simply encouraged the disintegration which he was fighting to prevent.

The question as to how Russia could be reunited was neither contemplated nor asked. Instead of providing a rallying point for the new governments, Denikin fought them. He insisted on a unitary Russia when the demand was for federation, and he appeared willing to make some concessions in the direction of autonomy only after the demand had passed to independence. The Bolsheviks admittedly achieved the reunification of Russia by force, but there can be little doubt that their espousal of the doctrine of self-determination and subsequent advocacy of federation greatly facilitated their victory.

A policy of federated reunification would have aided the Volunteers at least as much as it aided the Bolsheviks and probably more, since it would have gone far to dispel the fear of Great Russian chauvinism in the borderlands and would have made Denikin's claim that he wanted to establish a basically democratic union more convincing not only in Russia but also with the Allies. However, to have been really effective this policy should have been adopted from the beginning of the struggle, rather than after defeat. Denikin hesitated to accept such a policy not only because he felt that he was not competent to change the political *status quo,* but also because he distrusted politicians, and especially those of the left, who predominated in the most important border areas. Besides preferring the traditional non-involvement of the army with political parties, he believed that winning the civil war was the prerequisite to any political decision, and he believed he could win the war alone. A quick victory was the easy answer to his opponents, especially since the questions at stake were too complex to be resolved fully during the struggle. Once the victory had been achieved, every one, friend and foe, would see the necessity of cooperation in determining the future structure of the country through a Constituent Assembly. In holding these views Denikin certainly had a good case, but he was both unrealistic in his hopes for military success and obstinate in his demand that every one trusts his motives. When in the end military failure became obvious even his British allies lost faith in him and he was forced to resign and go into exile, surely a terrible fate.

It was clear even before the evacuation of Novorossiisk that General Denikin would not continue to lead the White movement in South Russia, even if he and his forces succeeded in extricating themselves from their predicament. Denikin irritated the British by becoming more and more reluctant about negotiations with the Bolsheviks, whom he naturally distrusted; in addition he feared assassination from his own men, if and when they found out about his 'betrayal'. At the very end he still hoped that by ridding himself of all the conservative generals, whom in any case he had suspected of plotting against him, he would be able to come to some sort of negotiated agreement with the Bolsheviks. But the British with their precise ideas on negotiations and agreement took rightly Denikin's vagueness as evasion and breach of promise. Fortunately for him, Denikin found that members of the British Mission, apart from its head, General Holman, who simply carried out his government's orders however unsavoury they might be, were aiding and abetting him. Thus, although Wrangel suspected General Keyes of implacable hostility towards the Whites, he was in fact the staunchest supporter of the White movement *vis-à-vis* his government. It was only thanks to him that Denikin could resign with dignity and not be dismissed like an errand boy. On the other hand General Holman negotiated Denikin's resignation with Wrangel and it was only the latter's reluctance to assume leadership which saved Denikin from dismissal by the British even before the evacuation of Novorossiisk.

II

Between January and March 1920 General Denikin had dismissed practically all his outstanding field commanders together with many bad ones; he exiled them mainly to Turkey together with his eventual successor. Whether these veteran soldiers realised fully under what pressures Denikin exercised his leadership is not known, but they must have realised that it was the British who were dismissing Denikin. When the White council of war met and formally appointed the new leader, all members were told that unless they began immediate negotiations with the Bolsheviks, the British government would withdraw its Mission, stop all aid and even abandon the White officers and their families, whom it promised to 'save' from the Bolsheviks. The British had no objection to General Wrangel being elected leader; in fact they 'recommended' his election, for both General Holman and Keyes considered Wrangel not only a capable field commander but also a shrewd politician who had learned some lessons from his predecessor's failures.

On 4 April 1920 the war council of the White movement in South Russia appointed General Wrangel as General Denikin's successor. Wrangel, only just arrived from Istambul, took stock of the situation in the Crimea and quickly realised that he and his movement were at the mercy of the British and the Red Army. In military terms he had General Slashchev's Corps, some 3,500 men and 2,000 cavalry, to protect the Crimea from Bolshevik onslaught, and that was very little. Politically he was under a British umbrella; Britain was actively negotiating with the Bolsheviks Wrangel's surrender, and that was worse. The Bolsheviks expected success in the Crimea without the intervention of arms and concentrated on mopping up the Whites in Northern Caucasus, Trans-Caspia and Turkestan. They were so sure of the fall of the Crimea through negotiations that they completely ignored this White bastion and transferred their armies to the western border against the Poles who, in conjunction with Ataman Petlyura, invaded the Ukraine. Ultimately the Bolsheviks had to pay for their miscalculation in the Crimea with the defeat in Poland.

Evidently the most urgent task of General Wrangel was to reconstitute his military forces, both for defence, and, eventually, offence. In the circumstances of the civil war this was quite realistic, especially since the Bolsheviks were making a cardinal error of relying on negotiation rather than force which they were capable of exerting at this particular junction. As soon as Wrangel could defend himself he was determined not to negotiate with the Bolsheviks and somehow replace the British by any other western ally. From the start this task was an uphill struggle: the British left in the Crimea only the stores evacuated from Novorossiisk, which were quite insufficient — especially to build up his offensive capacity. Given his policy decision not to negotiate he could not hope to get any further supplies from Britain and there was no obvious alternative ally. In addition he could not be sure of the armed forces which he inherited from Denikin and which were under strong British influence. Apart from the 'separatist' Cossacks, who openly detested him, two important Volunteer generals, Kutepov and Vitkovsky, publicly opposed

Denikin's dismissal. Before rebuilding his army Wrangel had to purge its command. He pounced first on the Don Cossacks, arrested their Commander-in-Chief, General Sidorin, and Chief-of-Staff General Kelchevsky, and after court martial proceedings, presided over by General Dragomirov, exiled them together with a large group of other officers, including such old comrades in arms as Generals Pokrovsky, Borovsky and Postovsky. In a similar way Wrangel bullied the Kuban Cossacks into submission, but since their armed forces were mainly on the Black Sea coast they could retaliate, and as soon as they were out of the Crimea some surrendered to the Bolsheviks, others joined the Georgians. Among the Russian commanders Wrangel retained all the successful field commanders, even if they were not in agreement with him, and dismissed practically all the HQ generals either outright or by sending them as his representatives abroad.

After making sure of the armed forces he next had to resolve the problem of British aid and supplies, or lack of it. General Percy, who succeeded General Holman as head of the British Military Mission in the Crimea, continued to press Wrangel to resume negotiations with the Bolsheviks, but he successfully delayed negotiations and instead launched intensive talks with the French and American allies. His representative in Paris, Maklakov, was soon able to inform Wrangel that for internal reasons the French government opposed peace with the Bolsheviks and was against a surrender in the Crimea. Albeit the reason for the French opposition to negotiations with the Bolsheviks was Poland, Wrangel's Crimea found at last a replacement for Britain; henceforth Wrangel dropped all pretence of negotiating with the Bolsheviks and concentrated on the organisation of armies and preparation of the offensive.

In order to secure his Crimean base, defended so far only by General Slashchev's mini-Corps, Wrangel ordered the construction of massive defence works on all the isthmi of the Crimean peninsula. With the control of the Black Sea by the White and Allied ships these fortifications could have made of the Crimea an impregnable fortress. General Yuzefovich was in charge of the works which were, however, frequently interrupted, either by the lack of materials, or because of military operations. Though the works were never completed, they did in the end provide a protective shield which enabled the Whites to evacuate the Crimea in good order.

As for the organisation of the armies themselves Wrangel made them up into four Army Corps. He placed the 1st Corps, consisting mainly of veteran volunteer units, under General Kutepov, supposedly his opponent. This decision was a calculated risk which came off well; Kutepov was no politician but an outstanding field commander who served Wrangel faithfully and brilliantly until the bitter end. General Slashchev commanded the 2nd Corps, which incorporated all sorts of units evacuated from the Kuban, Sochi and Tuapse. Slashchev, who had made special appeals of loyalty to Wrangel, was a bad choice: he was quite mentally unbalanced, was a drug addict and his command suffered correspondingly. The Don Cossacks were formed into a corps and placed under an efficient but undistinguished general — Abramov. Finally a Joint Corps consisting of bits and pieces found all over the Crimea came under General Pisarev, a figure comparable to Abramov. With these scratch forces ready he was immediately faced with a limited Red Army offensive, which he withstood well; and then to everybody's surprise he was able to launch his own limited offensive.

Early in June 1920, while the bulk of the Red Army was engaged in fighting the Poles in the West, Wrangel's forces broke through the line of the 13th Red Army, ripped Zhloba's cavalry to pieces and spilled out of the bottleneck of the Crimea into Northern Tauride. The Red Army retreated in a hurry, abandoning to the Whites substantial stores and a rich territory, but then it quickly regrouped and held another line against the Whites when they reached a point of exhaustion. This predictable though unexpected success posed Wrangel the most acute problem, which he never resolved: he evidently had to exploit the Red Army's preoccupation with Poland and elsewhere, in order to put himself into the best strategic position before the final showdown if he was to have a chance at all. His human and material resources were though so limited that he never succeeded in breaking out of Northern Tauride and thus sealed his own fate when the Red Army could concentrate against him alone.

Strategic experiments have always been considered the undoing of the White armies in the Crimea; they certainly sounded implausible given the limitations of Wrangel's forces. However, Wrangel had no other option but to probe and experiment. No-one, not even Wrangel himself, ever thought seriously that his movement and armies in the Crimea could defeat the Bolsheviks: thus Wrangel's operations in the Kuban and Don areas were desperate attempts at ameliorating the relative military and political positions before the final confrontation with the Red Army. It was natural that these desperate military efforts should fail, but they turned into terrible political blunders which pointed clearly to the final defeat. Wrangel was as blind politically as Denikin before him, when he decided to send a small expeditionary force under Colonel Nazarov into the Don region after he had failed to break through himself. It was a small miracle, after the purge of the Don officers, that Nazarov and his force agreed to go. They were successfully landed on the northern shore of the Sea of Azov, but immediately afterwards, contrary to their intelligence reports, ran into a large force of the Red Army which completely scattered them. Nazarov himself was captured, but later managed to escape from captivity, reach the Crimea and tell the tale. The force was lost and the region did not stir in the least; the political lesson and conclusion drawn from this failure had melancholy implications for the Whites in Russia.

Nonetheless Wrangel tried another operation in the Kuban region. The Kuban operation was a greater disaster than the Don one, although Wrangel remained convinced that it was less desperate and had a greater chance of success. After the Kuban Ataman Bukretov negotiated a surrender of his forces at Sochi his successor, Ataman Ivanis, found refuge in the Crimea together with a few men and many generals who refused to follow Bukretov. Wrangel disliked Ivanis and wanted to replace him with his protégé, General Ulagay, but failed because the Kuban Rada in the Crimea had no quorum and could not dismiss or elect any one. In these circumstances Wrangel attached exaggerated importance to intelligence reports from the Kuban region: these reports spoke of Kuban Cossack dissatisfaction with the Bolsheviks, of local uprisings and partisan fighting in the region. Thus Wrangel succumbed to the temptation of interpreting these phenomena as seething disorder and readiness of the Kuban population to rise and drive the Bolsheviks out as in 1918. As a consequence, under the overall command of General Ulagay Kuban, Terek and Astrakhan Cossack units were landed in the region to destroy the Red Army garrisons. In a two-pronged attack Ulagay was intended to seize Ekaterinodar and start a general uprising. However, it soon transpired that both the military and the political intelligence was faulty – no Kuban Cossack was prepared to rise and fight, and shortly after landing General Ulagay, who kept quarrelling with his Chief-of-Staff, General Dratsenko, discovered Red Army forces many times stronger than his own. Rather than even attempt a raid on Ekaterinodar and get himself cut off from the coast, Ulagay retreated and asked to be taken back to the Crimea. General Babiyev, who lost contact with the main Ulagay force, had to extricate himself fast and retreat as well. The operation was a final failure which proved beyond any doubt that not even the wealthy Kuban Cossacks were prepared to fight for a White Russia. In addition it was a useless military diversion, for now the Red Army launched a counter-attack in Northern Tauride and Wrangel's depleted forces all but collapsed.

Throughout August 1920, while Wrangel was sending away his forces on futile raids, the Red Army pressed hard the 1st Corps, which he rather superfluously renamed the 1st Army. Only after the withdrawal from the Kuban was he able to reorganise his forces into the 2nd Army, in whose command he put the garrulous General Dratsenko. The combined forces of the 1st and 2nd Armies managed to beat off Red attacks and Wrangel responded with his own offensive. In September 1920 he tried to break through the Red Army lines into the Don, in the direction of Gulay Pole, the Green anarchist capital. Once again it was a political nonsense, for the Greens were ready to support the Red Army rather than let the Whites through. Wrangel's breakthrough attempts at Alexandrovsk and Mariupol also failed, and in October his Trans-Dniepr operation, a breakthrough into the Ukraine, came to a similar conclusion. Still Wrangel tried out everything.

It is obvious that given the limitations of the Crimea Wrangel was doomed to failure from the very beginning, but he was determined to try his best against whatever odds, and at least in politics he proved a little more successful. He was determined not to repeat Denikin's internal political errors and tried to share power with politicians. Like Denikin he considered the army his sole responsibility, but unlike Denikin he wished to hand political power almost exclusively to the politicians. But he found it hard to implement this intention. To start with he inherited from Denikin his government and Premier Bernatsky, and distrusted them too much to hand power to them. Next he found out that there were few able politicians left in the Crimea and he had to go abroad and invite exiled politicians to join the South Russian government which he wanted to form. However, exiled politicians either refused his invitations outright or took some considerable time to arrive, and he thus found himself exercising absolute power much longer than he really wished. It was obvious that Russians had little faith in his military success. and even less in his government. Ultimately he did succeed in luring to the Crimea from Paris A.V. Krivoshein, a capable tsarist minister of agriculture, who consented to become his Prime Minister. Krivoshein was a success and was given quite considerable powers by Wrangel. He gathered round himself capable administrators, who took over the administration of the Crimea and conquered territories from the army, which never really happened under Denikin. Even before Krivoshein's arrival Wrangel set up several commissions which attempted to sort out immediate problems and draw up long-term plans: Senator Glinka's commission looked into agricultural problems, the Shatilov commission examined administration as a whole, the Vilchevsky commission looked for ideas as to how to remove conflicts between the army and the population, while the Matusevich commission looked into finance and the complex problems of self-sufficiency. When Krivoshein finally assumed office he had the land decree ready and as an old expert modified only slightly the Glinka commission proposals. This land reform was one of the few political successes of the Wrangel regime.

Like Denikin Wrangel was also full of good intentions, but with the rest was much less successful. After witnessing the terrible abuses of the legal system under Denikin Wrangel became convinced that without a legal system his regime would come to the same end as Denikin's. He therefore re-established civil procurators and judges, and gave them teeth by suppressing all the judiciary and executive powers of the counter-espionage departments of the army. All criminal cases, except straightforward military espionage, had to be brought before civilian tribunals after investigation by a civilian procurator. Special military courts dealt with cases in the army only and could not judge civilians. Moreover he put in charge of political security an experienced tsarist policeman, General

Klimovich, and as a result the Crimea never witnessed political difficulties from the left or even the Bolsheviks, as under Denikin; nor were summary executions made use of. Still the weakness of the Wrangel system was that criminals, even murderers, in the army found themselves protected against civilian complaint, and while the general state of lawlessness prevalent under Denikin ceased, numerous lawless acts could be and were perpetrated. Thus, for example, General Slashchev should have been court-martialled for exceeding his powers, and his counter-intelligence officer, Sharov, tried for murder. In any case Wrangel himself invariably changed any capital sentence on soldiers into the punishment of fighting in the ranks. Again, sadly enough, like Denikin the supreme commander was not above lawlessness: he ordered large-scale deportations from the Crimea of people suspected of pro-Bolshevik sympathy. Arbitrary arrests of leaders who opposed him were also widely practised and the Wrangel regime never really rid itself of the old Volunteer reputation that it preached law and order and committed far graver excesses than the Bolsheviks, who at least scrupulously controlled them.

Apart from the problems of administration in general, and law and order in particular, Wrangel had to tackle the tricky problem of finance, food and other supplies. Denikin never tried and though Wrangel also failed to solve the financial problem he tackled it very seriously. He convened a large conference of Russian financial experts, including former ministers of finance, and intended to implement all its proposals. However, in October 1920, when the conference finally met, it was too late and the proposals remained on paper. Wrangel also tried to negotiate a loan in France, but these negotiations came to nothing: French terms were so tough that the Russians rather leaked them and got no loan at all. Food supply problems were more or less solved after the conquest of Northern Tauride, which was a rich agricultural region. Premier Krivoshein even thought of exporting surplus grain, bartering it for arms and ammunition, of which there were chronic shortages. But the international conditions were not right for this type of trade and the idea was never realised. Despite this failure Wrangel managed to get a trickle of military supplies from the former Russian stores in Romania and the Caucasus with a few French shiploads thrown in. On the whole Wrangel had enough basic equipment for his armies, though he was short of men. Thus he could offer war supplies to his partisan allies such as the varied Ukrainian factions, Caucasians and minor Cossacks. This was a marked improvement on Denikin, who had had immense surpluses of everything but helped no-one.

Despite the relative political-administrative achievements Wrangel still remained the absolute dictator that his predecessor had been. He relied almost exclusively on the armed forces and dismissed civilian administrators at a whim whenever he suspected that things were not going well. Most often he simply scared the officials, especially the elected ones, into resignation and exile. Even though he desired a free election of local government, and just before the collapse of his regime did carry out one, he probably would not have been able to deal with such elected representatives successfully. He and his army were hyper-sensitive to any kind of criticism and clashes of interests occurred even under the old unrepresentative system. Wrangel knew of only one remedy for dealing with criticism: dismissal and the arrest of the culprits.

Because of the personal type of Wrangel's regime the few conspiracies that were hatched aimed at the removal of the supreme commander; one assassination attempt failed only accidentally when a huge mine was found by chance on the line where his train was due. However, the conspiracies were ridiculous: a monarchist conspiracy wanted to replace him by Archduke Nicholas, then on the Riviera in France. Duke Leichtenbergsky was to represent the Archduke in his absence and naval officers from Sevastopol were to buttress this regime. Wrangel had them all arrested. contemptuously sent the youthful Duke to his father in Germany and the naval officers to fight in the army as soldiers. Only one *éminence grise* of this affair, one Pinkhus-Logvinsky, was executed. These conspiracies proved again that the White movement contained too many fantastic adventurers who were prepared to snatch power and life even from a clearly doomed leader.

A little paradoxically it was in August 1920 as Wrangel wasted away his meagre resources in useless operations that he scored his greatest international success — his regime was suddenly recognised as the *de facto* government of Southern Russia by France and the United States of America. The French told Foreign Minister Struve that Wrangel 'restored democracy, gave land to the peasants, and now it was our turn to recognise and help you'. Wrangel was rather surprised by this international windfall, but soon realised that it meant nothing. The French would not follow the recognition by granting him loans and the Americans did not even begin to think of practical aid. The recognition was clearly the result of inter-Allied disagreement; the French, because of Poland, wanted to take over from the British, but as soon as the conflict in Poland came to an end they also lost interest in the fate of Wrangel. In the meantime they used the White ploy in their own negotiations with the Bolsheviks. They had many Frenchmen in Bolshevik prisons under threat of execution, and as early as April 1920 the Bolshevik plenipotentiary, M. Litvinov, had a solemn French promise that France would not intervene in South Russia against the Bolsheviks if the arrested French were repatriated to France.

In September 1920 the British government, whose influence with the Whites was supplanted by France, had a top secret report from the Crimea indicating that the Wrangel regime and its armies were on the point of collapse. However, it was only in October 1920 that the French High Commissioner, Comte de Martel, and General Brousseau arrived at

Sevastopol to put into effect their government's recognition and start studying the problem of aid. In fact they only arrived to survey the ruin of Wrangel and re-embarked twenty days later to report in Paris on the final hours of the White Crimea.

Although in October 1920 Wrangel made yet another effort at breaking out of Northern Tauride across the Dniepr into the Ukraine, his forces kept a weary eye on the landing strip which the Red Army ominously occupied and kept against all White counter-attacks on the left bank of the Dniepr. On 26 October 1920 the Red Army crossed the Dniepr in force and two days later launched a general offensive against the two armies of Wrangel. It almost cut off Kutepov's army from the Crimea, but in the end both White armies squeezed in and installed themselves on the prepared fortified lines across the approaches to the Crimean peninsula. There, for a week, the operations came to a halt.

Both sides regrouped and Wrangel put Kutepov in charge of the defences. On 3 November 1920 the Drozdovsky Division, now a battalion, beat back the attack by the Red Army but suffered such heavy casualties that it practically ceased to exist. Then Wrangel, on Kutepov's recommendation, put into effect his emergency plan of evacuation. Throughout the next three days the Red Army's attacks were beaten off, but on 8 November 1920 Red forces, after a risky manoeuvre, turned the White flank and Kutepov had no alternative but to sound a general retreat. Though beaten the Whites did not panic as at Novorossiisk or Odessa, but retreated in good order to the points of embarkation.

The Wrangel regime did prepare well at least this last operation: Russian and French ships were ready in all the ports of the peninsula and began to evacuate civilians and wounded first. The South Russian government was told of the Red breakthrough on the 8 November and was evacuated next day. Wrangel made his last inspection of the front and even had time to refuse a Bolshevik offer of surrender. By 14 November 1920 some 145,693 soldiers and dependents had sailed into exile; organised military resistance to the Red Army and the Bolshevik regime ceased. The Crimea and the rest of Russia was cleared of White armies and the civil war came to an end.

Civil War in North Western Russia

The civil war in the Baltic provinces of Russia was particularly complex and quite different in character from the rest of Russia. Before the armistice in November 1918 Germany occupied all the three provinces, Estonia, Latvia and Lithuania, on the strength of a supplementary agreement with the Bolsheviks signed on 27 August 1918. In this agreement the Bolsheviks renounced all their claims to these provinces and in return Germany guaranteed that Finland, newly independent, would not attack the Bolsheviks. Thus the German occupation and presence in the provinces inevitably dragged the Allies in after the armistice.

The majority of the population of these provinces was non-Russian and they were naturally more interested in seizing independence for themselves than in Russian civil war. However, there were also White Russian forces in these provinces, some formed by the Germans, others by the Allies, and their presence easily transformed the struggle for independence into civil war. Moreover, the Bolsheviks had on their territory large military forces consisting of Latvian, Estonian and Lithuanian nationals, whom the native communist leaders intended to use to lay claim to the provinces once the Germans withdrew.

In these circumstances it was not surprising that, when German troops began their withdrawal, power passed at first into the hands of the nationalists. On 11 November 1918 Poska (Ptas) proclaimed himself Prime Minister of Estonia; almost at the same time Ullman (Ulmanis) did the same in Latvia and Professor Waldemar in Lithuania. However, it was far from clear how long they could maintain themselves in power, whether they had any armed forces to insure their security, and what the Bolsheviks would do.

The Western Allies, France and Britain, had initially no interest in these provinces of the Russian Empire. They were left out of their Convention on Russia, but because they were under German occupation they had to be dealt with, and Britain, without any objection from France, seized the initiative. On 4 November 1918 the Admiralty was asked to send ships into the Baltic Sea and a few days later the War Office defined the British position vis-á-vis the Baltic area:

'no particular responsibilities were allocated nor accepted by the British in the Baltic. The ultimate fate of these provinces would be settled by the Peace Conference in Paris. In the meantime German evacuation should be procured and the Baltic provinces should be aided with arms and foodstuffs, and encouraged to establish their own administrations.'

However, almost immediately the Admiralty contradicted these vague proposals by despatching a squadron of British ships for the purpose of isolating the centre of Bolshevism in Russia: the ultimate aim of this Admiralty initiative was the defeat of the Bolsheviks in the area by aiding particularly the Estonians who were the most exposed.

Thus even before any action was undertaken in the provinces British policy was in a muddle and during November 1918 additional complications arose. The Foreign Secretary, Lord Balfour, endorsed the decisions and measures already taken, and then recommended rather ambiguously that the Baltic states should be helped to independence, albeit their progress towards it may be halting and their situation imperfect; he claimed that in the circumstances this was the only possible policy for Britain in the area. However, Balfour also promised British support to all the pro-Allied Russians in the old provinces and thus created a new problem which would have not arisen, since the Russian Whites were extremely weak in the region.

All this was a purely British initiative and neither ally nor foe were consulted. A fortnight after the armistice a British squadron consisting of five light cruisers, nine destroyers and seven other ships sailed for the Baltic and brought food and military supplies to Reval for the Estonians. Rear-Admiral Sinclair found the situation in the Baltic area very bad, but since he had no precise instructions he decided to stay on at Reval until spring, when the ice would break. With a British squadron icebound the British government tried to force the Allied peace conference, as soon as it convened, to come to some sort of decision about the Baltic provinces, for in the meantime the Bolsheviks, seeing Allied indecision and impotence, invaded the region, especially Latvia.

Perhaps a little paradoxically the Latvian Rifle divisions had stood the Bolsheviks in good stead during and after the Bolshevik coup in November 1917. Now the Bolsheviks were simply sending them home and they marched on Riga without much resistance from the nationalists. On 3 January 1919 British ships had to evacuate the Latvian government from Riga, which fell to the Bolshevik Latvians. The Latvian Prime Minister, Ulmanis, from his refuge H.M.S. *Phaeton* asked the British government for help. Similar requests were received from Estonia, where the army was short of ammunition and had no oil.

With the situation rapidly deteriorating and without an Allied decision

Britain decided to act on her own and took decisions and measures in anticipation: on 31 December 1918 the British cabinet considered the situation in the Baltic provinces and decided to increase its naval involvement. A second British squadron under the command of Admiral Sir Walter Cowan sailed almost immediately for the Baltic Sea. The aim of this operation was even more restricted than that of Rear-Admiral Sinclair, who in view of the Bolshevik advance changed his mind and was on his way back to England. The purpose of Cowan's mission was to keep the British flag flying, control the Estonians and Latvians and generally behave passively (retaliate only if attacked). However, the new commander, Cowan, was a completely different man from his predecessor: it was clear that he was much more belligerent and that he would interpret his instructions to suit his own ideas. Thus immediately on his arrival the Admiral spent January and February 1919 helping most 'actively' the hard-pressed Estonians and Latvians against the Red Army 'which was contrary to his instructions'.

In the meantime France also took a decision and early in 1919 several French ships joined the British in the Baltic Sea. Then suddenly, on 3 March 1919, the Allied Supreme Council decided to blockade the Eastern Baltic area in order to force the German occupation forces out. The decision, taken in peaceful Paris miles away from the Baltic, seemed though unrealistic to the Allied men on the spot. Rear-Admiral Hope on receiving orders to that effect immediately pointed out the difficulties: the withdrawing Germans would have to be replaced by Allied troops, unless the Allies wished to abandon the Baltic states, and above all Latvia, to the Bolsheviks. The Allies came face-to-face with an insoluble dilemma.

Although the Allies were present in these provinces the German army was still the decisive factor. In Latvia there were only some 1,000 pro-Allied Letts with 3,000 Baltic Germans who could not be relied on and only some 200 non-Bolshevik Russians. Even with a further 4,000 Letts mobilised the situation was grave and it was foolish to try and force the Germans out. Moreover, Hope warned, the Germans were themselves badly demoralised, and if their collapse was to be avoided the Allied blockade should not be applied to the supply ports of Libau and Windau. These were strong words from the man on the spot, but the British at least decided that the Allied decision on the blockade of the Baltic was impracticable. Both the Admiralty and the Foreign Office were in agreement with Rear-Admiral Hope's suggestions and told him so. It was hoped that suitable arrangements would be made on the spot, which meant that the British, as the only Allied force in the area, would tolerate German troops as long as 'they behaved and did not act against Allied [British] interests'. The blockade was therefore ignored and the priorities on the spot were as follows: the local forces were to be built up to replace eventually the Germans who would then finally withdraw. If the Germans 'behaved', they could possibly stay for quite a long time.

So far the British had no trouble with the Germans in Estonia, for they promptly withdrew after the armistice leaving the Estonians to face the Bolsheviks on their own. However, in Latvia the situation was different; the Iron Division, which held the province before the armistice, also began a slow evacuation. But in Latvia, in contrast to Estonia, the withdrawing Germans practically handed over the territory to the Red Army, driving away the armed forces of the Latvian National Council. Since its independence (proclaimed on 18 November 1918) the Latvian government, which was in fact the peasant-dominated National Council of Valka, was desperately trying to gain control over the Latvian territory, but the task was hopeless. The Latvians were deeply divided: apart from the peasant National Council, the towns of Riga, Libau and Windau were under Latvian socialist control. On the Bolshevik side there were the pro-Bolshevik Latvian Rifles and given the weakness and division of their opponents the outcome of the struggle was clear. The British had no choice but to bargain with the Germans.

First of all the Allied representatives on the spot (mainly British army and naval officers) argued with the Germans that under the conditions of the armistice agreement they were obliged to slow down their own evacuation until such time as a substitute force, approved by the Allies, could be found. Both the German commissar for the Baltic territory, Winnig, and the general commanding troops in Latvia, von Esdorff, rejected these arguments, but all the same were undecided as to whom they should aid. The Latvian nationalists were accusing them of favouring the Bolsheviks and even handing them arms on withdrawal. But before the fall of Riga Winnig and Esdorff tried to bargain with the British representative, Bosanquet: they asked for certain privileges for their aid against the Bolsheviks and requested fresh troops. But even if the Latvian government agreed to these proposals Bosanquet could not have sanctioned them; they could only have been approved by the Allied Council and that body could not bargain with local German forces. With the Germans passively looking on the Red Army marched into Riga and Bosanquet, the Latvian government and Captain Smyth, who commanded the British ships at Riga, withdrew.

On taking Riga the Bolshevik advance slowed down, for German evacuation had also slowed down. In February 1919 General Rudiger von der Goltz arrived to take over from the tired Esdorff, and paradoxically trouble for the Allies really started. On taking stock of the Latvian situation von der Goltz became convinced that he could succeed where Esdorff had failed: he even thought that he could re-establish German influence in the three Baltic states despite the lost war. The situation was certainly complex and Goltz thought that it would be sufficient to sabotage Allied efforts at consolidation and use local factors to his advantage to achieve his aim. On 9 February 1919 British war supplies finally arrived for the Latvian army at Libau, but the British ships which brought them had to dash off to Windau to bombard the Latvian Red Army and prevent it from taking the town. Then they returned to Libau to supervise the arming and training of Latvian forces. Ulmanis, the refugee Prime Minister, was back in town together with his government and military HQ. However, the greater part of Latvian forces consisted of local Germans (Baltisches Landwehr), who on Goltz's encouragement attempted a coup against Ulmanis. On 2 March 1919 this attempt failed only thanks to the prompt action by the British ships stationed in the harbour. Four days later the British retaliated and though Goltz disclaimed any responsibility for the attempted coup the British placed him under blockade. But he quickly called their bluff: if the blockade was really applied to him and his troops, he would be forced to withdraw. With the Latvians untrained and not even properly organised and with the Red Army still at Riga the British seemed in a tight corner.

However, von der Goltz never even entertained the idea of withdrawing. He simply wanted to get rid of the blockade which caused him and his troops plenty of difficulty. Because of the lack of supplies his own troops began to show signs of mutiny. Still before Goltz's troops had time to disintegrate the Allies changed their minds and made fresh concessions. On 5 April 1919 Lord Curzon told Balfour that if the Germans were allowed by the Allies to hold the Bolsheviks the Allies would have to allow them reinforcements. Nine days later von der Goltz was informed that the Allied blockade was provisionally lifted and that he was allowed reinforcements. Goltz's troops survived and he became a primary factor in the Baltic area both locally and internationally.

The Allied blockade proved to be a fiasco and henceforth General von der Goltz had everything his own way. His next move was to prove to the Allies that his German troops were the only armed force capable of resisting the Red Army in Latvia and driving it out of the province. This move though necessarily entailed the elimination of the local rivals, above all Ulmanis's Letts. During the night of 16 April 1919 the German Balts, this time aided directly by German troops attempted another coup against Ulmanis and his government, and this time they succeeded. After a lot of confusion and fighting a compromise was ironed out by Prince Lieven, leader of the local Russian troops: Colonel Balodis's Letts and Baron von Manteufel's Balts joined a fighting coalition to drive the Red Army out of Latvia. With his troops deserting him Ulmanis was left stranded on the British ship and the new coalition prepared for an offensive against the Red Army.

Needless to say it could not launch an offensive without German help and in the end the British discerned clearly Goltz's planning and execution behind these Latvian moves. The impotent local Allied representatives reported everything to their capitals and Paris, and Allied reaction was swift. On 3 May 1919 Marshal Foch, Supreme Allied Commander, instructed the Allied representatives in Berlin to request the recall of General von der Goltz from his command in the Baltic provinces. The German government however acted much less swiftly and Goltz continued to implement his carefully planned objectives. On 10 May Pastor Niedra was proclaimed Prime Minister of Latvia and the Balts with Balodis's troops moved against Riga. Twelve days later Riga fell to the combined onslaught of the Balts and Balodis, without German participation. Goltz thought that faced with such favourable *fait accompli* the Allies would acquiesce and leave him to pursue his further objectives unhindered.

But he overplayed his hand. The Allies would have probably forgiven him the coup against Ulmanis, but after the fall of Riga he moved the German Balts further north until they came into contact with nationalist Estonians and Latvians jointly fighting the Red Army. It was obvious that the Balts could easily strike either way, against the nationalists or the Bolsheviks, whichever von der Goltz desired. Goltz thus made his intentions clear: he was indispensable for the balance of power in the Baltic area. This the Allies could not tolerate. In view of the successful outcome of the Riga operation they dropped their demand for Goltz's recall, but with his moves in the North they immediately renewed their demands for evacuation from and no interference in the Baltic area. On 11 June 1919 the Supreme Allied Council dealt with the Baltic situation and two days later the German government was requested to stop all operations in Latvia. German troops were not to move any farther towards Estonia; Libau and Windau, and all the Russian territory were to be evacuated as soon as possible.

Obviously General von der Goltz miscalculated. The Allies were prepared to tolerate him and German troops in the Baltic as long as they could be used against the Red Army, but even then with reluctance. When Goltz seemingly revealed that he also wanted to manipulate the future pro-Allied Baltic states he ruined his mission. In order to deal with the Baltic problems more directly the Allies now decided to send there a high-powered mission under General Sir Hubert Gough. The General's task was not only to implement Allied policies and decisions, but also supervise German withdrawal. In addition to the mission Marshal Foch sent concrete military instructions to the German government: German troops had to withdraw from the three Baltic states and were to be replaced by local national forces; military supplies and equipment left behind had to be handed over to the latter. On 29 June 1919 General Baron von Hammerstein replied in a conciliatory manner that Germany would comply with the Allied requests concerning the Baltic area, and pointed out that the withdrawal would be much quicker if the Allies lifted the blockade of Germany. The Baltic problem seemed to have been resolved.

Moreover the military situation in Latvia now turned against the Germans. Throughout June 1919 German troops acted so menacingly that Commander Duff, who was in charge in Latvia before Colonel Talents's arrival, decided to move two of his destroyers out of Riga harbour for fear of having them captured by the Germans. In addition to this menace Goltz transferred his HQ to the Latvian capital and continued his operations against the Estonians in the north. Then on 16 June 1919 the newly arrived Colonel Talents took charge of the situation and arranged an armistice between the Estonians and von der Goltz. Under pressure from Berlin Goltz also evacuated the important port of Libau, but instead of handing it over to the Latvians Goltz let the pro-German Russian Whites to take over.

Two days after these German setbacks the frightened puppet Latvian government of Pastor Niedra resigned and on 27 June Ulmanis and his government disembarked at Libau and were warmly welcomed by the population. Von der Goltz's diplomatic defeat was coupled with the military one: his German Balts were defeated by the Estonian Army and Colonel Zemitan's Latvian troops. Since the Germans were still in control in Riga the victorious Estonians and Latvians combined and advanced on the capital. In order to avoid most probably bloody fighting Colonel Talents arranged another armistice and then ordered Goltz to evacuate Riga by 5 July. He also appointed a military governor in the city to hand over to the legitimate government when it arrived. The Baltic Germans (Landwehr) were taken from Goltz and incorporated into the Latvian army to fight the Bolsheviks. They were placed under the command of Lieutenant-Colonel Alexander (later Field-Marshal Lord Alexander of Tunis) and fought bravely until the end of the civil war. Goltz complied with the ultimatum and Ulmanis and his government landed in Riga on 7 July.

Still this was not the end of trouble with General von der Goltz, who persuaded his government in Berlin that the Allies had no suitable troops to replace his division if withdrawn. The German Foreign Ministry representative, von Lersner, put it quite forcibly to the Allies: by compelling the Germans to withdraw from the Baltic area the Allies were inviting a Bolshevik takeover, but by then even Clemenceau was exasperated by Goltz's machinations and intrigues and demanded German evacuation. On his instructions Marshal Foch sent the German government another request for the completion of the evacuation by 30 August 1919.

It was at this stage that the Germans pulled out another card to continue their presence in the Baltic provinces. Apart from the German division and the local Baltic troops the three former provinces of the Russian empire were honeycombed with Russian partisans and paramilitary militia. One of the most important of these units in Latvia was under the command of General Prince Lieven and consisted of Russian loyalists, such as the Prince himself, and Russian prisoners of war who had somehow reached Latvia and enlisted in the Lieven Corps. Another unit, more partisan in style, was under the command of Colonel Bulak-Balakhovich, who had deserted from the Red Army, and operated mainly in north eastern Latvia and southern Estonia. While the Lieven Corps remained passive at Libau Balakhovich's partisans were raiding Soviet territory and even took part in an operation against Pskov. Until General Yudenich's arrival in Finland late in 1918 no one was in overall command of these heterogeneous Russian units. Then General Yudenich simply proclaimed himself the commanding officer of these forces and proceeded to organise them all into the North Western Army Corps with a view to conducting military operations against the 7th Red Army, whose task was to protect that part of the Soviet territory.

General Yudenich took on the heavy task of organising the North Western armies with surprising simplicity, but he was the most senior Russian soldier there. From the start he had great difficulty in communicating with his scattered forces while he himself and his HQ were in Helsinki. He was not discouraged by setbacks and gradually was recognised as the supreme commander in the North West by practically all the local Russian commanders which, of course, did not mean that Yudenich could actually command them all. Yudenich's greatest asset was political: as a former Russian front commander he was known to Allied generals and diplomats and recognised by them. This Allied 'recognition' was in fact responsible for his acceptance by the Russian commanders, but it could not enforce unity within the minute Russian North West. As long as some Russians remained pro-German, Yudenich's command was worthless and the North Western armies could not be a serious threat to the Bolsheviks.

The tacit Allied recognition was turned into an official recognition when the Allies finally found out about Yudenich's army and its existence. He was immediately supplied with arms and ammunition, but it also became clear that Yudenich on his own could not hope to defend the Baltic provinces against the Red Army. Only a combined effort of the North Western Army and Estonians, Latvians and Lithuanians could prove effective in the defensive sense. As for offensive purposes against Russia absolute unity was a precondition together with Allied aid and Finnish participation. If the Whites and their allies could not achieve these requirements they could not even start thinking in offensive terms. However, exactly the opposite happened. As soon as Allied supplies arrived for the Russian North Western army, Yudenich began to plan an offensive. He was not deterred by the fact that the Estonians strongly objected to Allied supplies going to the Russians rather than to themselves. The implications of this disunity were apparent, but they made no difference to Yudenich's offensive plans. Both the General and the Allies had an excellent intelligence network in the North West and Petrograd, and both knew full well of Bolshevik weakness in this area. With active Allied encouragement Yudenich speeded up his preparations and decided to launch his offensive in May 1919, although his armies were far from ready. This was to be a combined operation with the Estonians (stiffened by Finnish volunteers) who hoped to push the Red Army from the part of Estonia still occupied by it. Under the protection of British naval guns the Estonians were to attack from Narva along the coast, while the North Western Corps was to strike at Yamburg and Pskov and into Russia proper.

On 13 May 1919 the offensive was unleashed on the unsuspecting Bolsheviks. British naval guns, amphibious operations and Bolshevik desertions all combined to enable the Estonians and Whites to reach their first objectives. Yamburg and Pskov were taken within a few days and the Estonians also advanced significantly. Twelve days after the start of the offensive General Yudenich arrived from Finland to take over the command of all operations. This was obviously premature and a tactical error: the Estonians could not admit that Yudenich was in overall command and British naval squadrons could not possibly place themselves under Yudenich's control. Thus General Gough had no choice but to advise Yudenich to return to Helsinki and leave the offensive to get on under its own steam. Yudenich left and put General Rodzianko in command of the Russian forces, who immediately attempted to tackle field problems. To effect a deeper penetration into Russia and eventually take Petrograd Rodzianko required the Estonians, who formed the left flank of the offensive, to take the coastal fortresses whose guns now prevented British ships from affording the Estonians artillery cover. Although the two fortresses, Sedaya Loshad' and Krasnaya Gorka, mutinied, the Estonians were unable to relieve them and they were retaken by the Bolsheviks after some bloody fighting. This proved decisive for the fate of the May offensive, although the Allies tried hard to weaken the Bolsheviks and engaged them round Murmansk and even in Karelia, where the Finns launched a diversionary attack. The Red Army was alarmed enough by the initial successes of the combined forces in the North West to transfer its crack 2nd Division from the Eastern front to the North West, which stabilised the military situation. During the fighting round Sedaya Loshad' and Krasnaya Gorka everything went wrong with Estonian-White liaison: General Rodzianko failed to come to the aid of the Estonians and instead pressed on with his useless advance which had to be turned into retreat as soon as the fortresses fell back into Bolshevik hands. Moreover, since the fortresses were garrisoned by local, non-Russian soldiers who were massacred by the Red Army after the reconquest, the Estonians began to cry treachery and accused the Whites of disregard for human life. It became clear that the failure of the combined offensive was caused by fundamental disagreements and by incompatible interests. For the future the failure meant that unless Estonian national independence could coincide with the reconquest of Russia the White cause in the North West was doomed.

With the collapse of the offensive and Bolshevik counter-attacks political lessons had to be drawn and much tidying up, long overdue, had to be done. General Yudenich was blissfully unaware of the political implications of his armed struggle in the North West. He had his eyes on Petrograd and nothing else mattered. He chose to ignore the political aims of his allies, Estonians, Latvians and Lithuanians alike, and busied himself with the preparation of the next offensive. However, all other people involved in the armed struggle, including his immediate entourage, began to pursue political aims: the Baltic nationalities began openly to demand independence; the Germans were also exerting themselves to regain some influence. The confused Allies suddenly found out that Yudenich's Russians decided to rid themselves of the Baltic separatists (allies) by turning for support to the defeated Germans. Somehow this seemed natural, since the Allies supported the separatists. On the German side the defeated generals were more than sympathetic to the Whites: General von Seeckt encouraged them, Groener took steps to aid them and von der Goltz was actively engaged in the combat against the Bolsheviks. This was obviously a disastrous policy, but in mitigation it must be said that the Russian politicians who embraced it were third-rate provincials who were completely lost in the complexities of the civil war struggle in the North West.

However, what influenced most the North Western Russians in choosing the pro-German policy was the fact that the Germans in Germany were encouraging Russian Whites there to organise themselves for the struggle against the Bolsheviks and were in fact supporting the White movement financially. But this German support was limited and would be forth-coming as long as the Allies tolerated it. Among the German politicians who enthusiastically advocated support for the Whites was the Zentrum leader, Erzberger, and the Social Democrat Minister of the Interior, Noske. Noske granted the Whites permission to recruit prisoners of war for their armies. The chief organisers were Rittmeister von Rosenberg and Colonel Bermondt who also interested the German Association of Industry and Commerce in the scheme and obtained money from them. With this aid Russian prisoners of war in Germany were trained, equipped and sent off to join the Russian Corps at Libau. The Allies seemed uninterested in what the Germans did in Germany with the Russians: on 31 May 1919 when the first Russian soldiers left Germany for the Baltic provinces there were no formal protests by the Allies, but when the Germans also tried to erect a political front to this military force and formed the Russian Anti-Bolshevik League, the Allies became restless. At first the League attracted practically all the Russians in Germany. Even General Potocki, the White representative in Berlin and former head of the Russian intelligence section against Germany, joined. But when it became clear that this would be a German-dominated organisation frowned on by the Allies, the pro-Allied element quickly left it.

The Allies began though to object to German and pro-German policies when they began to bear fruit on the spot in the Baltic provinces in August 1919. Throughout that month Bolshevik advance in the North West continued and by the end of the month the Red Army captured not only Yamburg but also Pskov, thus separating the Whites from the Estonians. At the same time General Burt reported to London that General von der Goltz was in a subdued mood awaiting Marshal Foch's orders for evacuation. Then the Germans burst their first political bombshell: on the advice of the Auswärtiges Amt a West Russian Government was formed in Berlin. Baron Knorring was its Premier and the military plenipotentiaries were General Biskupsky and Colonel Durnovo. This indeed was a setback for the Allies, for the West Russian government had its armed forces in Latvia at Libau, while the North Western Army was without political leadership.

It became imperative that the Germans evacuate the Baltic area, otherwise the Allies may as well hand the region over to them. General von der Goltz was called to Berlin for consultations and reported that German evacuation was proceeding satisfactorily which was, of course, untrue. Baron von Av-Wachendorf used this Goltz report to reject Allied requests for speeded up withdrawal and Goltz's recall from the command. The Germans were not prepared to meet the Allied deadline for evacuation and von der Goltz said so publicly as soon as he returned to Latvia. The new deadline was 15 September and the Germans were becoming unnerved. They arrested two Allied officers and fired on two others, as if to show that they would not tolerate Allied interference with their evacuation. Then the second bombshell exploded: Russo-German financial agreements became known to the Allies and it was clear that even if the Germans evacuated from the Baltic area they would continue to exercise considerable influence through their Russian ally. But then even the evacuation came to an abrupt stop when German troops concentrated at Mittau to be shipped home suddenly mutinied. The Allies were defied again and the German presence in the area continued.

The mortal blow to the North Western White cause came from the pro-German forces and not from the Germans themselves. Allied observers noticed arrivals of Russian soldiers from Germany early in August 1919; General Malcolm reported from Berlin that the Germans wanted to get rid of them. But when they all went to Libau and were incorporated into the Lieven Corps (which now became the Bermondt Corps) the Allies became disquieted. Moreover German soldiers began to arrive from Germany in Latvia, where they claimed Latvian nationality and land grants much to the surprise of the Latvian government. Latvia seemed saturated with these new arrivals from Germany who appeared very keen on fighting the Bolsheviks. General Gough found himself in a difficult situation: he followed closely German moves and knew that Generals Arsenief and Rodzianko, Yudenich's field commanders were intriguing with the Germans in order to obtain direct aid from Germany through the West Russian Government. At the same time the Estonians, Latvians and Lithuanians declared quite openly that they would not help the Whites, if they were not promised independence.

To counter all the German intrigues and moves and to re-establish control on the spot General Gough decided to act decisively. He also needed a Russian government which could take control of the armies and grant concessions to its allies. But it proved rather difficult to collect enough Russian politicians to form a government in the Baltic provinces. In the end General Marsh simply rounded up all available Russians, marched them into the British consulate at Reval, announced them the terms on which they would become ministers and gave them forty minutes to make up their minds. Only S.G. Lianozov, who had been in the Baltic provinces since the Bolshevik coup and conducted negotiations with the British before anybody else did not hesitate and agreed to become Prime Minister. He had the confidence of the British and also became Minister of Finance. All the other Russians hesitated and some experienced politicians (Senator Ivanov, Suvorov, Kartashev, Krusenstern) refused to join the pro-Allied government, thus defeating its purpose in advance since the North Western government was to be a representative Russian government giving independence to the Baltic provinces. The resulting government was full of obscure figures, utterly unrepresentative, whose promises of independence could not be taken seriously. General Yudenich was Minister of Defence as well as Commander-in-Chief. The first declaration of the government was the recognition of Estonian independence, which also called on the Allies to recognise Estonia *de jure*. This political move by a British general immediately misfired.

The first victim of this new government was General Gough himself: he was peremptorily recalled. On 18 August 1919 Lord Curzon made it clear in Paris that the North Western Government was formed without prior consultation and approval of the British government. A few days after this declaration Curzon informed Tallents that the British government would not recognise the North Western Russian government and local Allied initiative and attempts at sorting out the problems in the Baltic states collapsed. But the Allies were now determined to eliminate German influence completely, even if it meant certain tactical disadvantages. Immediately the Russian Whites in the region were forbidden to accept German aid. Next the Allies made a determined effort to combine all the anti-Bolsheviks and convoked a conference at Riga for 26 August 1919. But once again the conference proved politically inconclusive. In the military field it was decided to launch a combined offensive against the Red Army; representatives of General Yudenich, Premier Ulmanis, General Laidoner and Colonel Bermondt (Avalov) agreed to participate and the Finnish government would also be asked to join. However, the two last factors proved ultimately inoperative and were the cause of the final débâcle.

By August 1919 the old Lieven Corps, now commanded by Colonel Bermondt, was an important military force in the Baltic. In fact General March was so impressed by its organisation that he proposed that Allied aid should go to Bermondt rather than to Yudenich. However, it was too late to divert supplies to Libau, where the Corps was stationed and Bermondt revealed himself politically shortly after General Marsh's inspection. On 9 September 1919 Colonel Durnovo sought out Major Thorburn in Berlin and announced to him that since the Allies could do nothing decisive for the Whites, they would accept German aid; Yudenich's troops (like those of Kolchak) were semi-Bolshevik, hence they could not be relied upon to fight the Reds. Bermondt would therefore stiffen his Corps with German volunteers and then, supported by von der Goltz's troops, would strike against and take Petrograd. Although Durnovo was consulting the Allies about this project, on the spot it was already being executed. Both the Whites in Germany and the Germans in the Baltic thus explicitly rejected the combined offensive and decided to act on their own. All seem to have lost their sense of reality.

General von der Goltz halted German evacuation altogether, believing that Berlin would clear this point with the Allies. Then suddenly a large number of German troops awaiting evacuation were incorporated into the Bermondt Corps until it was swelled into a genuine army corps of some 50,000 officers and men. It thus became the principal anti-Bolshevik force in the Baltic, which moreover could have also taken on the Baltic national forces. Colonel Bermondt now declared that he was ready to strike against the Bolsheviks and proposed to move his HQ to Dvinsk in Eastern Latvia. This alarmed the Latvians considerably, for Dvinsk could only be reached via Riga and they had no troops there to protect it. But the Estonians and Yudenich's troops were equally alarmed, especially since the real intentions of Bermondt were not clear. In any case Bermondt's moves disrupted the final preparations for the combined offensive.

By September 1919 the Allies made it quite clear that they would not tolerate German interference in the Baltic region, even on behalf of the Whites. The German government was told to stop even contemplating supporting the Whites, to resume evacuation and dismiss von der Goltz. Although it complied with all the requests it was determined to make use at least of the Bermondt Corps for which it was largely responsible. General von Eberhart replaced von der Goltz and evacuation was resumed. However, the Bermondt Corps, still containing many Germans, appeared to have run amok: even today it is not known who advised Bermondt to act as the green anarchist leader, Makhno, did in Southern Russia. In August 1919 Yudenich tried twice to get Bermondt under his command and join the offensive. When finally Bermondt's Corps moved up to Mittau, Yudenich thought that he had won, but instead Bermondt once again supplemented his units with German volunteers. Then Yudenich issued a concrete order – he wanted Bermondt to join his 1st Corps and drive to Narva. On 27 September 1919 Bermondt formally rejected Yudenich's call, refused to be subordinated to him or join the 1st Corps and instead made preparations for the taking of Riga. Yudenich could not postpone his offensive and only the weak 1st Corps launched the offensive against Narva. Bermondt moved against Riga, which he took after a drawn-out battle, thus threatening the rear of Yudenich's armies as well as those of Latvia and Estonia.

The first week of the combined offensive (10 – 17 October 1919) went off well: Pskov fell earlier in October and by 16 October 1919 Gatchina and Tsarskoye Selo were in White hands. But afterwards the Whites failed to advance. Once again they surveyed Petrograd from the heights at the south, but could not make up their minds whether to take the city. In any case they were much in advance of the combined offensive, and had to wait for their allies to accomplish their tasks first. The Estonians were stuck in front of the coastal fortresses and not even the British monitors and their huge guns could make them fall. The Estonian army was simply incapable of taking such terrible obstacles and once again the Russian Whites, who might have, were not there to help them. Above all the Finnish drive from Finnish territory, which was to seal the fate of the city of Petrograd, does not seem to have materialised. The combined offensive, after so much preparation, negotiation and effort, was coming to an inglorious end.

The final impulse for the collapse came from Bermondt's Russian-German Corps. With its move on Riga the British had to detach a number of ships, so much needed by the Estonians, and rush them off to Riga, where a full-scale battle developed for the city between them and Bermondt. On 3 November 1919 the Red Army suddenly launched its counter-attacks and both the Estonians, without naval guns and rein-forcement, and the Whites, so dangerously exposed near Petrograd, had to fall back. The inevitable drive by the Red Army from the coast into the interior cut off the exposed North Western Army from its retreat into Estonia, and changed the orderly retreat into panic and rout. By the end of November 1919 the North Western Army ceased to exist as an organised body and the small remnants which succeeded in reaching Estonia were disarmed and interned by the Estonians. Only Bermondt was left to be destroyed.

Supported by the Germans Bermondt held on to the territory he had occupied round Riga, but failed to expand or reach the front against the Red Army, which was his avowed *raison d'être*. The Allies, since the Estonians, Latvians and Lithuanians were fully extended fighting the Red Army, thought first of calling in Polish troops to deal with Bermondt and the Germans, but the Baltic allies seemed as worried about the Poles as the Russians, and the idea was not pursued. Then the Estonians offered the Latvians aid to expell Bermondt jointly, but since the Estonians were also hard pressed by the Red Army and their retreat was already destroying General Yudenich's armies the Latvians refused, withdrew temporarily their own troops and supported by British naval guns (joined also by the newly arrived French ships *Garnier* and *Marne*) advanced on Riga. By 12 November 1919 Bermondt and the remains of the German Iron Division were beaten and began to withdraw; at Libau British monitors pounded Bermondt's forces into surrender. Five days later General von Eberhardt dismissed Bermondt from his command and asked for an armistice. Now it was the turn of the Latvians to refuse and General Balodis continued to push the combined German-Russian forces out of Latvia. By the end of November 1919 the Bermondt Corps practically dissolved itself and the Russians either withdrew to East Prussia or split up into small partisan units. The Iron Division also continued to withdraw under Latvian pressure, but from time to time it mutinied or turned against the Latvians, rudely checking them. However by 6 December 1919 General Turner, who was in the Baltic to supervise German evacuation, reported from Tilsit that the Iron Division was at Memel, a port in Lithuania, and on its way to Germany. General Eberhardt had already left Shavli for East Prussia and German intervention and evacuation from the Baltic had come to an end. On 22 December 1919 the North Western Army was officially dissolved and the Baltic states were left to face the Red Army and the Bolsheviks on their own.

From the very beginning of the war in the Baltic provinces the Finns played an important role in the fighting and the most decisive role in the planning of the taking of Petrograd. The Finnish nationalist régime, after its victories over the Finnish Red Army in April 1918, felt strong enough not only to defend itself against the Bolsheviks, but also to aid the other Baltic nationalists with highly trained and tough volunteers. General Mannerheim, a tsarist officer who assumed the command of Finnish forces, thought in offensive terms. He wanted to annex Karelia and in November 1918 offered to take Petrograd for the Allies; in return he asked Allied recognition *de jure* of nationalist Finland. The Allies declined Mannerheim's offer and explained that Finnish independence together with that of other Baltic states would be granted by the Peace Conference and not by individual allies. Still, the Finnish offer was retained and its execution was simply postponed.

The Finns also permitted the Russians to organise themselves in

Finland, and above all allowed them to use Helsinki as a sort of capital for the North West. General Yudenich established his HQ in the city and many Russian politicians also operated there. Where Finnish intervention became more meaningful their demands on the White Russian allies also increased. The Finns wanted public recognition of their independence and the problem was simply from which of the White régimes they should obtain it. The Bolsheviks had recognised Finnish independence implicitly and were careful never to dispute this *fait accompli*. In the end Admiral Kolchak obliged, and henceforth the Finns were officially on their own, no longer part of the Russian Empire or any of the succeeding régimes. Now it was the turn of Finland to repay the Whites for their political kindness and negotiations were immediately started about a joint Yudenich-Finnish drive to Petrograd. In June 1919, just as the White offensive was halted, Yudenich and Mannerheim reached an agreement, but the Allies insisted that the agreement be ratified by Admiral Kolchak as without it no combined drive to Petrograd was possible. The Finns feigned suitable surprise and became convinced that General Yudenich was held in such low esteem by the Allies that it would be foolish to become his ally. On 23 June 1919 Kolchak ratified the agreement but negotiations continued, for the Finns raised the price of their participation in taking Petrograd. To probe Allied intentions more clearly they demanded military equipment for their armies to the tune of £15 million and an Allied announcement sanctioning Finnish intervention in Russian affairs. The Allies found their way out of the announcement – they assured the Finns that they had no objection to their intervention in Russian affairs, if it was the result of Admiral Kolchak's orders. However, they felt unable to supply the Finnish army with the required equipment for these purposes. Yudenich, Kolchak and the Finns continued their negotiations, but it became increasingly clear that the Finns would never get involved in the civil war in the North West.

Everything seemed to hinge on the resolution of military aid. General Gough, when he arrived in the Baltic area, also negotiated with the Finnish government and confirmed the importance of aid for Finnish cooperation with Yudenich. A few days later though on 23 July 1919, Gough must have changed his mind, for when military aid actually arrived, he recommended that it be given to Yudenich exclusively and the Finns were left high and dry. Still without the Finns no decisive success against the Red Army in the North West could be achieved and in the light of this Allied decisions sound most baffling. In the end the combined offensive was launched in October without a firm agreement with the Finns, though it was hoped that they would be coerced somehow to join in. On 22 October 1919 the Finnish government proclaimed partial mobilisation and had an offensive followed the Red Army would probably have been unable to defend Petrograd, at whose gates the North Western Army was poised to strike. It is still unclear for whose deception Finnish mobilisation was proclaimed, though it seems probable that it was the result of an appeal by General von der Goltz, who had helped the Finns militarily in April 1918. Goltz forced Colonel Bermondt to offer unconditional recognition of Finnish independence if the Finns would join in the offensive against Petrograd, but the final result of this initiative as well as that of Admiral Cowan, who asked his government to intervene directly in Helsinki, was the same. The Finns never directly refused any request, but instead of joining the fight skilfully relied on other means. At the height of the fighting they released rumours that they were favourably disposed towards the Bolsheviks and would come to an agreement with them. This should have killed any hope that the Whites still entertained *vis-à-vis* Finland, but the Allies refused to believe it, until it became a fact. On 4 December 1919 Lord Acton, British Ambassador in Helsinki, asked Curzon, now Secretary of State, whether the British would permit the Finns to recognise the Bolsheviks and raise the blockade. The British did not object and the Finnish problem was solved. By refusing to be drawn into the civil war by either side and by exploiting the situation round Pegrograd to their best advantage the Finns succeeded in withdrawing from the Russian Empire more permanently than the other Baltic states. Although negotiations with the Soviets took a long time and peace was only concluded on 14 October 1920, the Finns effectively solved their problems themselves and were first out of the morass of the civil war in the Baltic region.

The Estonian problem was obviously much more complex, but after the defeat of Yudenich and Bermondt not insoluble. Since the Bolsheviks were as exhausted by the civil war as the Estonians, the time had come to negotiate. In fact the Bolsheviks approached the Estonians about negotiations well before the October offensive; on 12 September 1919 the Estonians informed the Allies about the approach, but they were advised to postpone negotiations until after the outcome of the offensive. It was natural that after the collapse of the Whites, the Estonians would ask again for Allied permission to approach the Bolsheviks. On 25 November 1919 they were told to resume their talks and on 1 December 1919 negotiations were started at Dorpat. They were to prove long, tortuous and successful.

Even prior to negotiations the Soviets had declared that they were prepared to recognise Estonian independence subject to a few qualifications. The most important qualification was the North Western Army, but certain territorial problems also figured high on their list of qualifications. As for the defeated Russian armies the Estonians were not free agents and could not satisfy the Bolsheviks immediately. The Allies, especially the French, wanted to reconstitute the North Western Army from the surviving soldiers and the Bermondt Corps troops who refused to withdraw to Germany. This the Estonians opposed most resolutely, for they feared that once reconstituted the North Western Army would simply topple their nationalist regime; backed by the British they prevented the Allies from executing this plan. However, they needed the White army as a counterbalance to the Bolsheviks and if the Allies implemented their other plan, which meant that the Whites were evacuated elsewhere, they would have been seriously weakened. The Finns resolutely refused to send troops to Estonia to replace the Whites and as if to drive in their points, the Red Army counter-attacked several times on the Narva front. But these attacks were beaten off with the aid of British naval guns, another reminder of how precariously independent the Estonians were.

Throughout December 1919 the Allies could not decide what to do with the North Western Army. The French in particular hoped for some sort of agreement between the Whites and Estonians, who obviously needed each other. General Niessel, who was in the area as the head of the second Allied mission, reported to Paris several times that a compromise was possible, but when on 16 December 1919 he convened a conference to Riga to force the Estonians to tolerate the reconstitution of the North Western Army on their territory, he failed in his effort. The Allies hesitated, studied all sorts of alternatives and in the meantime asked the Estonians to delay their negotiations with the Bolsheviks, until final decisions were made by the Allies. Only on 24 December 1919 did the British finally decide that the North Western Army should be dissolved and the Russians given a free choice of staying in the country or emigrating. This British decision was accepted as a solution by the other Allies on 1 January 1920 and the Estonians could really start peace negotiations with the Bolsheviks.

In Estonia Allied decisions were anticipated. In order to speed up negotiations the Red Army attacked again on the Narva front and though the Estonian army beat off the attacks, it had to ask the British, who were taking part in the fighting, to be allowed to conclude an armistice with the Bolsheviks. When this was granted the Bolsheviks insisted on a precondition – the Estonians had to guarantee to disarm and expel from their territories all Russian Whites. Fortunately this guarantee coincided with the Allied decision and on 31 December 1919 an armistice was signed which came into force on 3 January 1920. Negotiations continued throughout January and on 2 February 1920 a peace treaty was signed at Dorpat, which finally made Estonia an independent state.

The solution of the Latvian problem was even more difficult than the Estonian. After the withdrawal of Bermondt and German troops the Latvians had no counters and could not hope to face the Red Army successfully on their own. They thought at first that they could restore the military balance by combining with the Lithuanians, but this was really no solution, for the Lithuanians were propped up by the powerful Polish army which had just routed the Red Army. General Niessel therefore suggested to Marshal Foch that the Poles should be called in to restore the situation in Latvia. This idea was vehemently opposed by the British, who feared all sorts of complications – the Poles were already quarrelling with the Lithuanians and they could easily overextend themselves. However, in the end this was the only practical solution; both Lithuania and Estonia agreed to it, and Latvia quickly signed a military convention with Poland before its fronts against the Red Army had time to collapse. As a result a combined operation against the Red Army was launched and Dvinsk was taken. To everyone's surprise the Polish army, which did most of the fighting, promptly handed the city to the Latvians.

With the front stabilised the Latvians could concentrate on retaking their country from the Germans and Russians. By 9 December 1919 German evacuation was practically completed and the Russians also disappeared without much intervention by the Latvian army. Although they were approached by the Bolsheviks at the same time as the Estonians they could not start negotiations because of the internal situation. However, with their territory now clear of Germans and Whites and after the success of their combined offensive they were ready to renew contacts with the Bolsheviks. The Red Army, also duly impressed, agreed to an armistice on 1 February 1920 and a peace treaty was finally signed at Riga on 11 August 1920. Only Lithuania waited for a peaceful solution, which was to be achieved within the Russo-Polish context.

Thus ended civil war and intervention in the Baltic region, former provinces of the Russian Empire. As everywhere else the Whites proved so weak and divided that they appeared doomed from the beginning. In contrast local nationalists emerged from the struggle victorious – Finland permanently independent and Latvia, Lithuania and Estonia with 20 years of that experience. The struggle was complicated by the intervention of great powers, the Allies, chiefly the British, and Germany. It was largely British military aid and political skill which ultimately forced the Bolsheviks to deal with and recognise the new Baltic states. It was Britain, too, which prevented Germany from gaining a power footing in the region and maintaining its influence there. But all this was achieved only because both Germany and Russia were defeated in and worn out by the world war, and in this sense the solutions were temporary ones.

Otherwise the Baltic problem was insoluble. If either of the two powers, Germany or the USSR, really wanted to dominate the Baltic littoral, no other power could really prevent them from doing so. On 16 September 1919 the British Prime Minister, Lloyd George, put it quite succinctly: 'We cannot recognise Baltic independence, for would you [W.S. Churchill] fight for it, if our allies, the Russian Whites, won and claimed the provinces for themselves?' And while for the Baltic nationalities the solutions seemed honourable, for the Whites they smacked of betrayal, and the Allies were as embarrassed as anywhere in Russia.

Red and White Civil War

When summing up the civil war in Russia, 1917-1920, it would be easy, though inaccurate, to affirm that the Bolsheviks and the Red Army were superior to their White opponents and therefore won. It would be difficult to substantiate such a simplified summary and before anything of that sort is attempted, it is most meaningful to analyse the Bolsheviks and the Red Army at greater depth. The aim of this analysis is to isolate a few decisive factors which operated in their favour and enabled the Bolsheviks to emerge from the struggle victorious.

From the very beginning, November 1917, the Bolsheviks, led by Vladimir Ilyich Lenin, had one significant factor favouring them: they seized power by design in the imperial capital, Petrograd, and succeeded in consolidating their power in the central regions of Russia. It is equally significant to note that in practically all the border areas, in the *Okrainy*, Bolshevik attempts at imposing their power had collapsed under the slightest show of opposition. Moreover, these *okrainy* were largely inhabited by dissident nationalities, which instead of being interested in retaking power in Russia rather wanted to leave the Russian Empire and become independent states. Thus because of the victory of the Bolsheviks in the central Russian regions, all the opposing Russians, the Whites, had to build up their bases of resistance to the Bolsheviks in these largely non-Russian territories.

Thus from the beginning of the struggle the Whites were at a disadvantage. While their Red opponents controlled the central mass of Russia which was thickly populated and contained most of the large cities and industry as well as fertile agricultural land, the Whites were perched precariously in non-Russian regions with local separatist interests operating strongly against them. In the South the Caucasus actively resisted any encroachment on its territory by either the Whites or Reds. The Caucasian peoples – the Georgians, Armenians, Adzerbeijanis and others – aimed at achieving independence and as a consequence mainly damaged the White cause. The Whites who had their base in South Eastern Russia needed the Caucasus as their rear, but such needs cut no ice with the dissident nationalists, who did not want to have anything to do with Russia, Red or White. However, the Whites continued to claim the Caucasus as a Russian territory and thus made sure of the enmity of the nationalities as well as of mutual damage. In turn the Caucasians tried to influence the Allies and others to check and moderate White claims and ambitions, and this in concrete terms meant that they tried and succeeded in limiting the extent of Allied aid on which the Whites so vitally depended. The Whites could never become so strong as to destroy the Caucasian states to enforce their claims. In addition the Caucasians openly supported any dissidents in White territories and fought the Whites in their rear whenever they felt threatened. Apart from these independent nationalities the Whites in the South had the problem of the autonomists, that is, people who did not aim at independence and were ethnically Russians. These included chiefly the various Cossack voyska (territories), especially the Don and Kuban, as well as 'loyal' Caucasian tribes – Crimeans, Tartars, etc. These autonomists also resisted White encroachment, but were either too weak or too disorganised, and had to submit, albeit very reluctantly. They also weakened the White movement and perhaps even more fatally than the independent nationalities: their morale tended to collapse during the decisive battles of the civil war.

In the West it was Poland, which had left the Russian Empire as soon as it began to crack up. Back in 1917 the Provisional Government had granted it independence after the war, but while Poland marched on independently thereafter, the Ukraine was not so fortunate. It was much less united than Poland, its social fabric collapsed altogether as the result of the war and it also made the cardinal mistake of asking for protection from Germany, a power which was defeated in the war. Both the Red and White Russians made their bids in the Ukraine, both were resisted tooth and nail, but in the end the Reds won because of the weakness and division of the Ukrainian nationalists. An additional reason for their defeat was the number of large-scale anarchist movements in the Ukraine, the principal ones led by Ataman Grigoriev and the peasant Makhno, with whom no-one could come to terms. Thus the western okrainy were even more precarious as bases than the South; it was no wonder that both South and West, with the exception of Poland, were reconquered by the central Russian power, the Bolsheviks.

In the North and North West of Russia the struggle in the civil war was as confused as in the South and West. In the North West the Whites had interminable conflicts with the three nationalities, the Lithuanians, Latvians and Estonians, who aspired to independence, and who as a consequence did their utmost to prevent the Whites from organising themselves properly. Up to the armistice in the West this region was occupied by German armies, whose withdrawal after November 1918 complicated the situation for the Whites even more. As the withdrawal was gradual and German troops were not replaced by Allied troops the Russian White movement split into two groups: one seeking aid from the withdrawing Germans and the other from the Allies who had not yet arrived in strength. After this division the position of the Whites in the North West was clearly hopeless. In Finland internal conflicts between Reds and Whites were resolved decisively in April 1918, when the Finnish Whites, with German aid, defeated the Finnish Reds, established themselves firmly over the whole of Finland and eventually become independent. Finland was the exception in the North as Poland was in the West. Though after the defeat of the Whites the Baltic nationalities did become independent, they were not stable enough to survive another upheaval some 20 years later, when they were incorporated into the USSR.

The Whites owed their existence in the North entirely to the Allied landings at Murmansk and Archangel. At Murmansk the Allies were invited to help the local Soviet to defend itself against the Bolsheviks, while the landing at Archangel came as a result of the Allied policy of helping the Czechoslovak Legion in June 1918. Both bases were most unsuitable for any White movement and clearly Russia proper could not be conquered from and by these thinly inhabited regions. In fact the Allies and Whites in the region were purely of nuisance value and quite weak Red Army forces were able to contain them. As elsewhere the Whites in the region were also hopelessly divided, intent on seizing power from each other rather than defending themselves against the Bolsheviks. Thus when the Allied forces were evacuated from the two bases in autumn 1919, both Murmansk and Archangel almost immediately fell to the Red Army, while the Whites withdrew on available ships to other White-held territory.

In the East, which in this context includes Siberia and the Far East, but not Central Asia, Trans-Caspian territory, or Mongolia, the Whites seized power from the Bolsheviks as a result of direct foreign intervention, i.e. the revolt of the Czechoslovak Legion in May 1918. For a relatively long time the Legion maintained these regimes in power and the collapse of the White regimes coincided with the withdrawal of the Legion from Siberia and the Far East. However, the weakness of Siberia stemmed from the fact that this was no Russia but a continent on its own, containing hundreds of nationalities, which though insufficiently organised to obtain independence were sufficiently powerful to subvert any power they disliked. Thus it was these nationalities which in any case precluded a real internal unity, even if it were not for the basic Russian division between the Social Revolutionaries and the others (liberals, conservatives, monarchists, regionalists, etc.). Unity there was well nigh impossible, for even the Cossack voyska (Urals, West Siberian, Amur, etc.) jealously guarded their autonomies, the Urals voysko keeping completely separate from White Siberia. It only occasionally entered into Siberian affairs confusing them still further. However, in the end these antagonistic forces weakened the

White regime politically to such an extent that it collapsed in chaos; militarily these same forces were the direct cause of the White Army's defeat. The defections of the Ukrainian brigade and the Kirghiz cavalry during the Kolchak offensive in spring 1919 were the turning points of the battle. Farther East Ataman Semenov and the Far Eastern Republic could only remain in existence as long as the Japanese army remained in the Russian Far Eastern provinces; they fell to the Bolsheviks as soon as the Japanese withdrew.

Thus politically and demographically the Bolshevik central position was undoubtedly of tremendous importance, and it was meant to be. The Bolsheviks seized power in the two administrative capitals, Petrograd and Moscow, by design. These two capitals and the regions between them practically controlled the whole of Russia. What was even more important the Bolsheviks had time to establish themselves firmly in these central regions before the civil war started, and consequently fought the civil war from well-prepared defence positions, which made their task much easier compared to the Whites, who invariably had to attack. Moreover the Petrograd and Moscow regions were also the most heavily industrialised, which made the Bolsheviks less vitally dependent on foreign aid, which in any case no-one offered them. It is true that the Whites conquered the Donets and Ekaterinburg (Urals) industrial regions, but they found them devastated and disorganised, failed to reorganise them and in any case controlled them for too short a time to gain any appreciable advantage. Tactically it was probably easier to defend central Russia, although the Bolsheviks had to face practically the same problems as the Whites: local nationalities in revolt, peasant uprisings and White conspiracies. In contrast to the Whites they could afford to treat these problems differently. From the beginning Lenin and the Bolsheviks preached federalism in the future and never mentioned the reconstitution of imperial Russia. They never employed national forces of their allies in battles and operations which could have resulted in decisive Red defeats and would have brought about their allies' autonomy or independence. Nationalities fought in the Red Army as auxiliaries who, as a result of Red victories, came to power in their regions and provinces within the future Federal Union of the Soviets. With the exception of Red Ukrainians and Red Don Cossacks, the Bolsheviks preferred the Kirghiz cavalry to fight in the Ukraine and Poland, the Chinese units as security forces, the Latvians in the Volga region, the dissident Caucasians in the South against Denikin, etc. Hence the Bolsheviks had much less trouble with nationalist dissidents than the Whites and could make better use of them in the military sphere. As with the Whites the various peasant uprisings caused the Bolsheviks considerable headaches and tactical defeats, but they were never allowed to spread and disrupt the whole rear, and when negotiations failed, sharp, decisive counter-measures, usually carried out by Cheka detachments, proved extremely efficient. The Whites never came to grips with their peasant rebels, who were allowed to organise themselves into partisan and para-military units. Too late the Whites tried to hunt and destroy them, while usually fighting the Red Army at the same time. The peasant rebel armies did play a significant part in the Whites' downfall; the Reds destroyed them after the civil war.

The central position of the Bolsheviks gave them many tactical advantages. Thus they could coordinate their military operations in a more rational way than the Whites. They could make better use of the only vehicle of locomotion in Russia, the railways. In contrast all the White operations had the appearance of improvisation and haphazard execution: Denikin's operation against Moscow was launched after Kolchak's offensive had failed; Yudenich's second drive on Petrograd followed the failure of Denikin's operation. With the exception of the revolt of the Czechoslovak Legion, which was a surprise to every one, all the White operations were predictable, and even when their timing proved a surprise, they invariably permitted the Red Army to re-group and check them one after the other. The Whites seemed to thrive on improvisation and in their eagerness to get to Moscow first they absolutely refused to coordinate their offensives and operations. Of course, there were also objective difficulties which prevented the Whites from acting in a more rational way: Kolchak's envoy to Denikin, Tolstoy-Miloslavsky, took four months to arrive from Siberia to the South, while Denikin's envoy, Grishin-Almazov, never arrived, for he was captured by the Bolsheviks and perished on the Caspian sea. The Whites depended for their lines of communication on foreigners, mainly on the French and Paris, though the Athens embassy was also used as a relaying post. On the other hand the Red Army was from the beginning under an unified command and used the internal railway network to transfer troops from one front to another as the military situation required. Moreover, when the Red Army finally destroyed the okrainy bases of the Whites, they destroyed with them the separatist nationalist movements, and destroyed them so well that the Bolsheviks were not hamstrung by these nationalities either in the pacification of the whole country or in the future federal arrangements.

Thus tactically and strategically the White armies were probably at a disadvantage. However, because of the solid backing that the Russian officers had given to the White cause, it could reasonably be expected that they would be at an advantage in matters of organisation, training and supplies. On closer examination it appears that the concentration of senior officers in the White armies had in fact proved a drawback rather than an advantage. Paradoxically it was the Red Army which developed and retained the best aspects of the Imperial Army, while the White armies had to make do with the worst, corruption included. It was the Red Army, created by political amateurs, which inherited the Imperial Army's administration, barracks and depots. Without these the White generals seemed lost and their recruitment and training proved inferior to that of the Red Army. While the Whites tended to rely on volunteers and their mobilisation orders were improvised, came late and were not observed, the Red Army, by contrast, proved most methodical, strictly enforced mobilisation orders and proved much more successful than the White. Thus In May 1918 the Red Army consisted of some 306,000 men, while in December 1920, at the end of the civil war, the command and administrative staff alone amounted to 446,729. In fact between May 1918 and October 1920 the Bolsheviks succeeded in mobilising some 5,498,000 men, which was several times more than the Whites. Naturally, most of the Bolshevik recruits never saw active service: 2,587,000 served in reserve armies and 391,000 in labour units. However, 1,780,000 men were drawing military rations, of whom at least 800,000 were actual combatants. This tremendous organisational achievement was due to the closest coordination and cooperation of political, military and security organisations and without this close cooperation the Bolsheviks would have lapsed into the same chaos as the Whites, with their recruits turning instantly into deserters, and subsequently into dangerous partisans.

Trotsky, as Commissar for War, was primarily responsible for the organisation of the Red Army and to make his army really effective he was forced to discard many of the revolutionary innovations dating back to March 1917. Thus in the Red Army officers were not elected by their men, but appointed with their authority largely restored. Necessarily Trotsky had to appoint a large number of former imperial officers to command his army, and to control them politically and make sure of their loyalty he retained another innovation of 1917, the duality of command. A Bolshevik political commissar was attached to all Red Army units, from company to regiment, division to corps and army, up to the field command, the last being the Bolshevik replacement of the old general staff. Thus the Red Army not only had the ordinary structure of command, but was also subject to political control by the Bolshevik Party. To make the control real the Bolshevik Party stiffened all units with its own members. This stiffening of the army by Bolshevik cadres and the efficient use of security forces, the Cheka, was largely responsible for keeping the Red Army together, at least until the end of the civil war. To prevent large-scale desertions the Bolshevik government restored capital punishment at the fronts and mercilessly enforced it. Moreover to retain the loyalty of the former imperial officers Trotsky instituted a system of hostages — for treason and desertion an officer's family was executed — and on the whole succeeded in forcing the officers, called specialists (*spets*), to fight for his cause. However, despite these draconian measures many an officer did desert and betrayed the Bolsheviks; men also mutinied, some newly formed units refused to go into battle, and others left the front without permission even with their commissars and all. Still the scale of desertions and betrayal was not comparable to that of the Whites. In any case in such occurrences of indiscipline Trotsky did not hesitate to apply supreme punishment to all and sundry. Summary courts martial were kept busy and the Chinese internationalist units, reserved for security tasks, carried out executions by firing squad without halt. At least once Trotsky himself took part in a summary execution when in August 1918, in order to stop the Red Army's precipitate retreat from Kazan, he ordered executions of every twelfth man in a regiment which was running from the battlefield. In this instance the executions included regimental commissars — Bolshevik Party members. There were very few instances of such determination and ruthlessness in the White Armies, but it was this merciless terror as well as intelligent organisation that had kept the Red Army in the field fighting under Trotsky and the field command.

Although the Bolshevik Party disliked the idea of reconstituting the general staff and general headquarters (Stavka), or field command, it was forced into coordinating the fighting on the civil war fronts as they arose, and inevitably had to form the Stavka. At the early stages of the civil war the Supreme Military Soviet, whose chairman was Trotsky and whose deputies were Podvoysky, Sklyansky and Danishevsky, all experienced soldiers, had acted as a command centre. However, in April 1918 the All-Russian Supreme Staff had to be set up to deal with the worsening military situation. Still later the Republican Revolutionary Military Soviet was formed and became the top political council of war with Trotsky as chairman and Sklyansky, I.N. Smirnov, Rosengolts, Raskolnikov, Muralov and Yurenev as leading members. This body then appointed the ex-imperial colonel, Vatsetis, so far commander of the Latvian Rifle Division, as Commander-in-Chief of the Red Army, and Vatsetis collected his field staff which became the nucleus of the general staff. He selected other imperial colonels, B. Shaposhnikov and P.P. Lebediev, for his Stavka and they became responsible for operations, planning and coordination of the five Red Armies and five fronts then in existence.

After the formation of the field staff, when real military operations were re-established, Trotsky had to dismiss most of the self-appointed Bolshevik commanders, who proved unable to carry out military orders or conduct military operations. Their places were taken up by the *spets* — imperial officers and the Red Army's generalship began to measure itself with the White's. On the Eastern front, where five Red Armies were concentrated, the overall command fell to the former imperial colonel S.S. Kamenev, who proved himself so well that he subsequently replaced Colonel Vatsetis as C-in-C, a post which was clearly above the intellectual capacity of the latter. Of the five armies fighting in the East, three were commanded by ex-imperial officers (1st by Tukhachevsky, 2nd by Shorin and 4th by Baltiysky and later Khvesin) and one by an ex-imperial NCO

(3rd, by Lashevich); only Blyumberg, in command of the 5th Red Army, was a Bolshevik commander without imperial antecedents. Although the 'wild' Bolsheviks had been eliminated the operational performance of the Red commanders varied widely. In December 1918 Admiral Kolchak's conquest of Perm proved to be one of the greatest disasters suffered by the Red Army, despite Commissar Gusev, who had kept a close eye on this front. The 4th Red Army had to be reorganised altogether and Gusev proposed for its new commander not a professional soldier, but a Bolshevik intellectual, M.V. Frunze, which turned out to be an excellent choice and the 4th Army soon redeemed its tarnished reputation. Still it was Admiral Kolchak's White Armies which struck first in the spring of 1919: again initially they split the Red fronts wide open forcing the Red armies to retreat. In these conditions the relations between the field command and the Eastern front became strained and the Red Army lived through its first crisis of command. Trotsky left Moscow to supervise operations on the Eastern front in person. Inevitably command reshuffle followed: Frunze took over the command of the Turkestan Army, but also retained the 4th; G.D. Gai became the commander of the 1st, Shorin of the 2nd, Mezheninov of the 3rd and Tukhachevsky of the 5th. Frunze also formed a separate Revvdensoviet for his southern group of armies and placed V.V. Kuybyshev on it as his commissar. On 28 April 1919 the reorganised Red armies went into the attack, and completely out-fought and out-generalled the White armies.

Even while victorious and advancing the Red Army went through a series of crises, which invariably resulted in changes in operations and personnel. Vatsetis, who insisted on directing the operations on the Eastern front, transferred Colonel Kamenev, who persistently opposed him, to the Northern front, and put the Northern front commander, General A.A. Samoilo, in his place. The new commander, however, hesitated too long, changed his orders for a general offensive several times, and after objections from army and political leaders he was sent back North and Kamenev was restored to his command. All these moves and the power struggle went on while the Red Army was fighting one of its most important battles and success came despite the trouble. This was mainly due to the excellent performance of the Red Army on the divisional level: hard fighting continued unabated with capable commanders and commissars, such as Kashirin, Mamontov, Zhigalin, I.N. Smirnov and others, scoring great victories.

As a result of the political struggle on the Eastern front Trotsky registered his first political defeat in his career as Commissar for War. Through his nominee, Vatsetis, he was in fact responsible for all the changes in the East, and since they all proved rather unfortunate Trotsky's political opponents, had a pretext for censoring the arrogant commisssar. Stalin, Gusev, Kuybyshev and others finally persuaded Lenin that Trotsky had to be checked and their proposals were accepted and implemented. These proposals entailed the sacking of the Commander-in-Chief, Vatsetis, and his replacement by S.S. Kamenev; they also contained the continuation of offensive activity on the Eastern front, while the old command favoured a halt to operations and concentration in the South against General Denikin. By July 1919 Trotsky had to yield on all points and even saw his republic Revvdensoviet reorganised and his personal enemies, Gusev, Smilga, Rykov and S.S. Kamenev, added to it. Still the Eastern front gamble came off and Western Siberia was overrun. By then, however, Trotsky and the new high command had to concentrate their attention on the Southern front, where the military situation deteriorated with incredible rapidity late in 1919.

While early in 1919 the Bolsheviks concentrated all their military power in the East they only really had the 10th Red Army in the South facing the Don Cossacks and General Denikin. The men who led this army were quite bizarre characters and it was with them that the Caucasian Bolshevik, Stalin, struck up a friendship, after interrupting his original mission of procuring food supplies for his native Caucasus. The local commander was the ex-imperial NCO Voroshilov, with ex-tailor Shchadenko as commissar, and local orator Minin thrown in. It quickly became obvious that instead of conducting military operations this new-style leadership of the Red Army at Tsaritsyn (later called Stalingrad and still later Volgograd) indulged in card-playing and vituperative denunciations of Trostsky and the field command. They certainly aroused antagonism and in the end Trotsky succeeded in dispersing them: Stalin was transferred elsewhere and even Voroshilov had to leave the Tsaritsyn army for the Ukraine. But even then Trotsky's problems in the South were not solved, for suddenly General Denikin struck against the 9th Red Army in May 1919 and scattered it: Vsevolod, the commander, preferred to join the Whites, and Trotsky once again found himself in disagreement with Kamenev as to how the Southern crisis should be tackled. Kamenev favoured a drive into the Don region and another drive along the Volga to prevent a Denikin-Kolchak junction. He hoped that this dual drive against the Whites would destroy their bases in the Don and Kuban and thus knock them out of the conflict. However, the Kamenev plan meant that the 10th Red Army would be given top operational tasks and Trotsky had not yet forgotten his quarrels with Stalin-Voroshilov about this army. He was reluctant to favour such a troublesome army with such important operations and also objected to the proposals of Kamenev, with whom he was not on the best of terms. In the end he had to give in and work out a compromise: he appointed V.N. Yegorov to command in the South and carry out the Kamenev plan. The result was not brilliant: the two army commanders, Shorin and Selivachev, failed to achieve the objectives of the Kamenev plan and both Trotsky and Kamenev had grounds to complain about each other. When in turn the

Whites struck back and their cavalry proved particularly effective in the struggle, it became clear that the Red Army would have to reorganise and employ the same arm to check the Whites. Still Trotsky opposed the development of the cavalry, for once again the two Don Cossacks, Dumenko and Budyonny, who had initially organised it, were friends of Stalin and Voroshilov.

It is curious to see that the organisation of the Red cavalry, whose importance vastly increased with Denikin's breakthrough, was hindered because of bad personal relations. Budyonny, who took over the Red cavalry corps from Dumenko after he had fallen ill, was Voroshilov's friend and was therefore detested and underestimated by Trotsky. Trotsky opposed the development of cavalry for this reason alone, even when it became clear that it was a tactical weapon of immense importance. Still after November 1918 the Red cavalry was re-equipped and began to be used against the Cossack cavalry of the Whites. Ultimately, and a little paradoxically, all the significant military leaders came from this force: the future Marshals Timoshenko, G.K. Zhukov and Rokossovsky. More immediately it became a counter to the White cavalry forces led by Generals Mamontov and Shkuro, who with their raids into the Red rear were creating a particularly heavy havoc there and deciding many a battle waged in the proximity of Moscow between July and November 1919. Although the deployment of the Red cavalry meant the complete abandonment of the Kamenev plan and the re-adoption of Trotsky's original proposals both Kamenev and Trotsky had to compromise, for the situation became very serious indeed: the Whites were at Orel and Voronezh and another cavalry raid could have caused a complete collapse of the Red Army. The Southern front was therefore split into two groups of armies placed under Yegorov and Shorin: they were to strike simultaneously to the north west of Orel and east of Voronezh; Budyonny and his cavalry had to defeat Mamontov's cavalry and then drive a wedge between Denikin's Volunteers and Don Cossack armies. In November 1919, when this offensive was finally launched, it was carried out brilliantly and was immediately successful, the cavalry deciding most of the battles. With Mamontov's defeat Budyonny's raids caused in turn panic in the White rear and the White armies fell rapidly back to Rostov, their original base. In December 1919 Budyonny's cavalry corps became the 1st Red Cavalry Army with a separate Revvoysoviet, which not surprisingly comprised not only Voroshilov and Shchadenko but also Stalin. The Red Cavalry continued its triumphant advance far ahead of the supporting 8th, 9th and 10th Armies, until it reached the Bataisk Heights of Rostov, which were heavily invested with Don Cossack cavalry and the rest of Denikin's artillery. This was the Whites' last stand, blocking the Red Army from the Kuban base and North Caucasus. Shorin, the new commander in the South, ordered Budyonny to attack these prepared positions frontally and the

Red cavalry experienced its first defeat in battle. Still Shorin persisted with his orders and refused to allow Budyonny to take the heights from behind. After another unsuccessful attack Budyonny and the entire Revvdensoviet wished to resign in protest against Shorin's orders. In the end a political intervention and command reshuffle resolved this dangerous deadlock. Tukhachevsky, recently transferred to the South from the East, assumed the command, and he and his commissar, S. Ordjonikidze, finally permitted Budyonny to take the heights in his own way. Afterwards the fate of the Whites was sealed. They split into two groups: the one in the Crimea was isolated from the other on the Don and in the Kuban. The latter, after losing the heights, completely collapsed and simply ran off before the Red Army, which continued its advance gradually mopping up the Whites in the Kuban and North Caucasus. Part of the Whites' forces, chiefly the Volunteers, were evacuated from Novorossiisk to the Crimea, which, though isolated, was relatively safe and at this stage not threatened by the Reds. It was obvious that its turn would come when the Red Armies completed their reconquest of the Northern Caucasus. However, instead the Red Army became involved in the Polish war and the Crimea had to wait until that conflict was resolved.

The Red Army's operations against Poland can hardly be classed as civil-war conflict, although Poland, like the Baltic and Caucasian states, was also part of the extinct Russian Empire. Moreover it gave refuge to great numbers of Russian Whites, made an alliance with Ukrainian nationalists and was openly hostile towards the Soviet regime. This war seems to have been the first Bolshevik experiment of using the Red Army in foreign affairs. Since November 1917 the Bolshevik leadership hoped that as a result of the world war the combattant countries would disintegrate and extreme left wing forces would come to power, thus bringing about the long-awaited world revolution. After the armistice in November 1918 grave difficulties did arise in both Allied and central power countries, but the countries did not collapse, and even when they did, as was the case of the Austro-Hungarian Empire, the left wing extremists failed to gain power and the succession states continued to be governed by liberals instead. Still chaos and disruption were widespread all over Europe and elsewhere, and to exploit these conditions and help the world revolution on its way Lenin and the Bolsheviks founded the Komintern, an international organisation of all the revolutionary parties of the left. But the Komintern proved an instant disappointment; instead of fostering the revolution at home the fraternal delegates preferred to hang about in Moscow, at best taking part in the civil war. When unexpectedly Hungary became a Soviet republic this was no result of revolutionary activity but of a political shift in which the right wing elements overthrew the weak liberal regime and threw their weight behind Bela Kun and the extreme left. Since the Hungarian Soviet regime appeared to be very unstable and threatened from all quarters (especially from Romania) and the Komintern offered no solutions, Lenin began to consider buttressing it with his own Red Army. In 1919, when the Bolsheviks were far from winning the civil war in Russia this external experiment would probably have meant virtual suicide; such a war would have involved the Red Army, apart from Allied pressures, with Romania and though the latter was no military giant, it would have found it easier to deal with the invading Red Army than with the German Army. Fortunately this experiment did not proceed farther than the planning stage; Romania disposed of the Hungarian Soviet Republic by invading it. However in 1920 the Polish situation seemed more favourable to the Soviets: the civil war in Russia was practically won, an actual conflict arose between the two neighbouring countries and the Polish delegates to the Komintern were enthusiastic and optimistic about the outcome of this conflict. Thus Soviet Russia was ready to destroy nationalist-bourgeois Poland.

Throughout 1919 Poland, which was considered by the Soviets as a puppet state of the Western Allies, had shown a marked tendency towards expansion, especially at the expense of its Ukrainian and Byelorussian neighbours. However, when the Red Army finally defeated the Whites and Ukrainians and drove them out of the Ukraine, the Poles, who seemed unconcerned about the Ukraine proper, effected a *volte face,* concluded an alliance with the defeated Ukrainian nationalists and in a surprise invasion expelled the weak Red Army from the Ukraine in May 1920. The Bolsheviks, whose leadership contained a number of Russianised Poles, had been considering the best way of seizing power in Poland for some time; with the Polish invasion of the Ukraine they had finally got the best pretext for decisive action in Poland itself. Military plans were worked out even before the Polish invasion and as soon as the Red Army mounted its counter-attacks the Bolshevik Poles gathered in the vicinity of the front, formed a Polish Soviet government and were prepared to install themselves in Poland as soon as the Polish army was crushed by the Red Army. Soviet Russia concentrated all its military resources on this war — operations were suspended everywhere else, massive transfers of troops took place, the high command worked out a final plan of operations and all the military power that the Bolsheviks possessed was directed against Poland and for its destruction.

Both sides seemed to have prepared for the final clash, the Bolsheviks as early as February and March 1920. The Red Army's plan envisaged first the conquest of the Minsk area; from there a classic pincer operation by the Northern and Southern group of Red armies would destroy Poland. Still the surprise Polish invasion of the Ukraine caught the Red Army off balance; above all it upset some operational plans whose centre of gravity moved from Minsk farther south. However, within a month Soviet counter-attacks resulted in precipitate Polish withdrawal from the Ukraine and the situation seemed redressed in favour of the Red Army. By then the Red Army's strength on the Western front (in Byelorussia) was considerable: some 92,393 infantry and cavalry; but the South Western front, which was to deliver the southerly blow, was still unready. It is curious to note that the operational plans against Poland had previously been approved by the Bolshevik central committee which appointed its special watchdog, Stalin, to coordinate them and supervise closely their execution. The army of the Western front, now commanded by Tukhachevsky, who had changed places with V.N. Gittis (sent to North Caucasus), was to strike out through Byelorussia towards Warsaw and destroy the Polish armies opposing it there. The South Western front armies, commanded by Yegorov and strengthened by Budyonny's 1st Cavalry Army, were to deliver a supporting blow in the general direction of Rovno-Brest. Ultimately both army groups and fronts were going to meet and finally destroy the Polish army near Warsaw.

After their panicky withdrawal from the Ukraine the Polish army seemed in disarray and it looked as if the Red Army would achieve its objectives. However, while the West sounded alarmed by the turn of events and the Reds were confident of success, the Poles reorganised their armies, prepared the defence of Warsaw and even worked out their own offensive plans, for the Red Army, after initial success, seemed to have gone wrong on several counts. Thus Tukhachevsky's modified plan in Byelorussia went awry and his operations were bogged down in local swamps; he had to receive reinforcements intended for the South Western armies. Coordination between the various Red Armies was poor, and above all, the supporting blow from the South West was slow to develop. However, the most elementary error committed by all the Red Armies was that while they defeated and forced the Polish armies to withdraw, they did not encircle and annihilate them, as the plan had envisaged. It became obvious that the Poles were saving their armies for the decisive encounter near Warsaw, where they would be fighting most desperately to save their country from the traditional Russian invader. It was equally obvious that at the battle of Warsaw the Red Army would be at a disadvantage: it would be exhausted and disorganised after the long fight on the way, badly coordinated and above all it was not certain that the South Western forces would arrive in time for the decisive battle.

The South Western timetable of operations was upset by several factors which were not taken account of in the original plan against Poland. Thus the Whites, taking advantage of the Red Army's engagements on the Western front, launched their first offensive on 6 June 1920. I. Kh. Pauka's 13th Red Army was routed and the Whites occupied Northern Tauride. Yegorov had to divert his 1st Cavalry Corps, commanded by Zhloba, to relieve the hard-pressed 13th Army, but General Wrangel's veterans swiftly dealt with these reinforcements and defeated them. Thus throughout the war against Poland Wrangel's White armies remained a threat to the rear of the South Western armies. With the extension of operations into Poland Romania also became a potential threat. Yegorov had to divert forces from Poland to guard against this contingency. It was therefore no wonder that the supporting blow from the South West was so slow developing and it was a miracle that it came at all. The Northern group of armies were under the impression that the Polish armies were practically destroyed and taking Warsaw would be a joyride. Then the South Western front command misunderstood or misinterpreted instructions from field headquarters and instead of sending the weakened 1st Cavalry Army directly to Lublin and Warsaw it diverted it to Lwow. The rest of the South Western group of armies were detached from the Polish war area guarding against the Whites and Romania. The Southerly blow could not be delivered unless the South West received reinforcements, which it was refused. By then the Polish Commander-in-Chief, J. Pilsudski noticed the divergence between the Western and South Western fronts and decided to counter-attack at this spot. On 16 August 1920, with the Red Army quarrelling about orders, subordination and coordination, the Polish armies struck in the weak spot and within two days Tukhachevsky's Northern group lost its left wing; his moving wheel of advanced armies near Warsaw saw itself suddenly cut off from the rear. In subsequent operations the Poles trapped and destroyed practically all the Red armies of Tukhachevsky's group, while the élite Red cavalry forces never reached the battlefield near Warsaw. In turn they had to extricate themselves from encirclement and retreat into the Ukraine without achieving anything.

Thus the first full-scale 'foreign' war of the Red Army ended in disaster. As a result Poland finally cut itself free from Imperial and Soviet Russia and like Finland and the Baltic states also gained independence. Learning a lesson from the failure in Poland, subsequent 'foreign' wars conducted by the Red Army in the Caucasus, Central Asia and Far East proved invariably successful. After Poland the most pressing priority became the destruction of the Whites in the Crimea. With the Polish mistakes fresh in mind the Soviet high command prepared the operations against the Crimea very thoroughly: the armies from Poland were concentrated against Wrangel and reinforced from the Caucasus, Turkestan and even Siberia. The 1st Red Cavalry Army was also sent South and by mid-September 1920 the Red Army massed there some 38,400 infantry, more than 7,000 cavalry, 288 guns, 1,067 machine guns, 45 aircraft and seven armoured trains. Reinforcement continued to pour in and the 6th and 13th Red Armies were completely reorganised: Uborovich was put in command of the 6th Army and Mezhin became his commissar; F.K Mironov, and later O.I. Gorodovikov, commanded the 13th Army with Shchadenko as commissar. On Lenin's insistence M.V. Frunze was appointed as front commander and the Red Army was ready for the final battle of the civil war.

On 28 October 1920 Frunze launched his final offensive against Wrangel: he had some 100,000 infantry and 33,600 cavalry engaged in the battle and outnumbered Wrangel's forces by four to one. Although skilfully executed the Red offensive failed to achieve its initial objective, namely cutting off Wrangel's forces in Northern Tauride and destroying them there. The Whites managed to slip through into the Crimea, where they took up prepared defensive positions. The Red Army had to storm these considerable obstacles if it wanted to conquer the peninsula. On 8 November 1920 Blyukher's 51st division from Siberia went into action against the White defences and only the following day breached them. The Whites finally gave in after they had found out that Blyukher's men had turned their flank by crossing the mouth of the river Sivash, on which a narrow path froze solid by a freak turn of the weather. The Whites hastily withdrew, embarked on prepared ships and left the Crimea altogether. The Red Army was also able to settle final accounts with Makhno and his Green Anarchists. On 16 November 1920 Frunze reported to Moscow that the Southern front had been wound up and all the significant fighting of the civil war had ended in victory.

Thus from this summary it can be seen that the organisation and functioning of the Red Army was far from faultless, though compared to the White Armies both were more than sufficient. Clearly the Bolsheviks mobilised more men than the Whites and controlled both men and officers better by means of political commissars and party cadres. Although they also had difficulties with political control, and commissars often confused or even paralysed military operations, they nevertheless solved these problems more efficiently and rapidly than the Whites and the Red Army was largely responsible for the victory.

In addition the Bolsheviks proved themselves more than sufficiently even in non-military matters. Although the Whites had virtually the monopoly of ex-imperial administrators, nonetheless the Reds turned out to be more successful administrators of conquered territories than the Whites. Since hardly any important governor or minister went over to the Bolsheviks they had to experiment with amateurs and did surprisingly well. On balance it seems that imperial administrators, despite their administrative qualities and skills, proved themselves to be a hindrance rather than a benefit to the Whites. In 'liberated' territories peasants who had previously risen against the Bolsheviks were rapidly disenchanted with the White Armies and administrators, for they usually brought in their wake former landlords whose lands they had seized and were working on. In the circumstances of the civil war no one was really sure who owned what, but the very presence of these dispossessed landlords made the peasants feel uneasy, so they rapidly switched their loyalties to the Reds and in the end longed for the Bolsheviks' return: only then could they be sure that the land settlement would not be reversed. Moreover, the Whites were given to chaotic reprisals once they seized territories from the Reds: thus the sons of murdered landlords would avenge themselves on the peasants in the village. By contrast the Reds were very selective and most efficient in eliminating potential leaders rather than disturbing the rank and file: their selected reprisals proved most effective for mass intimidation. Thus in the country the peasantry was relieved to have them back, although both armies practised looting, requisitions and confiscations.

Invariably something went wrong with the appointment of civil administrators in White-held territory: even when they proved administratively efficient they turned out to be politically disastrous. They never managed to collect enough executive officers, which in Russia meant largely policemen, to back them up. Thus most often the White armies remained in charge of internal administration and security and this formal division of power weakened both the army and the administration. At best the Whites ignored the workers, for they suspected them of Bolshevik sympathies even when they were members of the Menshevik and Social Revolutionary parties; most often they persecuted them needlessly, because of their baseless suspicions, thus making sure that the workers would rise against them at the first opportunity. Despite proclamations the Whites never brought back law and order: in the country they caused agricultural chaos because of the unresolved agrarian reform; in the towns they invariably caused economic ruin with unchecked inflation. In comparison Bolshevik plundering and requisitions of grain seemed relatively orderly, executions of hostages of White leaders always discreet and efficient. Their pacification policy in conquered areas was also superior: they searched efficiently for arms and summarily executed those who had concealed them.

If the Reds proved more efficient in practice than the White, in theory i.e. ideology and propaganda, they really excelled. Thus the Bolshevik Party seized power on behalf of the Soviets, the spontaneous politico-administrative bodies which sprang up all over Russia after March 1917. Although they were a party of the workers, the city proletariat, they claimed from the beginning that they based their power on the majority of the people, as represented by the Soviets. To control this majority the Bolsheviks purged the Soviets after November 1917 and replaced the non-Bolsheviks with their own men or sympathisers; thus they came to represent the Soviets in theory and practice. On the other hand they were not afraid to contradict their own ideological precepts: they handed over the seized lands to the peasants by official decree in November 1917, while the Whites proclaimed their 'reform' only in 1920, when they were already decisively beaten.

In the circumstances of the civil war the Bolsheviks quite realistically restrained themselves from making extravagant promises, but succeeded in convincing a majority of the Russian population that their way of governing the country would be to their advantage. Skilfully exploiting the divisions among the Whites the Bolsheviks paralysed White propaganda, which was never good in any case, and the stark reality in White-held territory nullified White ideology. In contrast to the Reds, the Whites never tired of making extravagant claims. They incessantly repeated that they intended to restore the Russian Empire, reconstitute old or new Russia, which meant the restitution of either the tsarist or the Provisional Government systems, both obviously lost causes, or else they spoke of democracy, freedom, elections, law and order, and all that was unrealistic in a civil war situation. The contrast between ideology and reality was such that Red propaganda could easily demolish any White claim or promise. On balance the Russian people probably came to the conclusion that the Bolsheviks were a lesser evil.

Perhaps most unexpectedly the Bolsheviks proved far superior in handling foreign affairs. They had two advantages in tackling these problems: 1. they were not saddled with old allies of the *ancien régime,* and 2. Lenin, Trotsky, Chicherin and Litvinov, who concerned themselves principally with foreign relations, were above all politicians and not civil servants-diplomats. Thus they had no previous experience (only Chicherin was for a short time a clerk in the tsarist Ministry of Foreign Affairs), no allies and neccessarily had to proceed in the trial-and-error way. Still 'revolutionary' common sense proved sufficient to paralyse their enemies by playing them off against each other. Immediately after the *coup d'état* Lenin used the Germans against the Allies and very largely succeeded in splitting the latter; later, during the civil war, Germans were used to paralyse Allied intervention. The Whites were no choosers, and though they had plenty of politicians and diplomats, experienced and skilful in foreign affairs, it was their generals and their narrow military interests which determined White allies and policies. The Whites therefore appeared as the undignified puppets of Britain and France, while the Bolsheviks seemed independent Russian patriots defending the country against foreign interventionists. Thus General Janin thought that he would run Siberia for France and Admiral Kolchak was supposed to run Siberia for Britain; General Denikin was a British general, while the others, Yudenich and Miller, were supposed to be British pocket generals. Whether they really were is immaterial now, but at the time such reputations made even their fellow imperial generals join the Red Army. Above all the Allied politicians treated them as servile satellites supposed to carry out Allied policies and incidentally also defeat their Bolshevik opponents. Only General Wrangel achieved a measure of independence by playing Britain against France, but then he was the very last White leader, with no hope of success. All the other interventionist countries had their puppets: the Japanese had their Atamans-Generals Semenov, Kalmykov and Horvat, while the Americans 'controlled' a much less distinguished bevy of Social Revolutionary politicians and colonels. Not only were these White Russians treated with disdain, but they were not permitted to act with the slightest independence, for invariably such actions would have contradicted Allied policies and interests. In their frustration many Russian generals and politicians turned in despair to Germany, their erstwhile enemy, thus making sure that they would be abandoned by both Allies and Germany alike.

Lenin and the Bolsheviks were more skilful: they never committed themselves to either side, treating them all as wicked imperialists to be made use of against each other. They also had a small power card, which forced all others to listen to the Bolsheviks: the world revolution. Though the card was little indeed, as Hungary and Germany had shown, it was ultimately sufficient to bring a peaceful settlement in international affairs. The exploitation of the basic division between Allied and German interests in Russia proved satisfactory, albeit precarious. In November 1917 the Bolsheviks turned to Germany to conclude a separate peace and thus force the Allies to do likewise. Although their attempt at general peace failed, the Bolsheviks gained a breathing space to reorganise and consolidate their power. During this period of consolidation the Allies failed to dislodge the Bolsheviks from power although the Germans almost did; they detested the new masters of Russia as much as the Allies. Still Germany was defeated before it could do anything decisive against the Bolsheviks and the Allies once again split as to the policies to be pursued in Russia after the war − Britain on the whole wanted to give support and intervene against the Bolsheviks through the Great Russian element, while France preferred to base herself and her policies of intervention on dissident nationalities. The inevitable conflict of policies confused all the Allied forces involved in the civil war on the White side, not to mention the Whites themselves, and only the Bolsheviks benefited from this confusion. Germany was also confused by the contradictions of Allied policies in Russia, and after the war tried to safeguard her own interests in Russia and in some of the former Russian provinces. German troops still occupied Russian territory and much depended on whom they would leave in control of these territories. However, Allied determination to liquidate all German interests in Russia led to the paradoxical *rapprochement* between the Germans and Bolsheviks in Russia: the Germans handed occupied territories either to the Bolsheviks or forces near to them rather than to the Allies or Whites fighting with their support. They also paralysed White movement and military operations by supporting their own forces, ostensibly against the Bolsheviks. The confusion was resolved by the final expulsion of the Germans from Russia, but once again the Bolsheviks proved the chief beneficiaries. Frustrated militarily and politically the Germans began to make economic offers to the Bolsheviks and inevitably split the Allies again. Since the Allied-sponsored White movements began to collapse and social unrest began to spread even in the victorious Allied countries, Allied policies in Russia were modified, the Whites abandoned and a *modus vivendi* sought with the Bolsheviks. After the victory in the civil war theirs was also a victory in international affairs and it sharply contrasted with White failure.

It is clear that all the Bolshevik victories were organised by their politicians and that politics was of paramount importance. It was above all their leader, Lenin, who had left a personal and indelible mark on all policies and who could be called without exaggeration the chief architect of Bolshevik victory in the civil war. Of course it can be said that his political intransingence caused the civil war in the first instance; however, once the civil war became reality all the policies that he formulated and advocated led to victory. One of his most important policies was the tactical alliance with the peasantry: Lenin gave the confiscated land to the peasants by an official decree thus substantially influencing the eventual outcome of the civil war. In international affairs it was again Lenin who was largely responsible for the policy of non-commitment, although he left others (Chicherin, Litvinov) to apply this policy as skilfully as possible. In contrast to the White politicians Lenin considered that politics and policies came first and that civil war was just another means to carry them out. From his study of Clausewitz he knew enough of the practice of civil war to refuse to be involved directly in it. Thus he and his party continued to exercise power normally in the interlude of consolidation, between November 1917 and May 1918, and even after, despite the open conflict. Lenin continued as head of the government trying to re-establish central administration in Russia: he held elections for Soviet congresses, reported to these congresses on the state of affairs and his governmental action, passed laws and through his administration organised the rear, especially war industries, and transport. Through the Bolshevik Party Lenin continued to mobilise its members for the struggle and to use party cadres in the civil war — one of the most crucial factors of victory. Lenin also continued his party work as if no civil war existed: the leadership met regularly, held elections for congresses and continued internal discussion of problems, though naturally most effort went into the civil war. Although Lenin refused to be involved directly in the civil war and aimed at political normalcy, he nevertheless kept a sure grip on the conflict. He created new institutions to cope with this emergency: he personally presided over the Supreme Council of Defence through which he coordinated all the policies and administrative measures concerning the conduct of the civil war, such as industrial production, transport and security. Through the Bolshevik Party and its central committee he had control over the armies in the field: his political followers and allies were invariably members of army Revvoysoviets, and through these Soviets he approved or blocked any action or even operation of the Red Army. Through this channel Lenin also issued political directives to the Red Army which it then translated into military operations (Hungary, Poland). Ultimately all major military decisions by the Red Army were subject to approval by the Bolshevik Central Committee, i.e. by Lenin himself. Indeed Lenin had proved himself an ideal politician for the civil war and the Whites never produced anyone comparable to him; he had everything under firm political control and at the same time gave others a free hand to organise Bolshevik victory: Trotsky in the army, Dzerzhinsky in security.

L.D. Trotsky, who became a Bolshevik only in August 1917, was also a politician, above all an orator, comparable to Kerensky whom he ousted from power. He could galvanise crowds, and even crowds of soldiers after a world war, and at the same time be an efficient and feverish organiser of the Red Army with clear and realistic ideas of immediate necessities and priorities. Lenin consistently supported him within the party and in practice made him a supremo in military affairs, confidence which Trotsky put to good use. When in March 1918 he became Commissar for War and surveyed the incredible instrument at his disposal he immediately made bold decisions. He would scrap completely what was supposed to be the Bolshevik army — the puny Red Guards, detachments of sailors, Latvian riflemen and German and Austro-Hungarian prisoners of war — and build a new army, the Red Army.

As soon as he made this fundamental decision a whole series of controversial decisions had to be made and carried out. Again Lenin supported him, although some of the decisions went against the revolutionary grain of the Bolshevik Party: the new army would be a real army in the traditional sense, commanded by officers. Since no other officers were available the Red Army's officers would be selected from among the imperial ones. This was a calculated risk, for the officer-specialists were known for their hostility towards the Bolsheviks and once employed on a large scale they could conceivably turn this new instrument of Bolshevik policy against the party itself. Futhermore there was the question of self-made Bolshevik commanders, mainly ex-imperial NCO's, who had risen to command after November 1917 and who would undoubtedly be displaced by the professionals. Still, with Lenin's aid Trotsky overcame the opposition to his schemes within the party and at the same time made doubly sure of the new officers' loyalty. Ultimately it was thanks to these fundamental decisions that after a disastrous start Trotsky and his Red Army won the civil war.

Immediately afterwards Trotsky set most energetically and systematically about organising his new army along the new lines. He set up training academies for NCOs and officers of the new type, though again he had to employ imperial officers as instructors. In the end Trotsky did build up a new army, but he also preserved the imperial army traditions in training and ideology: his Red Army never became a revolutionary army with indiscipline, partisan type of command and operations and other characteristics and innovations. The Red Army he created was a conventional almost 'professional' body of men, an instrument of the leaders in power, not even under his own control, as he found out subsequently to his detriment. This was perhaps a little surprising, for from the beginning Trotsky handpicked all the personnel in his ministry and field command as well as political commissars. Undoubtedly Lenin saw to it that Trotsky's power within the new army was nicely checked and balanced by his opponents within the Bolshevik political leadership, of whom the most redoubtable were Stalin and Dzerzhinsky. However, during the civil war it cannot be doubted that Trotsky served Lenin, the Bolshevik revolution and the Bolshevik Party loyally. In the performance of this service Trotsky was totally dedicated, ruthless and at the same time inspiring. After the rout at Kazan Trotsky discriminatingly executed every twelfth man of deserting units and had shot even political commissars, members of the ruling Bolshevik Party. At the same time he rallied demoralised soldiers, and persuaded them to go into action again and defeat the Czechoslovaks and the Whites who had routed them such a short time ago. Trotsky knew how to heighten his influence with the soldiers, for he was an accomplished actor who even dressed up with consummate skill for such occasions to look strange and impressive. He always travelled in an armoured train, which was not only his HQ but also the Ministry of War and Bolshevik Party propaganda department. On the train he had a platoon of personal guards, machine-gunners, motor cars, ammunition, medical stores, weapons, in fact everything to make it quite independent at the front or in the rear. With this train Trotsky rushed about Russia, from one sector to another, from one front to another, leaving in its trail Red victories. In time the man and the train became a symbol of victory and an unifying factor of the fronts: the Whites never found an equivalent to this man, this mobile GHQ or the symbol.

Two other Bolshevik politicians deserve a mention for their contribution to Bolshevik victory in the civil war: Stalin and Dzerzhinsky, both non-Russians, both specialists in their own field rather than soldiers. Stalin became Lenin's troubleshooter — he was entrusted with top military-political missions and investigations, which invariably resulted in significant improvements in the Red Army's performance, if not outright victories. Lenin, while using Stalin to counterbalance Trotsky, did not always support his views or his findings. Thus it was Stalin who espoused the cause of the partisans within the Red Army, supported them throughout and eventually lost, as Lenin put his support behind Trotsky in this matter. Still Voroshilov, Budyonny and Shchadenko, to mention the most important 'partisans', owed everything to Stalin and their significant contributions to Bolshevik victories on the civil war fronts were coupled with the name of Stalin and not Trotsky, who only tried to eliminate them and prevent the development of the Red cavalry, which they advocated. It was Stalin who investigated the Perm disaster and brought improvements to the Eastern front; it was he who organised the defence of Petrograd against the first drive on the former imperial capital by General Yudenich. Stalin was also involved in countering Trotsky's appointments in the Red Army command, especially, the Commander-in-Chief, Colonel Vatsetis. Vatsetis was not a particularly brilliant soldier and his dismissal probably saved the Red Army from unpleasant reverses, especially on the Eastern front. Still Vatsetis was not dismissed on that ground but for political reasons, after Stalin and other Bolshevik leaders had fabricated evidence of high treason against him. Stalin also played an important part in the Polish campaign and was later accused of being responsible for the defeat of Tukhachevsky's armies: the latter was appointed and favoured by Trotsky. The charge is probably false, for Stalin was only a coordinator; still, it was his friends Voroshilov and Budyonny who had failed to turn up at the crucial moment of the battle of Warsaw. It is doubtful that Stalin would have sabotaged operations of the Red Army to win a political point or two, but not impossible. Subsequently, in 1938, he dealt with the generals involved in this failure most mercilessly and had them all executed. In his list of outstanding commanders and commissars of the civil war Marshal Bagramyan put Stalin at the top, although by 1958, when he compiled his list, Stalin had been politically downgraded, if not denigrated, and was dead.

Dzerzhinsky seems to have been neglected for the same simple reason as Lenin — he never took a direct part in the civil war. However, as Commissar, and head of the Extraordinary Commission (Cheka) he was vitally involved with security in the rear and at the fronts. In addition to transporting troops and equipment his Cheka detachments maintained food supplies in the rear and were in charge of security at the fronts. They formed special courts martial where they executed their own sentences. They did the same in the rear, but after the abortive attempt on Lenin's life they dispensed with courts altogether and applied indiscriminate terror 'in reply to White terror'. Dzerzhinsky was naturally involved in all the significant military decisions as a member of the government and of the Bolshevik central committee. In the end his detachments, led by Tukhachevsky, reduced the last important revolt against the Bolsheviks at the Kronstadt naval base in 1921.

Obviously there were many other political and military leaders who had contributed significantly to Bolshevik victory, but evidently at different levels from those of Lenin, Trotsky, Stalin and Dzerzhinsky. Of the commanders Soviet historians do not particularly relish speaking of the former imperial officers who had helped them to victory, even though they remained loyal servants of the Bolshevik Party, such men as S.S. Kamenev, P.P. Lebedev and B. Shaposhnikov, who even made a political career and was elected to the Bolshevik Central Committee. They preferred Bolshevik politicians as their commanders and the list of merit is headed by N.V. Frunze, a non-professional, who did well in the East and Turkestan, led the final assault against Wrangel and succeeded Trotsky as Commissar for War. Quite naturally he is followed by two 'Stalinists', Voroshilov and Budyonny, who in turn are followed by commanders purged in the 1930s — Apanasenko, Blyukher, Uborovich, Yakir, Timoshenko, etc. Trotsky's nominees are usually left out of these lists, although many of them had been rehabilitated in the meantime (Tukhachevsky, Yegorov, Eideman etc.). Of the commissars, such an important man as Sklyansky does not make the list because he was Trotsky's adherent, while such an unknown quantity in the civil war as N.S. Khrushchev was added to these lists during his term in power. Still the commissars did rather well subsequently: V.V. Kuybyshev became the USSR's chief planner and member of the Bolshevik Party's politburo; Ordjonikidze became Minister of Heavy Industry; Kalinin, President; Sverdlov, Kalinin's predecessor, died in 1919; Kirov became a top party official, as well as Gusev; Shvernik, President; Mekhlis, Party Controller of the Red Army. Thus most of them reached the politburo of the Bolshevik Party and top offices of the state. It appears that it was this leadership which was responsible in a decisive way for the victory in the civil war; only in a slightly less decisive way were the mistakes of the White opponents responsible for the final victory.

In comparison the Whites failed to produce such political leadership; their politicians were responsible for practically nothing in the struggle, and even failed efficiently to aid the armies fighting on their behalf. They also failed to produce a united political movement, not to say a political party, which might have provided the White armies with the cadres it so desperately needed in such a conflict. Ultimately the Whites also failed to produce the right military leaders-generals fit to fight a civil war, though like the Bolsheviks they also produced partisan leaders and a new type of commander. Thus on almost all counts the Reds seem to have been more successful than the Whites and therefore appear superior to them. However, the Red superiority must have been only marginal, for the inferior Whites kept up the struggle for some three years and won many a battle. The Bolsheviks must have been a tiny minority of the Russian population, which through superior organisation, ruthless determination and efficient propaganda snatched the victory from an inefficient, divided and silent majority.

Notes
to Bibliographical Introduction

1. A.S. Bubnov, S.S. Kamenev, R.P. Eideman (eds), *Grazhdanskaya voyna, 1918-1920*, Moscow, 1928-30, 3 vols.
2. S.F. Nayda, G.D. Obichkin, Yu.P. Petrov, A.A. Stuchkov, N.I. Shatagin, *Istoriya grazhdanskoy voyny*, Moscow 1957-60, vols 2, 3, 4, 5.
3. *V.I. Lenin v Oktyabre i v pervye gody Sovetskoy vlasti*, Leningrad, 1970; I.A. Bykhovsky, D.I. Voynolovich, *V.I. Lenin i baltiyskiye moryaki*, Moscow 1967; *O.Lenine*, Moscow, 1966; G.V. Tsvetkov, (ed.), *O voyenno-teoreticheskom nasledii V.I. Lenina*, Moscow, 1964; A.S. Zheltov, (ed.), *V.I. Lenin i Sovetskye Vooruzhennye sily*, Moscow, 1967; I. Kilesnichenko, 'K voprosu o konflikte v Revvoyensovete Yuzhnogo fronta (sentyabr-oktyabr 1918g.), *Voyennoistorichesky zhurnal*, No. 2, 1962.
4. *Partiya v period inostrannoy voyennoy interventsii i grazhdanskoy voyny*, Moscow, 1962; *Partiyno-politicheskaya rabota v Krasnoy Armii, Moscow, 1964; Kommunisticheskaya partiya Turkestana v period inostrannoy voyennoy interventsii i grazhdanskoy voyny*, Tashkent, 1964; *Latyshskiye strelki v borbe za Sovetskuyu vlast*, Riga, 1962.
5. *Ustanovleniye sovetskoy vlasti na mestakh v 1917-1918 gg.*, Moscow, 1959, etc.
6. G.F. Kennan, *Soviet American Relations*, 1917-1920, Princeton, 1956-8, 2 vols; R. Ullman *Anglo-Soviet Relations, 1917-1921*, Princeton, 1961-8, 2 vols; G.A. Brinkley, *The Volunteer Army and Allied Intervention in South Russia*, Notre Dame, 1966; J.F.N. Bradley, *Allied Intervention in Russia*, London, 1968 etc.; V.S. Vasyukov, *Predistoriya interventsii*, Moscow, 1968, etc.
7. *Pravda*, 5.8.1969,
8. A.Kh. Klevansky, *Chekhoslovatskiye internationalisty i prodanny korpus*, Moscow, 1965.
9. *Yuzhny front*, Rostov, n.d. (1962); *Yuzhnoye Zauralye v period grazhdannskoy voyny* Kurgan, 1963; *V Ogne grazhdanskoy voyny*

Odessa, 1962; *Inostrannaya voyennaya interventsiya i grazhdanskaya voyna v Sredney Azii v Kazakhstane*, Alma Ata, 1963; N. Dvoryanov, V. Dvoryanov, *V tylu Kolchaka*, Moscow, 1963; A.I. Krushanov, *Borba za vlast Sovetov na Dalnem Vostoke, i v Zabaykalie*, Vladivostok, 1962; B.O. Kashkayev, *Borba za Sovety v Dagestane*, Moscow, 1963; Ts.P. Agayan, *Veliky Oktyabr i borba trudyashchikhsya Armenii za pobedu Sovetskoy vlasti*, Ereban, 1962, etc.

10. M.I. Kulichenko, *Borba Kommunisticheskoy partii za reshenie natsionalnogo voprosa, v 1918-1920gg.*, Kharkov, 1963.
11. P.G. Sofinov, *Ocherki istorii VChK*, Moscow, 1960; *Sluzhim otchizne*, Moscow, 1968; *Direktivy Glavnogo komandovaniya Krasnoy Armii*, Moscow, 1968; I.D. Ochak, *Yugoslavskiye internatsionalisty v borbe za pobedu Sovetskoy vlasti v Rossii 1917-1921*, Moscow, 1966; S.S. Khesin, *Oktyabrskaya revolyutsiya i flot*, Moscow, 1971; *Moryaki v borbe za vlast Sovetov na Ukraine*, Kiev, 1963; L.I. Yakovlyev, *Internatsionalnaya solidarnost trudyashchikhsya zarubezhnykh stran s narodami Sovetskoy Rossii, 1917-1922*, Moscow, 1964.

Notes on Sources

Chapter 1
Primary sources used in this chapter are as follows: The Trotsky Papers (Harvard University): Miliukov Diaries; Denikin Diaries and Notes (Columbia University); Documents and papers belonging to the personal archives of General P.N. Wrangel (Stanford University); Auswärtiges Amt (captured German documents), British Foreign Office, War Office and Admiralty archives; Quai d'Orsay and Ministère de la Guerre archives.

Chapter 2
In addition to the documents mentioned in Chapter 1 the following were used: The Maklakov Papers (Stanford); The Birkin Papers; The Bogayevsky Papers; General Kazanovich Papers; The Makhrov Papers (on Savinkov); The Nikolayev Papers; the Shatilov Papers; General Kornilov documents – all at Columbia University. The Alexeyev Account Book; the Akaemov Papers; the Don Cossack Papers and letters by Generals Krasnov, Lukomsky, Kornilov – all at Stanford University.

Chapter 3
Primary documents consulted come from the archives of the British cabinet, Foreign Office, War Office, especially the Milner Papers (New College, Oxford), the Admiralty and the Curzon Papers; Ministère des Affaires Etrangères and Ministère de la Guerre archives; the records of the Department of State in Washington. The Maklakov Papers (Stanford) as well as the Miliukov Papers (Columbia).

Chapter 4
The Janin Papers were used extensively (Ministère de la Guerre); also the Abrikosov Memoirs (Columbia University); Khagondakov Memoirs (Columbia University); the Dieterichs Papers (Stanford) the Melgunov Civil War Collection (Stanford).

Chapter 5

The Denikin Diaries were used as well as the Wrangel Papers; in addition The Shatilov Memoirs (Columbia University) were consulted, Ya G. Kefeli Memoirs, Sannikov Memoirs; the Makhrov Papers; the Maslovsky Papers; The Panina Papers; the Svechin Papers; the Tikhobrazov Papers all in Columbia University; the Terek and Don Cossack Papers; the Golovin Papers; the Rodzianko Documents; the Shcherbachev Papers; the Vinaver Memoirs – all at Stanford University.

Chapter 6

The Tomilov Memoirs were used as well as the Cowan Papers (Admiralty); archives in the Ministère des Affaires Etrangères and Ministère de la Guerre were consulted; also Adjutanture generalna naczelnego dowodztwa (Pilsudski Institute, New York); captured German documents: Auswärtiges Amt and Oberkommando der Armee.

Chapter 7

The Trotsky Papers were consulted. The following were also used: The Aprelev Papers (Columbia); S.P. Melgunov Papers (Civil War Collection, Stamford); captured Bolshevik materials (Stanford).

Select Bibliography

Agar, Captain, A., *Baltic Episode*, London, 1963
Aten, Captain M., with A. Orrmont, *Last Train Over Rostov Bridge*, London, 1962
Avalov, Z.D., *The Independence of Georgia in International Politics*, London, 1940
Bechhofer-Roberts, C.E., *In Denikin's Russia*, London, 1921
Beneš, E., *My War Memoirs*, London, 1928
Bennet, G., *Cowan's War*, London, 1964
Blair, D., and Dand, C.H., *The Adventures of a British Service Agent in Russia*, London, 1937
Bradley, J., *La Légion tchécoslovaque en Russie*, Paris, 1965
—, *Allied Intervention in Russia 1917-1920*, London, 1968
Brinkley, G.A., *The Volunteer Army and Allied Intervention in South Russia*, Notre Dame, 1966
Carr, E.H., *The Russian Revolution 1917-1923*, London, 1950-52
Chamberlin, W.H., *The Russian Revolution 1917-1921*, New York, 1935
Chernov, V., *The Great Russian Revolution*, New Haven, 1936
Denikin, A.I., *The Russian Turmoil*, London, 1922
—, *The White Army*, London, 1930
Deutscher, I. *The Prophet Armed: Trotsky, 1879-1921*, London, 1954
—, *Stalin: A Political Biography*, London, 1967
Efremoff, I.N., *The Cossacks of the Don*, Paris, 1919
Fleming, P., *The Fate of Admiral Kolchak*, London, 1963
Erickson, J., *The Soviet High Command*, London, 1962
Footman, D.J., *Civil War in Russia*, London, 1961
Fedotoff-White, D., *Survival Through War and Revolution*, London, 1939
—, *The Growth of the Red Army*, Princeton, 1944
Gough, General Sir Hubert, *Soldiering On*, London, 1954
Graves, General W.S., *America's Siberian Adventure 1918-1920*, New York, 1931
Hodgson, J., *With Denikin's Armies*, London, 1932
Kennan, G.F., *Soviet American Relations 1917-1920*, London, 1958
—, *Russia and the West under Lenin and Stalin*, Boston, 1960

Kournakoff, S., *Savage Squadrons,* London, 1936
Komarnicki, T., *Rebirth of the Polish Republic,* London, 1957
Liddell-Hart, Captain B.H. (ed.), *The Soviet Army,* London, 1956
Lockhart, Sir Robert B., *Memoirs of a British Agent,* London, 1932
Luckett, R., *The White Generals,* London, 1971
Lukomsky, General A., *Memoirs of the Russian Revolution,* London, 1922
Machray. R., *The Poland of Pilsudski,* London, 1936
Mannerheim, Field-Marshal Baron Gustav, *Memoirs,* London, 1953
McCullagh, F., *A Prisoner of the Reds,* London, 1921
Masaryk, T.G., *The Making of a State,* London, 1927
Manning, C.A., *The Siberian Fiasco,* New York, 1952
Mayer, A.J., *Politics and Diplomacy of Peacemaking,* New York, 1967
Page, S.W., *The Formation of the Baltic States,* Cambridge, 1959
Pipes, R., *The Formation of the Soviet Union,* Cambridge, 1964
–, (ed.) *Revolutionary Russia,* Cambridge, 1968
Price, M.P., *My Reminiscences of the Russian Revolution,* London, 1921
–, *Russia, Red or White,* London, 1948
Ransome, A., *Six Weeks in Russia in 1919,* London, 1919
Radkey, O.H., *The Sickle under the Hammer,* New York, 1963
Reed, J., *Ten Days that Shook the World,* London, 1961
Rodzyanko, Colonel P., *Tattered Banners,* London, 1938
Schapiro, L., *The Origin of the Communist Autocracy,* London, 1955
–, and Reddaway P. (eds), *Lenin; A Reappraisal,* London, 1967
Smith, C.J., *Finland and the Russian Revolution,* Georgia Press, 1958
Stewart, G., *The White Armies of Russia,* New York, 1933
Sukhanov, N.N., *The Russian Revolution,* London, 1955
Swettenham, J., *Allied Intervention in Russia,* London, 1967
Tallents, Sir Stephen, *Man and Boy,* London, 1943
Thomson, J.M., *Russia, Bolshevism, and the Versailles Peace,* Princeton, 1967
Trotsky, L., *My Life,* London, 1930
–, *Stalin,* London, 1968
Ullman, R.H., *Anglo-Soviet Relations 1917-1921,* Princeton, 1961 and 1968
Unterberger, B.M., *America's Siberian Expedition,* Duke University, 1956
Varneck, E., and Fisher H.H. (eds), *The Testimony of Kolchak and other Siberian Materials,* Stanford, 1935
Vining, L.E., *Held by the Bolsheviks,* London, 1924
Wandycz, P.S., *France and her Eastern Allies,* Minneapolis, 1962
Ward, Colonel J., *With the 'Die-Hards' in Siberia,* London, 1920
Wrangel, P.N., *The Memoirs of General Wrangel,* New York, 1930
Zeman, Z.A.B., *Germany and the Revolution in Russia,* London, 1958

Index